Two week loan

Please return on or before the last date stamped below.
Charges are made for late return.

D1321140

LAW AND ORDER AND BRITISH POLITICS

To R.N. Berki
who inspired the volume

Law and Order
and British Politics

Edited by
PHILIP NORTON

Gower

Published by
Gower Publishing Company Limited,
Gower House, Croft Road, Aldershot,
Hampshire GU11 3HR,
England.

and
Gower Publishing Company,
Old Post Road,
Brookfield,
Vermont 05036,
U.S.A.

British Library Cataloguing in Publication Data

Law and order and British politics.
   1. Breach of the peace--Great Britain.   I. Norton, Philip
   344.104'53   KD8035

Library of Congress Cataloging in Publication Data

Main entry under title:
Law and order and British politics.
   Bibliography: p.
   Includes index.
   1. Criminal justice, Administration of---Great Britain--Addresses, essays,
lectures. I. Norton, Philip.
HV9960.G7L38 1984   364'.941   84-18722

ISBN 0-566-00688-X

Typeset at the University of Hull
Printed by Paradigm Print,
Gateshead, Tyne & Wear

Contents

Preface

This book seeks to provide an inter-disciplinary contribution to the contemporary debate on Law and Order in Britain. It has its origins in a series of seminars held in Hull University Politics Department in the 1982/83 academic year. The seminars, on the theme of 'Law and Order', were organised by and the brainchild of Dr R.N. (Bob) Berki. The papers given explored different aspects of the subject. Contributions were made by political philosophers, sociologists, political scientists, criminologists, lawyers, and a politician. A number of papers addressed themselves to the problem of Law and Order in Britain and these have been brought together in this volume. The authors were invited to revise their contributions for publication and I undertook the task of editing them.

In Britain, 'Law and Order' is a contentious and much debated subject. As editor, my aim has been to produce a concise volume that informs and clarifies that debate. The book is not designed to offer solutions, nor does it adopt a particular ideological, methodological or professional position. It is written not in order to convince but rather to further understanding of a complex subject. If it forces the reader to think more deeply about and with a better grasp of the subject it will have fulfilled its purpose.

In editing the volume, I have incurred various debts. My thanks are owing to the authors of the chapters: they have been diligent in meeting deadlines and in revising their contributions. All have responded positively to editorial requests and recommendations. I am especially grateful to Howard Elcock, whose contribution was prepared specifically for inclusion in this volume. (In the seminar series, the paper on Labour policy was given by Alex Lyon, but other commitments prevented him from working on it for publication.) In respect of my own research, I am indebted to the Home Secretary, Leon Brittan, for interrupting a busy schedule to discuss the subject with me. My thanks are due also to Ken Batty for valuable assistance with various editorial tasks. Finally, my main expression of gratitude must go to Bob Berki. Without him, this book would not have been possible. I know my fellow contributors would wish to be associated with a tribute to Bob, whose fertile mind and personal commitment produced a stimulating series of seminars. It is to him that this book is humbly dedicated.

PHILIP NORTON

Department of Politics,
University of Hull.

1 Introduction

Philip Norton

At party conferences, on television discussion programmes, at election meetings, in the House of Commons, in the pub and across the garden fence, one of the few topics of political debate that can be relied upon to arouse genuine passion is that of Law and Order. Law *and* Order: the two words are so inextricably linked in popular usage that it is common to refer to them in the singular. All those who engage in debate on the subject appear to have some idea of what is encompassed by the term. The death penalty, allegations of police brutality, demonstrations on the street, acts of terrorism, fraud, violent crime, denials of civil liberties, harsh or lenient court sentences, police powers to stop and search, social security fraud, drug taking, corruption in the police force, burglary, shoplifting, the use of troops in Northern Ireland, legislation limiting or extending individual rights, and driving under the influence of alcohol: all are discussed under the rubric of Law and Order.

Given both the range and the substance of the topic, it is not surprising that it arouses public concern. No sensible person wishes to be burgled, mugged or murdered. Particularly brutal crimes heighten popular fear. The police are looked to for protection. Accusations of police corruption generate further worries. Who is to police the police? While one looks to the police and to the courts to deal appropriately with those who commit criminal acts, how is one to protect the innocent? What rights does and should the individual possess in the face of police demands to enter and search one's property or to detain and search the person? All are questions of genuine and legitimate public concern. 'Law and Order' appears regularly as a problem which a proportion of the population believes to be one of the most important faced by government.[1]

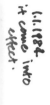

Law and Order, then, is a wide-ranging topic. It is a subject of popular political debate. It is, increasingly, a subject also of party political debate. The relationship between the parties has become a more adversary one.[2] Measures such as the 1983 Police and Criminal Evidence Bill have been the subject of partisan divisions in the House of Commons.[3] There is a popular perception of the difference between the Conservative and Labour Parties on the issue. The Conservative stance, seen as the tougher of the two, has been an electoral plus for the party. Of electors regarding the issue as an urgent one for government, an overwhelming majority have preferred the Conservative position.[4] In the 1979 general election, no other subject provided such a wide margin in the party's favour.[5] The Home Secretary, Leon Brittan, has stressed the extent to which Law and Order has been accorded preference in the Government's spending priorities.[6] On the Labour side, some writers have argued that the Conservatives have in effect 'stolen' the issue.[7] Roy Hattersley has argued that, to counter the Conservative advantage, the Labour Party 'must become the law-and-order party'.[8] The Alliance parties have sought to gain support by advocating the virtues of community policing.

The significance of Law and Order as a subject of popular concern can hardly be doubted. The most remarkable feature of the enduring, widespread and often intense debate as to the problem of Law and Order is, however, its lack of clarity. What is 'Law and Order'? Why are the two words so intimately conjoined? What precisely is the *problem* of Law and Order? Much has been written and spoken on the various issues mentioned already, yet few attempts have been made to provide a theoretical clarification of the concept of Law and Order or empirically to clarify and inform the debate on the subject. R.N. Berki, in a recent paper, has provided an incisive theoretical review of the subject.[9] The purpose of this volume is to clarify and inform the contemporary, practical debate in Britain.

The debate cannot be divorced from philosophical reflection and this introduction in part overlaps with, and has been informed by, Dr Berki's penetrating discourse. What the book does not seek to do is to provide solutions. It attempts solely to contribute to a clearer and more informed debate. If 'Law and Order' is to continue as a topic of popular debate and to be considered a problem, it is surely helpful to know what we mean by the term and why and in what way it is considered a problem.

Law AND Order

Law, order and the concept of 'law and order' are rarely the subject of precise definition. The Home Office, for example, has found no operational need to define the concept.[10] What then do we mean by law and order and what is the relationship between them? Do the two terms enjoy a discernible harmony?

Law, simply put, may be defined as constituting formally prescribed rules having applicability to all within the confines of the state or territory under whose aegis they are promulgated. All persons are bound by them and the state or territory is vested with the coercive power to ensure their enforcement.[11] Discussion of 'the law' in Britain encounters two problems. One is the variety of sources from which it emanates. The other is one of further definition.

In Britain, there are various forms of law. At the apex stands statute law, enjoying a position of pre-eminence because of the judicially self-imposed doctrine of parliamentary sovereignty.[12] Able to claim a greater longevity and the greater affection of many jurists is common law, 'a lawyer's law of universal application', according to Lord Scarman.[13] Law-making powers may be vested in subordinate bodies: delegated legislation is now a significant feature of British law.[14] Judicial interpretation adds the flesh to the skeleton provided by formal legislative enactments. Membership of the European Communities has added a new body of law, and an additional law-making process, to that which previously existed. For anyone seeking to discern and study the law in Britain, recourse to the *Statutes Revised* and the annual volumes of statutory instruments is not sufficient. Law emanates from different sources and is expressed in different forms.

More central to discussion of the concept of law and order is the further definitional problem. Law in the context of 'law and order' is often asserted to refer to 'the rule of law'. This assertion, far from clarifying one's understanding of the concept, raises further problems. What constitutes 'the rule of law'? It is a concept with a long history — reference to the rule of law is to be found in Aristotle[15] — but with little agreement as to its definition. Dicey, in the nineteenth century, identified it as one of the two pillars of the British constitution. (The other was parliamentary sovereignty.) He contended that it encompassed 'at least three distinct though kindred conceptions'. First, 'that no man is punishable or can be lawfully made to suffer in body or goods except for a distinct breach of law established in the ordinary legal manner before the ordinary courts of the land'. Second, 'no man is above the law, (and) every man, whatever his rank or condition, is subject to the ordinary law of the realm and amenable to the jurisdiction of the ordinary tribunals'. Third, 'the general principles of the constitution (as for example the right to personal liberty, or the right of public meeting) are. . . the result of judicial decisions determining the right of private persons in particular cases brought before the courts'.[16] The extent to which these 'kindred concepts' hold good today is open to much dispute. Dicey's assertions have been variously dismissed.[17] Many discretionary powers are vested in officials and public bodies, as indeed many were at the time that Dicey wrote. In so far as Dicey's second point infers that all persons have equal rights and duties before the law, it is of doubtful value: local authorities, ministers, police officers and others have many powers that the ordinary citizen does not have.[18] In so far as it inferred that it excluded any exemption of officials from the duty of obedience to the law which governed other citizens, then various exceptions may again be recorded.[19] Dicey's third point has been challenged because it is not clear why it is 'kindred' to the other two and because certain rights have been enacted in or modified by statute. It has been characterised as an expression of the nineteenth-century liberal obsession with the liberty of the individual.

Dicey's definition, then, has not enjoyed universal assent and no agreed definition has yet been formulated. Various attempts to find an internationally accepted definition have been made. The secretary of one international colloquium gave voice to the opinion that 'the rule of law is an expression of an endeavour to give reality to something which is not readily expressable'.[20] Some authorities subscribe to definitions posited by international bodies, such as the International Commission of Jurists' Declaration of Delhi,[21] while others stipulate their own definition. Within Britain, contemporary usage of the term would appear to imply a broad and a narrow definition. The broad definition, more common among jurists, implies certain substantive and procedural rights, as well as that government must be subject to the law and that the judiciary must be independent. The problem remains of determining what those substantive and procedural rights are. The narrow definition, more commonly employed by politicians and writers on the subject (including in this volume), is that of the universal enforcement of law. If a law is broken, then the transgressor must be apprehended and punished. It is this narrow definition which would appear most relevant in defining the concept of law and order in contemporary usage. In popular perception, the 'law' in law and order means the enforcement of law. For many, the strict enforcement of law and 'the rule of law' are synonymous.

Law and order, in contrast, are not synonymous terms. Law is an artificial creation. It is 'made'. Order refers to a particular state of being. It may be said to imply not only a state of tranquility but also a 'settled' society, one in which each person has a recognised place in the hierarchy of that society.[22] Philosophically, the two concepts (law and order) are distinct and separable. Empirically, the relationship is more complex.

Students of the House of Commons have assumed that disciplinary powers are wielded by the whips in order to ensure party cohesion. As more perceptive observers have noted, the effective use of discipline depends upon the prior existence of a high degree of cohesion. In the event of perfect cohesion, no formal discipline (or disciplinary rules from which it flows) is necessary. In the absence of any cohesion, no discipline is possible. The relationship between law and order is similar. In a state of perfect order, law would be superfluous. In the absence of order, law cannot be enforced. Law, to be effective, requires some prior degree of order.

Law needs order and law may be promulgated and enforced to ensure some degree of order. However, in as much as law and order in popular perception means the enforcement of law and the maintenance of order, there exists the potential for conflict. In certain circumstances, the enforcement of law may threaten the maintenance of order. In Brixton on 11 April 1981, for example, an apparent attempt by police officers to enforce the law precipitated public disorder.[23] As some of the contributions to this volume reveal, where sub-cultures have norms (and hence a form of order) which run counter to the norms of the dominant culture, and where the norms of the dominant culture are embodied in law, then the potential for conflict will remain and, as recent experience has shown, be realised.

In the event of the enforcement of law and the maintenance of order comprising mutually exclusive choices, there is no authoritative agreement as to which should be pursued. John Alderson has argued, in *Policing Freedom*, that the first duty of the police is to maintain the Queen's Peace, not to enforce the law.[24] The police should use their discretion to enforce the law in such a manner as to maintain public tranquility and prevent crime. As John Rex observes (ch. 6), this may entail the police winking at violations of the law relating to such matters as drink and gambling in certain homogeneous sub-cultures. Taking a contrary view to Alderson, P.A.J. Waddington (ch. 5) contends that such toleration should not be permitted. 'It would be contrary to *the rule of law*, and to the long-term detriment of the police themselves, if they were to adopt a policy of tolerating greater lawlessness in some areas than in others.' Disparate enforcement of the law, it could be argued, may constitute a greater long-term threat to order than its universal and consistent enforcement.

Between the two extremes (the enforcement of law versus the maintenance of order), the present Home Secretary, Leon Brittan, has taken a pragmatic stance, probably typical of his predecessors.

The enforcement of law, he contends, takes a high priority, but there may be occasions which justify *in the circumstances* a *temporary* giving way to the need to maintain order.[25] Such occasions, clearly, are presumed to be rare but there is a recognition of their existence.

In most instances, it is assumed that law and order are compatible, particularly when order is defined as encompassing a settled society (with stipulated relationships between those who comprise it) and not just as a tranquil existence. Nonetheless, there exists not only a law and order problem but also, on occasion, a problem of law versus order. Assuming, though, a compatibility between the two components, what of the law and order problem?

The problem of law and order

Identifying 'the' problem of law and order is not an easy task. In many respects, the problem is seen differently by different groups. At the popular level, and probably among most politicians, the problem is perceived as a problem *for* government. For some groups, such as civil libertarians, the problem is seen as being one *of* government.[26]

For those who see the problem as one for government, the task faced by government is to ensure that law is enforced and order is maintained. The challenge to law and order takes essentially two forms: law breaking and order defiance. The two challenges may involve similar or identical acts, but such acts (for example, murder or bank robbery) constitute means to very different ends. What we may term simple law breaking, whether done wilfully or out of ignorance, is engaged in for the purpose of benefitting the individual or individuals involved. It may be motivated by greed (robbery), by a desire for vengeance (grievous bodily harm, murder), by anger (ditto) or simply by a desire to get quickly from point A to point B (speeding). It is not motivated by some wider moral purpose nor is it a challenge (usually), nor is it meant to be, to the existing order, that is in the sense of a community with known and structured relationships. Indeed, as Dr Berki has argued, law breakers depend upon and expect known and structured relationships to be maintained ('how would you enjoy your ill-gotten fortune if there were no obliging waiters to fill up your champagne glass, and wouldn't you be indignant if the nightclub hostess were not law-abiding enough to give you your right change?') and, furthermore, by their unlawful acts they may serve to reinforce order.[27] When crime occurs, in Durkheim's words, 'everybody is attacked; consequently everybody opposes the attack'.[28]

Simple law breaking, then, comprises selfish acts by individuals *qua* individuals. It may involve the breaking of laws that are not regarded as of such importance as to incur popular wrath or heavy penalties (for instance, speeding or parking on double yellow lines) or it may take the form of acts that are so serious as to incur a public outcry and the imposition, if caught and convicted, of lengthy periods of incarceration (for example, mass murders). Though committed by individuals for selfish reasons, the incidence of serious acts of law breaking may reach such a level as to pose a threat to order. The problem then becomes a much more serious one, though how government responds may be motivated as much by ideology and public expectations as by a tempered evaluation of existing data.

Order defiance is of a very different nature to simple law breaking. It has a moral basis, however spurious others may regard that morality to be. It seeks consciously to disturb and destroy the existing order. It purports to be selfless, conducted on behalf of others (the poor, the proletariat or whatever). Pursuit of order defiance may be and usually does involve breaking the law and hence the unlawful acts of order defiers may overlap with those of 'ordinary' law breakers. Those seeking to destroy the existing order may rob a bank in order to provide funds for their cause; an ordinary criminal will rob a bank to line his own pockets. The motivation is different, the offence the same. Similarly with the offence of murder. A policeman killed by an ordinary bank robber, for example, is likely to have been killed because he sought to apprehend the law breaker. It could just as well have been someone else who suffered the same fate had they sought to do what the policeman did. Had the policeman stayed away or done nothing, the law breaker would have had no interest in him. For order defiers, the policeman is a target, representing as he does part of the agency of the state in existence to maintain domestic order. Hence, the policeman has to take no action (other than being a policeman) in order to constitute a target.

How is the state to respond? Should it distinguish between 'ordinary' law breaking and order defiance? In most cases, it does not. Bank robbery is bank robbery. It is a proscribed offence and if caught and convicted one may expect to be sentenced to a period of incarceration. However, the law is not altogether blind as to the distinction. The offence of treason (conspiring to kill the Queen or levying war against the Queen or adhering to the Queen's enemies) is unique in that it remains punishable by death. Various statutes recognise the existence of 'terrorism', for example, the 1976 Prevention of Terrorism (Temporary Provisions) Act. The present Home Secretary utilised the distinction also in arguing in 1983 for the return of the death penalty for those convicted of terrorist murders. Acts of terrorism, he declared, are crimes against civil society as a whole. Those who supported restoring the death penalty for terrorist murders did so, he said, because they regarded it as the duty of the state to signal its total repugnance for those who committed crimes that undermined its very foundation.[29] In addition, there is provision for the armed forces to be used in support of the civil power when the latter cannot maintain order. However, the use of troops reflects usually the scale rather than the nature of the attack upon order. In Featherstone in 1893, for example, troops fired upon rioters who, though considered a threat to tranquility, were most certainly not order defiers in the sense defined above. In Northern Ireland, in contrast, the threat does come from order defiers.

Furthermore, though order defiance in its *motivation* poses a more serious threat to the existing order than does simple law breaking, in recent British history law breaking has, in its *incidence* and in popular perception, constituted a more immediate threat. This is borne out in this volume by chapters 2 and 3 and by the chapters on the approaches of the political parties. The problem of law and order for government has been, and is seen by the parties as being, one of crime — that is, law breaking as opposed to order defiance. Order defiance in the form of terrorist acts constitutes clearly a serious problem but, for government and the political parties, 'law and order' problems are essentially those of the commission of crime, its prevention, and the detection, trial and punishment of those who commit it.[30] Order defiers may and, in their actions, usually do fall under this rubric but the primary focus is upon the incidence of crime as law breaking.

For government, then, the problem of law and order is one of dealing primarily with crime. The problem is seen as one for government rather than one of government. Some civil libertarians and politicians (the categories are not mutually exclusive) have, instead, seen it as much if not more so as a problem *of* government. Such a perception, generally stated, has not been confined to any one group: it has been expressed by writers on both the left and the right of the political spectrum.

On the left, there has been a tendency to see the response of government to apparent increases in crime and to public disorder as constituting a greater threat to order, and indeed to the rule of law in its broader definition, than that which it seeks to respond to. In recent years (criticism is not confined to any particular administration) government has responded to terrorist acts and popular fears about crime by the introduction of anti-terrorist legislation, by strengthening the police force (in equipment as well as numbers) and by increasing the maximum sentences possible for various offences. The courts and the police have contributed to this response. In the Spring of 1984, for example, the police prevented a number of miners leaving the county of Kent to picket coal mines in Nottinghamshire. The courts upheld the power of the police at common law to take such action. Such developments are seen by many on the left, as Martin Shaw observes (ch. 11), 'as creating a state which, if not "the strong state" in the fullest sense is demonstrably a dangerously stronger state'. Fears are expressed of an authoritarian consensus emerging which could contribute to a new order, that of a 'police state'. Though those who have expressed such fears, such as Patricia Hewitt, concede that 'civil and political rights have not been extinguished. . . . Britain is not a police state'[31] they nonetheless see inherent dangers in the way in which government seeks to respond to what it considers the problem of law and order. 'The danger', as Campbell and Wiles put it, 'is that the threats to the political order produced by. . . stresses will not, or not always, be met in a liberal way. A State under threat is not the best guardian of civil liberties.'[32]

On the right, the problem has been seen in a somewhat different but not altogether dissimilar way. Here the growth of government, the passage of more and more legislation and the pursuit of some idealised egalitarian goals are seen as threats to the traditional order and the liberties enjoyed by most Britons. Furthermore, the tendency of government to favour particular groups is seen as a significant threat to the rule of law, in terms of the law applying equally to all. More powers assumed by government, more legislation conferring rights and immunities not congruent with well established popular dispositions, legal privileges conferred upon special interests (notably the trade unions) all constitute a threat to order and the rule of law (see ch. 8). This perception was most forcefully expressed in the 1970s by Lord Hailsham. The growing concentration of power in the hands of the executive, he argued, had produced an 'elective dictatorship'. If the existing constitutional machinery was no longer sufficient to protect the traditional rights of the individual, then what was needed was a radical constitutional innovation. This, according to Hailsham, should take the form of a new constitution, with entrenched clauses, with the purpose of institutionalising the theory of limited government.[33] The aim was not to create some new idealised structure but rather to restore that which was presumed to have existed previously. In the latter half of the 1970s, the Conservative Party was united in its condemnation of the Labour Government for actions which it believed undermined respect for the law. In its view, the problem *for* government was one which had been contributed to *by* government.

The problem of law and order, then, is not a simple or easily discernible one. Indeed, it is not so much one problem as several. In a sense, how one sees it depends upon where you stand. One's ideological stance will often determine one's definition of the concept of law and order and concomitantly shape one's perception of the problem. As just delineated, it can be seen as a problem of government as well as a problem for government. Not only can there be a 'law and order' problem, there can be a problem of 'law versus order'. The very complexity of the problem, overlaid with ideological preconceptions, may have militated against a comprehensive and rational debate. Discussion has tended to be disparate, concentrating upon specific aspects of the problem. One may be sure that certain topics fall within the rubric of 'law and order'. Seeking to delineate precisely what the term encompasses is more problematical and much avoided. The very nature of the debate about the problem of law and order itself contributes to the problem.

The contemporary debate

The confused nature of the contemporary debate is reflected in some of the assumptions which underlie it and in the problems which political parties have in addressing themselves to it. To what extent are those assumptions valid? What are the problems faced by the political parties in seeking to deal with the issue of law and order? What are their policies on the issue?

One popular assumption concerns the incidence of crime and public disorder. There is a tendency to look back to the earlier part of the twentieth century and to perceive a period of tranquility and law-abidingness. Since that time, so the assumption goes, crime and public disorder have become rampant and each year the position gets worse. Yet to what extent is this popular perception borne out by the evidence? What are the implications of such a perception?

In the first section of this volume, 'Law and Order in Perspective', the contributors address themselves to these questions. David Dixon and Elaine Fishwick assess the extent to which the problem of crime and public disorder is not a new one for Britain. Historically, the country has been rent by various violent upheavals but such upheavals have not impacted themselves upon the national consciousness.[34] The nineteenth century was hardly a period of tranquility (hence the need for 'the Peelers'). In the 1860s, *The Cornhill Magazine* could complain: 'Once more the streets of London are unsafe by day or night. The public dread has almost become a panic.'[35] Nor, as Dixon and Fishwick show, were the early decades of this century free of conflict and disorder. Nor, as they (and P.A.J. Waddington in chapter 5) argue, were the police well trusted and supported in all parts of the community. Suspicion and distrust of the police among certain sections of the population is not a new phenomenon. As Waddington contends, it is somewhat fanciful to assume that the police enjoyed in the past some idyllic relationship with the local community.

The chapter by Dixon and Fishwick provides a useful corrective to popular assumptions. Their analysis can be utilised by those on the right as well as on the left of the political spectrum. For Conservatives, it shows that crime and disorder have been features of the landscape for some time; hence they may well contend that the riots of 1981 and preceding years should not be seen as demonstrating some novel and paradigmatic upheaval. The country has faced, and survived, similar problems before. Indeed, Conservatives may well find comfort in the comparative data. Government has not had to resort to the tactics employed earlier in the century (the despatch of troops, the use of the navy — a gunboat at one stage was sent up the Mersey) to maintain order.[36] Those on the left, for their part, can draw attention to the extent to which public disorder and crime appear to be consistent features of British society and, in their analysis, the need to deal with the structural roots of the problem.

In historical terms, then, the picture is a more complex one than is popularly assumed. Do not recent crime statistics help provide a much clearer picture? As Keith Bottomley and Clive Coleman demonstrate in chapter 3, the answer essentially is no. The official statistics reveal a steady increase in the incidence of recorded crime in earlier decades but a much more unpredictable pattern over the past ten years or so. Furthermore, as the authors show, the position becomes more complicated when one considers the means by which the data are compiled. There is a large area of unrecorded crime and this 'dark figure' has not necessarily grown at the same rate as that of recorded crime. The recording of criminal offences can be affected by changes in legislation, by a greater willingness (or reluctance) of victims to report criminal acts, and by greater activity on the part of the police. (As the authors mention, a more efficient and sympathetic police force can result in an increase in *recorded* crime.) As the Home Office itself has conceded, trends in serious offences recorded by the police may not reflect the trends in the total number of crimes committed.[37] To paraphrase the Home Secretary: the statistics *are* imperfect because the means of recording are imperfect; but they are the only thing the Home Office has to go on.[38]

However accurate the statistics for recorded crime, their publication can contribute to popular concern. In 1982, for example, the Chief Constable of Hampshire expressed the view that the statistics gave a false impression of the true level of crime and had unnecessarily inflated public anxiety about being victims of crime.[39] Bottomley and Coleman discuss the concept of 'moral panics' and the extent to which apparent increases in crime and incidents of well-publicised violence (for example, the Moors murders or conflict in Northern Ireland) contribute to such panics. They suggest that the law and order panic of the 1970s was the product of complex social processes with fear about crime being generated and reinforced by perceived notions about the incidence of crime rather than by personal experience of criminal acts. What was significant was the way in which the problem was portrayed. The authors also discuss the response to the problem in the sphere of penal policy. Here, they argue, policy is shaped less by established facts than by ideology and pressure from well-entrenched interest groups.

Again, such an analysis may be subject to different interpretations by Conservatives and Socialists. However well or badly founded the basis on which moral panics occur may be, Conservatives would tend to point to the need to take such panics seriously. While one may seek to deal with the roots of the problem, one needs also to acknowledge and respond to popular anxiety. Concrete measures may be necessary to respond to such anxiety. Increasing the maximum term of imprisonment possible for certain offences may not have any deterrent effect upon law breakers but what is important is that the worried law-abiding citizen believes that it does. Furthermore, public anxiety may be harnessed to help in the fight against crime.

For those on the left, moral panics help detract from fundamental social problems and, indeed, may serve to frustrate attempts to deal with them. Furthermore, such panics may be utilised as mechanism to legitimise an increase in the coercive powers available to the state. According to Hall, a moral panic is 'one of the principal forms of ideological consciousness by means of which a "silent majority" is won over to the support of increasingly coercive measures on the part of the state, and lends its legitimacy to a "more than usual" exercise of control.'[40] It can, to revert to our earlier discussion contribute to a 'dangerously stronger state'.

In the second section of the volume, the contributors address themselves to some of the specific contemporary problems of law and order. At times of public disorder and an apparent underlying increase in the crime rate, we look to the police to respond. However, one concern common to the contributions of J.L. Lambert, P.A.J. Waddington and John Rex is that the role played by, and expected of, the police is far from clear. Analyses of the role played by the police differ. Some writers have advanced a liberal model, positing that the police serve to enforce the law impartially and to protect the rights of the individual. Others have advanced a class model, contending that the police serve to maintain the rule of the dominant class. A third model is that of the police state, one in which the police are not ultimately subject to any political authority and decide for themselves what kind of law and order shall be enforced. John Rex (ch. 6) considers that the class model has become less applicable with the rise of working-class political power and the welfare state, but that the repressive class model may still operate in the policing of immigrant areas. J.L. Lambert,

12

though not advancing the police state model, points to the extent to which the police have become more directly involved in the debate on law and order. Chief Constables, he notes, no longer maintain a low profile and have lobbied unashamedly for greater police powers. Police staff organisations have become political pressure groups. The method of 'hard' policing adopted by some forces has come in for especial criticism.

The riots of 1981 and earlier years raised serious questions about police operations. In the wake of the riots, there were calls for more effective police accountability and, in order to avoid future clashes between police and local groups, 'community policing' and more extensive training of police officers. These proposals are variously considered in chapters 4, 5 and 6. The writers provide a cautionary note. John Lambert queries the extent to which official consideration of the problem of police accountability will be effective without a consideration of the wider issue of what society expects of the police. P.A.J. Waddington provides a cogent critique of 'community policing'. It constitutes, he contends, 'a romantic delusion. It harks back to a harmonious idyll, where the police were everyone's friend. It was never thus, and it is unlikely that it will ever be'. His chapter forces one to think more deeply about the concept and its application. John Rex addresses himself to the question of training and of consultation between police and local communities. Though not dismissing as insignificant the changes that have taken place, he nonetheless argues that more extensive reforms are needed. The police, he contends, must be part of a large-scale education programme. Some enlightened police officers seek to counter racialism within their ranks, but a much wider will must exist to deal with the problem effectively.

One further point that emerges from the chapters by Waddington and Rex is that, in many respects, society expects too much of the police. The police alone cannot deal with the problem of law and order. Improving police training and liaison with local communities will not solve the problems of the inner cities or of racial prejudice. Relying on the police, through the introduction of community policing or the provision of more resources, will not 'solve' the crime problem. There is a growing awareness that the community itself has to be more actively involved. The chapters in this section show that it is not sufficient for citizens to sit back and expect the police to deal with the problem of law and order or indeed of wider social concerns. To do so is both unfair on the police and unrealistic in expectation of what can be achieved.

Finally, in this section, Andrew Cox looks at a somewhat different aspect of the law and order problem. Trade union militancy has often featured as part of the debate on law and order. Strikes and mass picketing are seen sometimes as threats to public order. Some industrial action is interpreted as having a political goal. The overtime ban by the miners in 1974 is often credited with helping bring down the Heath Government. Dr Cox addresses himself to a number of popular assumptions about trade union militancy and its implications for law and order. He argues that changes in strike activity have been qualitative rather than quantitative. Strikes now occur more often in essential services and in sectors not regarded previously as strike prone. Most union militancy has tended to take the form of wage rather than political militancy. Only when government has sought to respond to severe economic difficulties by imposing legal restraint or a form of corporatism have unions responded by directing their action against the state. Both types of militancy pose potential threats to public order (several hundred irate pickets can pose a threat whatever their reason for gathering) but rarely do they constitute order defiers in the sense defined earlier. Dr Cox argues that government is likely to avoid union challenges to order by not resorting to legal restraint.

Dr Cox's analysis raises as many questions for those on the left as it does for those on the right. Conservatives can take comfort from the fact that industrial action is not pursued usually for political ends (though to present strikes as threats to order may prove politically expedient). The present Government would appear to be sensitive to the problems associated with attempting legal restraint. In the miners dispute in the Spring of 1984, ministers appeared content to leave it to the police to maintain order on the picket lines. Employers were not encouraged to resort to the courts to take action against the miners. Conservatives also appear to be aware that current economic conditions favour the Government in seeking to limit the number and impact of strikes. They are also likely to argue that, while trying to avoid industrial disputes is desirable, government has to take into account wider interests than those of trade unions. For them, therefore, Dr Cox's analysis constitutes something of a curate's egg. For those well on the left of the political spectrum, it constitutes a depressing analysis. It demonstrates the extent to which workers retain what Marxists would consider to be 'false consciousness'. At times of significant economic problems, workers in employment tend to demonstrate not militant tendencies but rather self interest. The preservation of one's own job is given priority over calls for union 'solidarity'. In the 1980s, on the basis of this analysis, it is difficult to see trade unions posing significant threats to the state.

What, then, of the position of the political parties? The contributors to the third section, 'Law and Order in Political Focus', address themselves to the political positions taken on the issue. The chapters reveal not only the differences between the parties but also the problems faced by them in addressing themselves to the issue of law and order.

Arthur Aughey and I draw out the problem for the Conservative Party in seeking to respond to an increase in crime that goes beyond a policy of 'more of the same'; for to pursue radical policies that accept that the problem lies with society rather than the individual is to run counter to Conservative perceptions of society. For Labour, as Howard Elcock shows, there are various problems, not least the fact that Labour's analysis runs counter to popular perceptions. For Labour, the task is as much an educative one as it is one of gaining office. In a sense, it has needed to undergo a process of self-education. Until recently, the party has not accorded much priority to promulgating policies in the field of law and order. 'The people's party', as Martin Kettle observed, 'has traditionally taken little interest in policing, prisons, criminal justice and the rest of established Home Office responsibilities. A party seeking social change — however limited — is obviously likely to concentrate on the economic and spending departments of government.'[41] Only recently has this begun to change. 'Today, with law and order issues now acquiring sharper party political edges, the Home Office is perhaps closer to the centre of the stage than for many years past. Labour. . . has taken a more radical stance.'[42] The extent to which the party has sought to generate a more radical and coherent policy is reflected in Dr Elcock's chapter. The problem of gaining popular acceptance of that policy remains. 'The belief that liberal Home Office policies are vote-losers is deeply held.'[43]

Stephen Ingle identifies the problems faced by the Liberal/Social Democratic Alliance in seeking to generate a policy. In his study, he discerns the basis for a distinctive Alliance stance on law and order. Commitment to community and participation generates Alliance support for 'community politics' and hence for the policy of community policing. Dr Ingle details some of the objections that can be levelled at the proposal for greater community participation as well as the Liberal response to such objections. The Alliance support for community policing, articulated by former police officers Alderson and Webb (see ch. 10), stands in sharp contrast to the view advanced by P.A.J. Waddington in chapter 5. For him, the policy is illusory, trying to re-create conditions of community that have never existed. As he mentions, the only effective community policing that did exist was in rural communities where the local policeman enforced the values of the local elite. Emphasis on community politics may also serve to detract from issues which may not be amenable to local resolution. For the partners to the Alliance, there is the need to hammer out a joint policy, one that addresses itself to such objections.

Martin Shaw considers the problems faced not by an organised party but by a specific though increasingly diverse political grouping. In chapter 10, Dr Ingle observes that the Labour Party, having failed to preside over a revolutionary transformation of society, has tended in the past to fall back on traditional Home Office wisdom. For Marxists, the absence of such a revolutionary transformation has been more traumatic. For both ideological as well as practical reasons (not being a party of government), they have not been able to descend to the level of formulating and debating specific policies. Instead, as Martin Shaw's chapter so ably demonstrates, they have had to grapple with the realisation that both law and order need to be seen in more sophisticated terms than has been the case with orthodox Marxists in the past and that there is a need to come to terms with the fact that existing British society is not going to disappear overnight in some miraculous Socialist revolution. Now, Shaw argues, there is a need to generate a strategy that does not dismiss existing institutions of the state but rather seeks to utilise them in achieving a socialist transformation. There is, he contends, a need to formulate a specific, democratic Socialist alternative to the 'law and order' policies of the right. The most obvious place for such a strategy to be developed is in the left-wing of the Labour Party rather than in the Communist Party. As the author himself concedes, his argument is not one that will find favour with orthodox Marxists. Indeed, his chapter bears witness to the extent to which the edges between Marxism, neo-Marxism, quasi-Marxism (often paraded as neo-Marxism) and non-Marxism are becoming increasingly blurred. One might be forgiven the observation that Marxists appear to be having problems maintaining order within their own ranks.

The chapters in the three sections of the book address themselves to particular aspects of the law and order debate. In the conclusion, Neil Elder draws out some of the underlying concerns of the chapters and puts them in the context of the modern state. Echoing a number of contributors, he draws attention to the changing nature of the debate, not least in terms of what is expected of government and the police in dealing with the problem of law and order, and the problem posed by popular perceptions and dispositions not being congruent with 'expert' opinion. The conundrum posed by Bottomley and Coleman remains. In responding to perceived problems of law and order, should government give priority to ideology, expert opinion, interest groups or popular anxieties and prejudice? The problem of law and order, and how to respond to it, is not peculiar to Britain. The conundrum is a familiar one in the modern state.

Notes

1. On average, one in twenty people regard 'law and order' as one of the two most urgent problems facing the country, though the figure has increased in the wake of outbreaks of public disorder. R. Webb and N. Wybrow (eds), *The Gallup Report* (Sphere Books, 1981), p.135.
2. That the relationship has become more adversary in recent years has been conceded by those on both sides of the political fence; for example, D. Downes, *Law and Order: Theft of an Issue*, Fabian Tract 490 (Fabian Society, 1983) and the Rt. Hon. Leon Brittan, Q.C., M.P. to author. Both sides tend to blame the other for this development.
3. See the division on the Second Reading of the Police and Criminal Evidence Bill, 7 November 1983, *HC Deb.* 48, cols. 107-11.
4. I. Crewe, 'Why the Conservatives Won', in H. Penniman (ed.), *Britain at the Polls, 1979* (American Enterprise Institute, 1981), p.284.
5. Ibid.
6. See his comments in the House of Commons on 23 June 1983, *HC Deb.* 44, col. 181. Between 1978/79 and 1982/83, he said, real spending on 'law and order services' had risen by almost a quarter.
7. See Downes, op.cit., and I. Taylor, *Law and Order: Arguments for Socialism* (Macmillan, 1981), pp.xiv-xv.
8. In 'Framework for a Labour Britain' in G. Kaufman (ed.), *Renewal: Labour's Britain in the 1980s* (Penguin, 1983).
9. R.N. Berki, *Reflections on Law and Order*, Hull Papers in Politics No.35 (Hull University Politics Department, 1983).
10. The Home Secretary, the Rt. Hon. Leon Brittan, Q.C., M.P. to author.
11. For a more developed definition, see Berki, op.cit.
12. See P. Norton, *The Constitution in Flux* (Martin Robertson, 1982), introduction.
13. Sir L. Scarman, *English Law — The New Dimension* (Stevens, 1974), p.2.
14. See P. Norton, *The Commons in Perspective* (Martin Robertson, 1981), pp.95-99.
15. *Politics*, III, 16.
16. A.V. Dicey, *An Introduction to the Study of the Law of the Constitution*, first published 1885, 10th ed. (Macmillan, 1959), pp.188, 193 and 195, also pp.202-203.
17. For conflicting comments, see E.C.S. Wade and G. Phillips,

Constitutional Law, 8th ed. by E.C.S. Wade and A.W. Bradley (Longman, 1970), ch. 5, and S.A. de Smith, *Constitutional and Administrative Law* (Penguin, 1971), pp.39-40.

18. O. Hood Phillips, *Constitutional and Administrative Law*, 6th ed. (Sweet and Maxwell, 1978), p.37.
19. See Norton, *The Constitution in Flux*, pp.15-16.
20. J.A. Jolowicz, quoted in E.C.S. Wade, introduction to Dicey, op.cit., p. cix.
21. See Hood Phillips, op.cit., pp.17-18.
22. Berki, op.cit., pp.14-15.
23. The details are well recorded in *The Brixton Disorders: 10-12 April 1981, Report of an Inquiry by the Rt. Hon. Lord Scarman* (Cmnd. 8427) (HMSO, 1981), Part III:B.
24. J. Alderson, *Policing Freedom* (Macdonald and Evans, 1979), cited in P.A.J. Waddington in ch. 5.
25. The Rt. Hon. Leon Brittan, Q.C., M.P. to author, interview.
26. This distinction is drawn and pursued in Berki, op.cit.
27. Ibid. p.20.
28. Quoted, ibid. p.20.
29. *HC Deb*. 45, col. 902.
30. See, e.g. 'Law and Order', *Politics Today*, 22, 19 December 1983 (Conservative Research Department, 1983). The Home Secretary has defined law and order in similar terms.
31. P. Hewitt, *The Abuse of Power* (Martin Robertson, 1982), p.xii. See also ch. 11 in this volume.
32. C. Campbell and P. Wiles, foreword to Hewitt, op.cit., p.x.
33. Lord Hailsham, *The Dilemma of Democracy* (Collins, 1978), p.226; see also Lord Hailsham, *Elective Dictatorship* (BBC, 1976).
34. See the comments in Norton, *The British Polity* (Longman, 1984), p.49.
35. Quoted in *New Society*, 25 March 1982, p.463.
36. See Norton, *The British Polity*, p.352, and S. Field and P. Southgate, *Public Disorder*, Home Office Research Study No. 72 (HMSO, 1972), pp.4-5.
37. Home Office, *Criminal Statistics: England and Wales 1980*, quoted by Bottomley and Coleman, ch. 3.
38. The Rt. Hon. Leon Brittan, Q.C., M.P. to author, interview.
39. *Sunday Times Magazine*, 26 September 1982, pp.51-52.
40. S. Hall et al., *Policing the Crisis*, p.221, quoted by Bottomley and Coleman, ch. 3.
41. M. Kettle, 'The Keepers of the Queen's Peace', *New Society*, 25 March 1982, p.473.
42. Ibid.

PART 1:

LAW AND ORDER IN PERSPECTIVE

2 The Law and Order Debate in Historical Perspective

By David Dixon and Elaine Fishwick

Introduction

This chapter seeks to challenge the uses made of history and the past in recent British debates about 'law and order'. Explicit or (more often) implicit in much talk about 'law and order' is a sweeping chronology which suggests that in the mid- to late-nineteenth century a previously tumultuous society was pacified in the 'conquest of violence'.[1] This installed a period of social harmony and stability which endured until the 1960s. Since then, Britain has become increasingly violent, disorderly and ungovernable. This history of a decline from civility which provides the explanatory coherence within prevalent views of 'law and order' is fundamentally and dangerously inaccurate. It misunderstands and misrepresents some crucial features of recent British history; consequently, it has implications for policies on 'law and order' which, at best, will be diversionary.

A general reinterpretation of modern British history is well beyond the scope of this brief chapter. Instead, two central components of recent 'law and order' debates have been chosen for closer examination because of their significance in interpretations of and reactions to the 1980-81 urban disorders. These are, firstly, a tangled thicket of myth and fiction about the part which 'traditional British policing' played in creating and sustaining the period of social order which is now regarded wistfully as Britain's 'peaceful past'; and, secondly, myths about the supposedly recent emergence of racial violence and disorder.

In presenting this historical revision, we are not suggesting that nothing ever changes, that the past and the present are identical. Rather, our intention is to reinstate important continuities which are too often ignored: the slowness of some historical change, the durability of social conflicts (political, sexual, racial), and the continuing reproduction of fundamental inequalities and disadvantage in which disorder is rooted.[2]

Dominant British culture is saturated with mythical images of the past. An obvious but important example is the constant reference in television drama to the decades before the First World War as a period characterised by order, stability, community and national cohesion.[3] Such myths have kept their hold on 'popular memory'[4] because of a remarkable historical amnesia, the persistent and insidious lack of a real sense of history in this country's dominant culture. There are a few fixed points such as the wars, but beyond that the past is little more than a few jumbled exciting events and personalities: there is, as Hoggart observed, 'little idea of an historical or ideological pattern or process'.[5] Of course, he was referring here to the working class, but his analysis is of more general cultural relevance. Hoggart argued that this ahistorical culture was the product of an ideology of progressivism with roots in the nineteenth century. Economic decline and social dislocation have undermined the faith in progress: it is no longer widely believed that the future will inevitably be better than the past. While the image of the future has been tarnished, there is no authentic sense of the past to which people can turn. A society without a sense of its own history is prey to being misled and exploited:

> The people of such a society may lack the will and knowledge to challenge statements about contemporary issues which are given apparent authority and indisputability by being cast in what purports to be a 'true' historical framework.[6]

Reasons for such historical amnesia are not hard to find. An ex-imperialist country has a great deal about its past which it is more comfortable to forget. Popular knowledge about the history of the Empire is negligible; the significance of this for racism in Britain can hardly be overstated. Secondly, British liberal democracy misrepresents its own history: a political ideology which insists on gradualism, evolution and all the other characteristics of constitutionalism finds inconvenient, and therefore forgets, the realities of conflict, struggle, violence and resistance out of which liberal democracy was born.

The deficiencies in this view of the past lead to a willingness to accept easy explanations and scapegoats for Britain's problems. Crime is particularly useful both as a comprehensible signifier of the breakdown of law and order onto which more complex, abstract fears and anxieties can be unloaded and as its explanation: public disorder can be discounted or 'tackled' as mere criminality.[7] Crime and disorder are supremely well-fitted to become the subject of the 'moral panics' discussed by Bottomley and Coleman (Chapter 3). As they point out, one of the weaknesses of the original sociological discussion of moral panics was its ahistorical approach. Pearson has shown that far from appearing merely 'now and then', moral panics about young working class males have repeatedly appeared in Britain. He traces a history of 'respectable fears' which consistently and unfavourably compare the present with an earlier generation:

> In these successive waves of anxiety about sudden upsurges in crime and violence, each pointing back to a previously untroubled era, we appear to glimpse a series of 'golden ages' nestling inside each other like a set of Russian dolls.[8]

Moral panics about crime and disorder are expressions of a more general concern about Britain's condition which has produced a plethora of studies in recent years claiming that Britain is 'In Decline', 'In Agony' or 'Against Itself'. An appropriate reaction comes from A.J.P. Taylor: 'All this talk about the decline of civilisation means only that university professors used to have domestic servants and now do their own washing up.'[9]

Our intention is not to deny that disorder, violence and crime are widespread. Quite the contrary: they are much *more* prevalent than standard accounts allow. In the following sections, we only spotlight a few aspects of disorder which are particularly relevant to recent 'law and order' debates. Many other types of disorder could have been chosen, such as that connected with leisure — for example, the racecourse disturbances of the 1920s, the results of the policing of black communities' clubs and meeting places, or the perennial disorder at football matches and seaside resorts. The point is that moral panics do not necessarily correspond to real increases in disorder, criminal activity or even recorded crime rates.[10] Nevertheless, they do have real social consequences, as the example of the 'mugging' panic discussed by Bottomley and Coleman exemplifies. Misuse of history and the past has vital policy implications: the clearest example is the 'community policing' debate in which so much time is spent discussing and planning the recreation of a police-community relationship which, as we will argue below, is largely an historical fiction. Such historical myths are dangerous because they obstruct a realistic approach to police and law reform. In addition, they have significant political implications. While invocation of historical myth is common across the political spectrum,[11] it is a particularly important feature of British neoconservatism.

Restoration of the standards of morality, discipline and respect for authority (which had allegedly been lost during the years of social democracy and 'permissiveness') is at the very heart of what Hall has described as 'authoritarian populism'.[12] Structural problems of economy and society are shifted onto ground where they can be dispelled by nostrums about 'law and order', the nation and Victorian values. There is no refuge from reality in a mythical past. It is evidence of a society in deep trouble when its dominant political force chooses to face the future by constructing and feeding off a series of myths about its history. As Ignatieff warns:

> This longing to return to a past when 'authority' was 'respected' only takes us one small step closer to the 'law and order' state. Against this use of the past, the historically minded can plausibly object.[13]

Public order and police—community relations

> During the weekend of 10-12 April . . . the British people watched with horror and incredulity an instant audio-visual presentation on their television sets of scenes of violence and disorder in their capital city, the like of which had not previously been seen in this century in Britain.[14]

According to many participants in the debates about the 1980-81 'riots', they were a direct challenge to the British way of life and an indication of the extent to which society had become increasingly disorderly and degenerate. This decline of civility was said to have manifested itself specifically in the deterioration of attitudes towards the police.[15] The exceptional nature of the 1980-81 events was frequently stressed[16], as was the alleged tradition of Britain as a peace-loving, homogeneous society. These interpretations of British history are our major concern, in particular the claims that such outbursts of disorder have never been seen before in this century and that at the heart of the problem is the deterioration of police-community relations.

By concentrating on the tensions and conflicts that have been a continuing characteristic of police-community relations, we do not intend to imply that all aspects of policing have been repressive and conspiratorial, but rather that a complex and often contradictory interweaving of experience and attitudes has determined that relationship.

The accounts of British history portraying a continuum of consensus argue that the disorderly and often violent society of the late eighteenth and early nineteenth centuries was transformed in the mid-Victorian period. Police historians, such as Charles Reith[17], claim that at the forefront of the growth of democracy and the 'conquest of violence' were the New Police. As Stuart Hall has pointed out,[18] this view of the leadership role of the police has been accepted as a 'commonsense' account amongst senior police officers:

> History shows us that before 1829 radicals and reformers were ruthlessly crushed by the army, the Establishment and big business interests. It is a fact that the 1829 creation of Sir Robert Peel's police service put an end to that repression. The police rigorously enforced the laws of the land. The Trade Union and Labour movements were given the freedom to grow and prosper.[19]

In such accounts, the part which the New Police played in preparing the way for democracy is presented as instrumental in their success in securing the consent of the public as a whole. In turn, that consent is regarded as the very basis of 'traditional British policing'.

A more realistic approach would show that, far from disappearing in mid-century, disorder permeated the late Victorian and Edwardian periods reaching peaks in the late 1880s and the years immediately before the First World War.[20] The end of the war saw major outbreaks of disorder of various kinds; in 1919 the Government's reaction was epitomised by the deployment of military and even naval power.[21]

However, an example deserving particular attention, because of contemporary references to them, are the inter war years of the Depression. The general recession and high rates of unemployment have prompted politicians to draw comparisons between the inter war period and the present day. One of Mrs Thatcher's reactions to the 1981 disorders was: 'we had much higher unemployment in the 1930s, but we didn't get this in any way.'[22] Similarly Norman Tebbit has told us that 'when his father was out of work he didn't riot but got on his bike and looked for work'.[23] Such comments overlook the considerable extent of disorder in this period which has been accepted even by revisionist historians who, in their attempts to argue that the 1930s have been misrepresented as the 'Devil's Decade', seek to play down the significance of this disorder.[24]

For some people the 1930s *were* years of wealth and plenty, while for others they were years of profound hardship and struggle. The message of Mrs Thatcher and Norman Tebbit is that such hardship which did exist was 'manfully' borne and that 'we had it rough but we were happy'. This message is supported by the images of the 1920s and 1930s which inform the collective memory. The famous football match between the police and strikers during the General Strike and the stolid dignity of the Jarrow 'Crusade' are persistently summoned up to represent the spirit of the times. Yet, far from being typical, these incidents were exceptions. Police conduct during the General Strike did little for the Force's image, and indeed left widespread bitterness and resentment: 'It is of course, a fable that there was no violence during the General Strike.'[25] The relationship between the police and public did not improve in the 1930s:

> Throughout these years (1929-1936), relations between the unemployed movement and the police were always strained. Glasgow, Manchester, Merseyside and especially London were all at various times the scenes of veritable 'battles' between unemployed demonstrators and the authorities: baton charges by the police were resisted by stone throwing on the part of the unemployed. Over the years, hundreds of arrests were made by the police and, in 1932, two men died from bullet wounds in Belfast when police opened fire on demonstrators.[26]

Further sources of serious disorder in this period were the activities of the British Union of Fascists and the ensuing conflicts between blackshirts, the police and antifascist demonstrators. The claims that recent concern about police powers and accountability is unprecedented overlook very similar expressions of concern about the police (and particularly the Metropolitan Police) in the 1930s. A notable product of this was the National Council for Civil Liberties, established in 1934 to monitor the policing of demonstrations.[27] It is no coincidence that so much of the modern law of public order derives from decisions made by Parliament and the courts in this period.[28] All this hardly justifies the presentation of the 1920s and 1930s as years of social harmony and tranquility.

Despite the fact that the Jarrow 'Crusade' was far from the largest or the most significant march, it remains as the dominant image of the 1930s. The reasons why it has received a disproportionate amount of attention link up with the broader question of why it is that only particular features of the period are retained in popular memory. There has been, and continues to be, a double repression of the past. During the turbulent years of the early 1930s, newspapers and newsreel companies cooperated with the Government by imposing self-censorship.[29] The BBC even offered to warn people away from the NUWM marches. However, since the Jarrow march emphasised its political respectability, by for example denying a platform to Communist speakers, it was filmed by Movietone News and was thereby immortalised. Both at the time and since, information and access to official records have been controlled.[30] This lack of information both contributes to and legitimises the way in which inconvenient aspects of 'our British heritage' are forgotten and ignored.

'Law and order' lobbyists are able to accentuate the allegedly pathological nature of recent public disorder by claiming the lack of precedents. Various explanations of disorder are proposed: inevitably among them are black immigration, political agitation and mindless hooliganism. Surprising mistakes are made even about recent history, as when Brixton 1981 rather than Bristol 1980 is commonly identified as the first of the recent disturbances.[31] These brief pathological biographies of the causes of disorder ensure that necessary, long term, remedies for the structural problems underlying the 'riots' are over-ridden in favour of short term solutions.[32] The Scarman Report did address itself to some of these deeper social issues (although the analysis was limited by e.g. the misunderstanding of institutional racism) but the proposals in this area have received much less attention than the discussion of policing.

Across the political spectrum, changes in policing have been regarded as the appropriate site in which to search for remedies to disorder. The dominant theme has been the wish to recreate the police-community relations of 'days gone by'. Its product is an intensification of the community policing debate. However, it is also responsible for legitimating extensions of both the police's legal powers and their riot control capability: these can be justified as necessary contingency measures until the ideal police-community relationship is 'restored'.

These references to an earlier and better age of police-community relations require critical examination. It is argued by traditional police historians[33] that the well known initial hostility towards the New Police soon disappeared other than among the 'criminal classes' and that the ideal of police-community relations to which contemporary debates so often refer was established in the mid-nineteenth century. However, the history of police-community relations has been more complicated than such writers allow. Opposition to the police, ranging from derisive comments to physical attacks persisted throughout the nineteenth century.[34] As a new school of police historians has shown,[35] the decline in opposition to the police was largely restricted to the middle classes whose concern about the growth of state power was allayed as they appreciated the benefits of the policing of working class areas. As the original mandate of the police was to regulate working class leisure and to enforce new standards of morality as well as to contain crime, it is hardly surprising that some sections of the public were rather more grudging in their acceptance of them. Opposition among the working class did not disappear, although it did come to be expressed in different ways:

> Moderation in the frequency of large scale anti-police
> eruptions in no way signified that the authorities had

27

succeeded in obtaining the full moral assent of the community . . . they were still regarded as unwelcome intruders in working-class neighborhoods, and were informed of the fact with some frequency.[36]

Storch argues convincingly that the decline in violence towards the police in the later nineteenth century was as much the result of general social changes as of any great improvement in police-community relations.

While it would be misleading to suggest that working class opposition to the police was total or undifferentiated, Roberts expressed a strain of antagonism which continued into this century:

Nobody in our Northern slum . . . ever spoke in fond regard . . . of the policeman as 'social worker' and 'handyman of the streets'. Like their children, delinquent or not, the poor in general looked upon him with fear and dislike . . . The 'public' (meaning the middle and upper classes), we know well enough, held their 'bobby' in patronising 'affection and esteem', which he repaid with due respectfulness; but these sentiments were never shared by the undermass, nor in fact by the working class generally.[37]

Working class autobiographies and oral histories[38] demonstrate that the police were only reluctantly accepted after a protracted and bitter struggle which resulted in 'a tentative, negotiated, truce'.[39] Resignation to the inevitability of the police presence was negotiated through the construction of an understanding of the limits to which they could penetrate into working class districts, and of the extent to which they could enforce particular laws.[40] This tenuous hold on public acceptance was inherently unstable even through what are generally considered to be periods of national harmony, such as the war years and the 1950s.[41]

Some sections of the population continued to experience the imposition of outside standards, heavy handed control of strikes and demonstrations and the maltreatment of individuals. However, they also received real benefits from the expansion of police work: the broad service aspects of policing[42] served in part to counter balance the continuing mistrust of the police. Further, the strength of particular ideologies of policing have produced a widespread ambivalence in attitudes to the police:

Public perception of the police varies by class, within the classes, over time, and within the same individual's image of the police in the abstract and in practice. Ordinary everyday 'common-sense' views of the police are therefore a medley of contradictions — constantly adapting new experiences to past images.[43]

This is an example of the general complexity of the relationship between dominant and subordinate cultures.[44] Abstract images of the police find expression in popular cliches about them being 'the best in the world' and 'the thin blue line between civilisation and anarchy' which do not necessarily coincide with popular experience of actual contact with the police.

Two examples illustrate these points. Firstly, presentation by the media of particular images of policing reinforce dominant values. Just as the under-reporting of the tensions and conflicts of the 1930s resulted in a partial account of policing, so in more recent times, television drama series have been purposively used to transmit various interpretations of the police role.[45] Secondly, opinion polls and surveys on public attitudes to the police have demonstrated the impact of dominant ideologies by consistently producing results which suggest that the police have (at least until recently) enjoyed the wholehearted support and consent of the public. Their crucial methodological weaknesses have obscured the ambivalence of popular attitudes.[46]

This section has shown the problems of uncritical and inaccurate references to the past in contemporary debates on 'law and order'. Only when the conjoint histories of public disorder and of police-public relations are discussed realistically will relevant and effective reform become possible.

Racial violence and disorder

After various initial attempts to dismiss the 1980-81 disorders as 'mere criminality' or the work of political agitators, commentators became virtually unanimous in pointing to the significance of race; although, of course, their interpretations of that significance varied. Indeed, race has been used to make sense of the whole 'law and order crisis' of the 1970s and 1980s.[47] Central explanatory elements in accounts of Britain's decline from social tranquility are postwar black immigration and the consequential undermining of cultural homogeneity. This has become so well established that references to race no longer need to be explicit for the message to be clear.[48] Black immigration is used to explain change and decline: by implication, violence and disorder connected with race are presented as new phenomena.

Historical distortion and error abound in such accounts. They reflect a general ignorance in Britain about the imperial past and consequently about the essential continuity of black-white relations overseas and in Britain. As Hall argues:

> The development of an indigenous British racism in the
> postwar period *begins* with the profound historical
> forgetfulness — . . . a decisive mental repression — which
> has overtaken the British people about race and Empire since
> the 1950s.[49]

Just as general assertions about British racial homogeneity can be
shown to be inaccurate,[50] the myth that black people first came to
Britain after the Second World War is being dispelled by the historical
rediscovery of black communities in Britain dating back to the sixteenth
century. Walvin's work is particularly valuable in showing that racist
reaction is one of the 'elements of continuity in black history in England
(which) are more striking than the historical breaks and more
significant than the distinctions marking off one generation from
another'.[51] It has been shown that the early black communities, like
other ethnic minorities including the Jews, the Irish and the Gypsies,
faced violence very similar to that of more recent years.[52] One of
Britain's crueller self-deceptions has been to treat disturbances and
disorder as an 'alien interruption of violence into (its) domestic affairs'
and 'as a break with tradition' when 'perhaps they are more usefully
understood as tradition itself'.[53] To illustrate this, the standard
chronology of the relationship between racial violence and public
disorder in this century needs to be examined in more detail. The point
to be made here is that neither individual racial violence nor larger scale
disorder with racial elements began during the period of postwar black
immigration: consequently, the 1980-81 disorders must be seen as only
one episode in a much longer history.

In the standard accounts, racial violence begins with the 1958 race
riots in Nottingham and London: '1958' is presented as a crucial
landmark in postwar social change.[54] It has attracted this attention for
two reasons: while one stresses and the other underplays the racial
significance of the disorders, both serve to 'externalise' the problems by
stressing that they were not products of 'true' British society.[55] Firstly,
they are explained as the result of excessive black immigration. The long
parliamentary consensus on immigration control was founded on the
belief that white British society is essentially tolerant and peaceful:
racial problems have sprung up because there have been too many black
immigrants to be 'assimilated' and because of perceived weaknesses in
black cultures and family structures. The black presence rather than
white racism is identified as the problem, and the inevitable remedy
advocated is a package of immigration and race relations legislation.
The 1958 riots played a key role in the production of this consensus and
provided a vital reference point for those who subsequently argued that
discriminatory immigration laws were indispensable for good

30

'community relations'. Secondly, the racial element is understated and the structural bases of racial violence ignored by claiming that black people were merely available targets for socially marginal, young deviants who were the products of 'affluence', a new type of adolescence and the influence of American culture. Racist violence is disconnected from society as a whole by categorising it as part of an essentially *new* youth problem, the work of 'rebellious youth in the welfare state'.[56]

In reality, '1958' was not nearly so significant a watershed as is normally claimed. The events of that year were perhaps larger scale, certainly more sensationally reported, examples of incidents which have occurred throughout this century ranging from cases of individual violence to major disorders. The incidence of individual racist violence has received some recent recognition: it is clear that it is an extreme example of the under-reporting and under-recording of crime discussed by Bottomley and Coleman.[57] Anything approaching a comprehensive history of racial violence and disorder remains to be written, but it is quite clear from the available evidence that there has been a long history of serious incidents: by implication, it is certain that one section of British society has never had a 'peaceful past'.

The only episode of pre-1958 racial violence which has attracted attention is the 1919 race riots in British ports, which involved several deaths.[58] The broader significance of these events is usually denied by marginalising them as the peculiar and unique problems of dockland or 'Sailortown' — universal phenomena without specific implications for race in Britain.[59] This has been encouraged by the attempts of the police and local authorities in Cardiff and Liverpool to forget these incidents and to propagate a complacent image of a peaceful and racially harmonious past.[60] This has amounted to a virtual 'conspiracy of silence', both about the past, and about continuing discrimination in policing practices, housing and employment.[61] This official amnesia is in stark contrast to the black communities' own view of the past. A succession of investigators have found that, for example, the Cardiff black communities did not forget 1919 or the subsequent discrimination: they were not forgotten because they formed part of a *continuing* history of racist violence and discrimination.[62]

This disparity between black experience and white society's perceptions had vital implications for more recent events. From the 1960s onwards, there were persistent warnings that increasingly serious conflict between black people and the police was going to boil over into major disorders. Official and unofficial reports and studies by journalists and academics consistently carried the same ominous message.[63] Nobody can have read such documents which charted the deepening crisis and still have been surprised by what happened in

1980-81: and yet, as the quotation at the beginning of the previous section shows, the Scarman Report could still begin with an account of public reactions to the Brixton disorders in exactly such terms. The complacency of some authorities before the 'riots' is now almost legendary: the Chief Constable of Merseyside reported only weeks before Liverpool 8 erupted that his Force's relationships 'with all sections of the community are in a very healthy state and I do not foresee any serious difficulties developing in the future'.[64] The consequence of such complacency was that little was done to avert the increasingly inevitable outbreak of major disorder. The police may have introduced community relations programmes: but the terms of such police-community contact were set unilaterally by the police, whose priority has been the management of legitimacy. It was low status police work and its marginal role was illustrated by the course of events in Southall in 1979 and in Brixton in 1978-81.[65] At least this shows that the police recognised the signs of trouble to some extent: but politicians did not and it is they, rather than the police, who must bear the primary responsibility for the 1980-81 disorders. Perhaps the worst effect of the myths discussed in this essay has been the consequences of the almost wilful misunderstanding of the real history of black people in Britain.

Conclusion

History shows us that, despite all the claims to the contrary, public disorder and law breaking are not new. Just as they have constantly recurred, so have similar reactions: expressions of fear and outrage, nostalgia for lost 'golden ages' and anxiety about the threatening future.[66] While conflict has been very much a part of the true British tradition, British society has nevertheless remained remarkably stable: the British state has an apparently limitless capacity for absorbing criticism, deflecting challenges and ignoring demands for reform. Part of the reason for this is that the worst *real* effects of crime and disorder are suffered by the very groups who are identified as their source and by those who lack the power to define what should be regarded as major social problems.[67] If these lessons are learnt, the way may be open for the origins of public disorder to be tackled. If they are not, then it is quite certain that conflict and disorder will continue to be permanent and characteristic features of the British way of life.

Notes

1. T.A. Critchley, *The Conquest of Violence: order and liberty in Britain* (Constable, 1970).
2. See G. Pearson, *Hooligan: a history of respectable fears* (Macmillan, 1983), part 4.
3. C. McArthur, *Television and History* (British Film Institute, 1978), p.40.
4. Centre for Contemporary Cultural Studies: *Making Histories* (Hutchinson, 1982), ch.6.
5. R. Hoggart, *The Uses of Literacy* (Penguin, 1958), pp.190-191.
6. J. Robottom, 'A history of violence', in N. Tutt, ed.: *Violence* (HMSO, 1976), p.40.
7. S. Hall et. al., *Policing the Crisis* (Macmillan, 1978), ch.6.
8. Op. cit., p.156.
9. Quoted in McArthur, op. cit., p.30. The references are to: A. Gamble, *Britain in Decline* (Macmillan, 1981); R. Clutterbuck, *Britain in Agony* (Penguin, 1980); S. Beer, *Britain Against Itself* (Faber and Faber, 1982).
10. Bottomley and Coleman, in this volume; Pearson, op. cit., pp.213-219; L. McDonald, 'Theory and evidence of rising crime in the nineteenth century' *British Journal of Sociology* 33 pp.404-420.
11. See criticism of recent 'socialist realism' for this by P. Gilroy, 'The myth of black criminality' *Socialist Register* (1982) pp.47-56 at p.53. See also the discussion of British political parties in this volume.
12. S. Hall, 'Popular-democratic vs authoritarian populism', in A. Hunt, ed., *Marxism and Democracy* (Lawrence and Wishart, 1980).
13. M. Ignatieff, 'Police and public: the birth of Mr. Peel's 'blue locusts'' *New Society* 30 August 1979 pp.443-445, at p.445.
14. *The Brixton Disorders, 10-12 April 1981:* Report of an Inquiry by the Rt. Hon. Lord Scarman (Cmnd. 8427) (HMSO, 1981).
15. Beer, op. cit., pp.217-218.
16. E.g. *The Times* 13 July 1981.
17. C. Reith, *British Police and the Democratic Ideal* (Oxford UP, 1943); T.A. Critchley, *A History of Police in England and Wales* (Constable, 1978). For analysis of these histories, see M. Brogden, *The Police: autonomy and consent* (Academic Press, 1982), ch.7; C.D. Robinson, 'Ideology as history' *Police Studies* 2 pp.35-49.
18. S. Hall, *Drifting into a Law and Order Society* (Cobden Trust, 1980) p.9.

19. D. McNee, 'Street riots', *Sunday Mirror* 31 October 1982.
20. V. Bailey, 'The Metropolitan Police, the Home Office and the threat of outcast London', in V. Bailey, ed., *Policing and Punishment in Nineteenth Century Britain* (Croom Helm, 1981); P. Addison, 'Winston Churchill and the working class 1900-1914', in J. Winter, (ed.), *The Working Class in Modern British History* (Cambridge UP, 1983), at pp.56-64; D. Smith, 'Tonypandy 1910' *Past and Present* 87 pp.158-184. For more general surveys, see S. Field and P. Southgate, *Public Disorder* (Home Office Research Study no. 72: 1982), at pp.4-5; F. Webber, 'Six centuries of revolt and repression', *Haldane Society Bulletin* 15 pp.6-9.
21. J. White, 'The summer riots of 1919', in New Society: *Race and Riots '81* (New Society, 1982).
22. Quoted in *The Times* 8 July 1981.
23. M. Kettle and L. Hodges, *Uprising* (Pan, 1982), p.167.
24. J. Stevenson and J. Cook, *The Slump* (Jonathan Cape, 1977), pp.190ff. Cf. C. Cockburn, *The Devil's Decade* (Sidgwick and Jackson, 1973).
25. C.L. Mowat, as quoted in Kettle and Hodges, op. cit., p.15. See C. Farman, *The General Strike: May 1926* (Hart-Davis, 1972), ch.12.
26. R. Hayburn, 'The police and the hunger marchers' *International Review of Social History* 17 pp.625-644, at p.627. See also: Cockburn, op. cit., p.64; A. Shallice, *Remember Birkenhead* (Merseyside Socialist Research Group, 1982); W. Gray et. al., *Unemployed Demonstrations: Salford and Manchester* (Working Class Movement Library, 1981); W. Hannington, *Unemployed Struggles 1919-1936* (Lawrence and Wishart, 1936).
27. See e.g. J. Curtis, *The Land of Liberty* (Secker and Warburg, 1938); W.H. Thompson, *Civil Liberties* (Gollancz, 1938); 'A Barrister': *Justice in England* (Gollancz, 1938). On the history of concern about the Metropolitan Police, see S. Bundred, 'Accountability and the Metropolitan Police', in D. Cowell et. al., eds., *Policing the Riots* (Junction Books, 1982), at pp.64-72. On the establishment of NCCL, see Cockburn, op. cit., p.78; P. Kingsford, *The Hunger Marchers in Britain 1920-1939* (Lawrence and Wishart, 1982) pp.192-193.
28. See S.H. Bailey et. al., *Civil Liberties* (Butterworths, 1980), ch.3.
29. Stevenson and Cook, op. cit., pp.222-223; J. Stevenson, 'The politics of violence', in G. Peele and C. Cook, eds., *The Politics of Reappraisal* (Macmillan, 1975), at p.149.
30. See e.g. the episode of the missing police files: R. Harrison, 'New light on the police and the hunger marchers' *Society for the Study*

of Labour History Bulletin 38 pp.17-49.

31. Beer, op. cit., pp.217-218, claims that the disturbances started in Liverpool in July 1981.
32. Kettle and Hodges, op. cit., ch.7.
33. See note 17 above.
34. R.D. Storch, "'The plague of the blue locusts': police reform and popular resistance in Northern England, 1840-1857" *International Review of Social History* 20 pp.61-90.
35. See Brogden, op. cit.; ibid., "'All police is conning bastards' — policing and the problem of consent", in B. Fryer et. al., eds., *Law, State and Society* (Croom Helm, 1981); P. Cohen, 'Policing the working class city', in NDC/CSE, eds., *Capitalism and the Rule of Law* (Hutchinson, 1979); Ignatieff, op. cit.; R.D. Storch, 'The policeman as domestic missionary' *Journal of Social History,* 9 pp.481-509.
36. Storch, op. cit. (1975), p.89. Cf. S. Reynolds et. al., *Seems So* (Macmillan, 1911), pp.85-86.
37. R. Roberts, *The Classic Slum* (Penguin, 1971), p.100.
38. E.g. R. Samuel, *East End Underworld* (RKP, 1981); Reynolds, op. cit.; Roberts, op. cit.; S. Humphries, *Hooligans or Rebels* (Basil Blackwell, 1981).
39. Brogden, op. cit. (1982), p.171; cf. Ignatieff, op. cit. p.444.
40. Samuel, op. cit.; Cohen, op. cit.
41. I. Taylor, *Law and Order* (Macmillan, 1981), p.67.
42. Brogden, op. cit. (1982), pp.206-219.
43. Brogden, op. cit. (1981), p.205.
44. M. Mann, 'The social cohesion of liberal democracy' *American Sociological Review* 35 pp.423-439.
45. A. Clarke, *Television Police Series and Law and Order* (Open University: Popular Culture: Block 5, Unit 22, 1982); cf. *Screen Education*, special issue on 'The Sweeney' no.20, 1976.
46. Brogden, op. cit. (1981), p.205.
47. J. Solomos et. al., 'The organic crisis of British capitalism and race', in Centre for Contemporary Cultural Studies: *The Empire Strikes Back* (Hutchinson, 1982), at pp.27-35; Hall et. al., op. cit., p.333 and *passim*.
48. Solomos et. al., op. cit., pp.31-33.
49. S. Hall, 'Racism and reaction', in Commission for Racial Equality: *Five Views of Multi-Racial Britain* (CRE, 1978), at p.25.
50. V.G. Kiernan, 'Britons old and new', in C. Holmes, ed., *Immigrants and Minorities in British History* (George Allen and Unwin, 1978), at p.23.
51. J. Walvin, *Black and White* (Allen Lane, 1973) p.217;

cf. A. Sivanandan, 'From resistance to rebellion' *Race and Class* 23 pp.111-152.

52. See K. Lunn ed., *Hosts, Immigrants and Minorities: historical responses to newcomers in British society* (Dawson, 1980); Humphries, op. cit., pp.192-200; R. Nugent and R. King, 'Ethnic minorities, scapegoating and the extreme right', in R. Miles and A. Phizacklea, eds., *Racism and Political Action in Britain* (RKP, 1979).

53. Pearson, op. cit., pp.209, 202.

54. E.g., A. Marwick, *British Society Since 1945* (Penguin, 1982), pp.166-167.

55. R. Miles, *The Riots of 1958* (Mimeo: Department of Sociology, Glasgow University, 1982); cf. J. Wickenden, *Colour Prejudice in Britain* (IRR/OUP, 1958).

56. This is the subtitle of T.R. Fyvel, *The Insecure Offenders* (Penguin, 1963). For his account of '1958', see pp.62-66. On concern about American influences, see Hall et. al., op. cit., p.21-28.

57. See F. Klug, *Racist Attacks* (Runnymede Trust, 1982); D. Hiro, *Black British, White British* (Monthly Review Press, 1973), pp.34,36-37.

58. N. Evans, 'The South Wales race riots of 1919' *Llafur* 3 pp.5-29; R. May and R. Cohen, 'The interaction between race and colonialism: a case study of the Liverpool race riots of 1919' *Race and Class* 16 pp.111-126; K. Little, *Negroes in Britain* (RKP, revised edition 1972), pp.57-60.

59. S. Hugill, *Sailortown* (RKP, 1967); A.D. Grimshaw, 'Factors contributing to colour violence in the U.S. and Britain' *Race* 3 pp.3-19.

60. Evans, op. cit., p.80; P. Scraton, 'Policing and institutionalized racism on Merseyside', in D. Cowell et. al., op. cit.; I. Law: *A History of Race and Racism in Liverpool* (Merseyside CRC, 1981).

61. D. Hiro, 'Three generations of Tiger Bay', *New Society* 21 September 1967 pp.385-387.

62. See L. Bloom's introduction to Little, op. cit., pp.23,26.

63. Scraton, op. cit., p.25. For examples, see *Report from the Select Committee on Race Relations and Immigration* (HC471:1972); *Final Report of the Working Party into Community/Police Relations in Lambeth* (1981); D. Humphry, *Police Power and Black People* (Panther, 1972); K. Pryce, *Endless Pressure* (Penguin, 1979). Finally, there was the unpublished 'Think Tank' report on Liverpool: see Kettle and Hodges, op. cit., p.157.

64. *Report of the Chief Constable to the Merseyside Police Committee for the year 1980* (May, 1981). See Scraton, op. cit. and A. and M. Brogden, 'Postscript: the Toxteth riots', in Brogden, op. cit. (1982), pp.238-250.
65. See *Southall 23 April 1979: Report of the Unofficial Committee of Enquiry* (NCCL: 1980); Kettle and Hodges, op. cit., pp.94-97. On police community programmes, see P. Gordon, *White Law* (Pluto, 1983) pp.60-64; J.M. Jones and J.T. Winkler, 'Beyond the beat' *Journal of Law and Society* 9 pp.103-114.
66. Pearson, op. cit., p.222.
67. Taylor, op. cit., ch.4.

3 Law and Order: Crime Problem, Moral Panic, or Penal Crisis?

By Keith Bottomley and Clive Coleman

Introduction

During the last decade, and especially since the run-up to the General Election of 1979, the theme of 'law and order' has come increasingly to the fore in public and political debate. The apparently straightforward idea that we have a problem of law and order gives way, on closer inspection, to the realisation that there are many different dimensions and interpretations of this theme in contemporary Britain. In this chapter we examine just three of these interpretations. The first is the widespread idea that we are experiencing problems of crime and disorder on a scale rarely seen before in our recent past. For anyone wishing to probe deeper into the validity of such claims and impressions, an obvious starting point must be a consideration of the evidence (for what it may be worth) of the official criminal statistics. This forms the first section of our chapter.

A second interpretation is that the concern with law and order is a 'moral panic', an unwarranted overreaction to the actual threat posed by crime and disorder. If such an interpretation can be sustained, to some extent at least, it raises important questions about the generation of social anxiety as a topic in its own right. In our third section we examine recent developments in penal policy and the penal system, which many have argued are in a state of crisis. Here we suggest that rising crime rates have not provided the only stimulus for the resurgence of more punitive 'law and order' responses. The three interpretations of the 'law and order' issue that we look at should not be regarded as mutually exclusive; instead the consideration of them together should lead to a recognition that there are complex reciprocal relationships between deviant behaviour and the various responses to it.

Law and order as a crime problem

Our analysis will focus primarily on the evidence from the last decade, but a brief review of trends in the official crime rate over a somewhat longer period will help to put it in perspective. The level of recorded crime since the beginning of this century starts at around 100,000 crimes recorded annually throughout the first two decades and rises to over 3 million at the present time. Since the 1920s, the picture has largely been one of steadily increasing crime rates each year, with only a relatively short period immediately after the Second World War (1945-54) showing an apparent stabilisation of the crime figures. Writing in the late 1960s, McClintock and Avison summarised the findings of their authoritative survey of crime in England and Wales as follows:

> . . . although clearly there have been fundamental political, social, economic and technological changes during the course of this century, the annual growth of recorded crime from the First World War onwards has been remarkably constant, accelerating from 5 per cent per annum in the 1920s to 10 per cent per annum in the 1960s. Such a long-term trend indicates the need for a cautious approach when considering general expectations based merely on recent social changes or economic conditions . . .[1]

It is important to note that the rate of increase between 1955 and 1965 (at an average of 10 per cent each year) was higher than ever before this century, including the period of social and economic upheaval in the 1930s. However, since McClintock and Avison completed their study, the trends in the official crime rate have been much less stable, with the overall rate of increase in crime declining significantly in comparison with the era of affluence and 'never had it so good' of the late 1950s and 1960s.

Between 1970-1980 the number of recorded crimes increased from approximately 1½ million to 2½ million. This represents a 60 per cent increase during the eleven year period, but with an average annual rate of increase of around 5 per cent, which is half that experienced during the late 1950s and the 1960s.[2] This average conceals fluctuations from year to year of a more unusual kind. For example, the figures for 1973 showed a *decrease* of 2 per cent on the previous year and, similarly, in

1978 the number of crimes recorded by the police was 2.7 per cent below 1977, followed by figures for 1979 which were almost 1 per cent lower again than 1978. So although the middle years of the decade, 1974-77, showed an annual average increase of around 10 per cent, in the years immediately before and after decreases were in fact recorded — making any sensible interpretation of crime trends in the 1970s more hazardous than usual.

Interpreting criminal statistics, particularly under the umbrella of 'law and order', is not simply a question of numbers — where one recorded crime is equally significant as any other — but it also involves the question of the nature of the different crimes that comprise the total. There tends to be an understandable stress on those crimes that are seen as posing direct threats against the person — especially violence and sexual offences — together with crimes such as vandalism. In the period 1970-80 (which, as seen above, witnessed an overall increase in the crime rate of 60 per cent) the statistics recorded increases in 'violence against the person' and robbery which were well above average, namely 136 per cent and 138 per cent respectively, and an increase in 'criminal damage' (the nearest legal equivalent to the popular concept of 'vandalism') of 970 per cent! In the face of such statistics, two points ought to be made by way of qualification. Firstly, when all the offences of violence against the person and robbery are added together (for 1980) they constitute only *4 per cent* of the total recorded crime rate. Secondly, within the overall category of violence against the person, the Home Office distinguish between the 'more serious' and the 'less serious'. In the period we are examining the more serious offences increased by less than one third (32 per cent), whereas the *less serious* offences increased by 143 per cent, so that in 1980 only 6 per cent of all offences of violence were in the 'more serious' category compared to 11 per cent in 1970.

The number of recorded sexual offences actually *decreased* by 13 per cent between 1970 and 1980, but the relatively small number of recorded rapes *increased* by almost a third, from 884 (in 1970) to 1,170 (in 1980) — still, obviously, far from reflecting the number of rapes that are actually committed each year throughout the country.

We can also analyse the seriousness of property crimes such as burglary and theft, which increased by 44 per cent and 54 per cent respectively between 1970-1980. In burglaries, for instance, during 1980 nothing was stolen in 23 per cent of cases; the value of stolen property was less than £25 in 22 per cent of cases, with a further 21 per cent of cases in which the value was under £100. Similarly, in the large category of offences of theft (dominated by thefts of and from motor vehicles, and shoplifting) in 1980, the value of property stolen in 40 per cent of all cases was less than £25 and more than £25 but less than £100 in a further 25 per cent.[3]

It should perhaps be noted at this point that all our analyses so far, like the official crime rates themselves, are based on what used to be called indictable offences. Reference is rarely made in these discussions to the large number of motoring offences and non-indictable or summary offences, many of which are arguably just as serious and certainly represent major social and economic costs to the community and the administration of justice. Partly because of the circumstances of the commission and discovery of such offences, no record is submitted to the Home Office by the police unless a person is proceeded against. In 1980, 1½ million persons were so proceeded against, of whom three-quarters were involved in motoring offences. There was a 13 per cent increase in the period 1970-1980, and 45 per cent increase since 1960, when just over 1 million persons were proceeded against for motoring and other summary offences. It is perhaps a significant comment on contemporary social and political values that numbers and trends of this sort are not the stuff of which campaigns for 'law and order' are made.

The difference in the way indictable or 'serious' *offences* are processed by the police and the Home Office, compared with the process for recording motoring and other summary *offenders*, highlights two further questions surrounding the meaningful interpretation of official information on crime and criminals: (i) What proportion of the 'serious' crimes actually committed in the community become known to the police and are recorded by them to constitute the official crime rate? (ii) What can usefully be said about the personal characteristics of offenders when only a minority of recorded crimes are cleared up by the police and the identity of those responsible established?

The existence of the so-called 'dark figure' of unrecorded crime has been recognised by criminologists and social statisticians since the early part of the nineteenth century. Whatever was believed about the absolute size of this 'dark figure', its significance for the interpretation of crime trends was minimised by making the (unwarranted) assumption that the *proportion* of all crimes that is hidden from official view remains constant, so that any increase in the known crime rate is assumed to reflect a similar increase in crimes committed. What is now becoming clear, however, as a result of research surveys in America and other countries (including, quite recently Britain) is that the number of unrecorded crimes is many times greater than the recorded crime rate, and that, for a variety of reasons, changes are taking place in the extent to which victims and witnesses of certain crimes report them to the police. As the vast majority of crimes recorded by the police become known to them through the direct initiative of victims and other members of the public, rather than through independent discovery by the police themselves, any such changes in crime reporting behaviour are of crucial significance for the production and interpretation of official crime rates. The Home Office has acknowledged this:

> It seems likely . . . that the proportion of all offences committed which are reported to and recorded by the police varies, as in certain other countries, according to a number of factors such as the type, circumstances and severity of the offence, whether or not a suspect is known and, if so, the relationship with the victim, social attitudes to the offence and insurance claim requirements . . . The propensity to report offences to the police could change over time and be influenced by changes in legislation, e.g. changes in the law to protect the anonymity of rape victims in reports of court proceedings, so that trends in serious offences recorded by the police may not reflect the trends in the total numbers of crimes committed.[4]

Surveys of crime victimisation carried out in the United States have shown that even in many apparently very serious crimes, more victims decide not to report them to the police than do. In Britain, a similar study carried out in London during the 1970s by Richard Sparks and his colleagues revealed the startling fact that more than ten times as many crimes were being committed in the boroughs of Brixton, Hackney and Kensington, than the numbers recorded in police statistics for the same areas.[5] The researchers concluded:

> . . . for every type of crime, in all three areas, the numbers estimated on the basis of our survey data are very substantially in excess of the numbers recorded by the police: for all types of offence . . . the ratio of survey — estimated to recorded crime is no less than 11.1 to 1. The ratio is less in the case of burglaries — for the sample as a whole it is 4.2 to 1 — but in the case of offences against the person (assaults, robbery and theft from the person combined), and of other thefts, the disparity between the two sets of figures is enormous by any criterion (about 22:1 and 48:1 respectively).[6]

In 1982 the Home Office embarked upon the first nationwide crime victimisation survey, which should produce interesting data to compare with the official statistics.[7] Some idea of the potential value of regular national surveys of this kind can be gauged, in a small way, from a brief report in the 1980 volume of *Criminal Statistics* of the findings of a question about burglary and theft from dwellings included in the

General Household Survey in four separate years: viz. 1972, 1973, 1979 and 1980. From the replies of the 10,000 households sampled it appeared that the number of such offences remained fairly constantly at around ½ million each year, from 1972 right through to 1980; official statistics, on the other hand, indicated an annual average increase of about 4 per cent throughout the same period, with the number increasing from 239,000 at the time of the 1972-73 surveys to about 307,000 in 1979-80, suggesting that 'the recorded increase for these offences appeared to be largely due to an increase in the proportion of such crimes that were reported and subsequently recorded by the police, rather than due to any actual increase in the number being committed.'[8]

The perceived seriousness of a crime is obviously a significant factor in determining whether or not it is likely to be reported. However, there are other equally important and often more subtle factors influencing public behaviour in this respect. Such factors include the level of personal or community 'tolerance' for certain kinds of illegal behaviour, so that an increase in certain recorded crimes could be a sign of a decreasing tolerance of that behaviour on the part of those primarily affected by it. Moreover, to the extent that the relevant public gain an increased confidence in the law enforcement agencies and have ready access to them, with few deterrents to reporting crime, to that extent will an augmented, more efficient and sympathetic police force be likely to *create a crime wave* of tidal proportions!

When we turn, finally, to the question of the characteristics of known offenders, systematic information is restricted for the most part not only and quite obviously to crimes known to the police, but only to those persons deemed responsible for a minority of these recorded crimes. In 1980, only 40 per cent of recorded crimes were 'cleared-up'[9] by the police, and indeed for most of the period since the Second World War the clear-up rate has been within the range of 40-45 per cent. There is considerable variation between offences, so that whereas for offences of burglary and robbery only 3 out of every 10 are cleared up, for offences of violence against the person and sexual offences the clear-up rate has always remained at the much higher level of 75-80 per cent. For some crimes (such as shoplifting, handling stolen goods, and certain frauds) the 'clear-up rate' is particularly meaningless because so often the reporting and recording of such offences occur simultaneously with the discovery of the offender.

Having noted these variations and idiosyncracies, the important general point remains that most official statements about the age and sex of contemporary offenders are based on a relatively small and quite probably very unrepresentative sample of known offenders. The Metropolitan Police Force, which is very prone to publicise the extent to which crimes in London are committed by young, male (black?)

offenders, is particularly guilty of this abuse of statistics as the clear-up rate for 'serious offences' in London is well below the national average, and currently (1981) stands at just 17 per cent.[10]

The main attempts to remedy our very serious lack of knowledge about the characteristics of offenders 'at large' have been 'self-report' delinquency studies, which seek to elicit reliable information about the extent of the 'hidden' delinquencies of those surveyed. Despite the extent and considerable sophistication of much of this research[11] it has been mainly directed at juveniles who admit to frequent and varied delinquent activities, more or less irrespective of social class, intelligence, and so on. Hardly any studies have been undertaken using random samples of adult populations. So, for the time being, we are left to speculate on the characteristics of most of the criminals in our midst, with the official information at our disposal more likely to confirm existing stereotypes than to question their validity.

Moral panics and law and order campaigns

In the previous section we have attempted to qualify some of the anxieties about the growth of crime and disorder by the use of the official (and some unofficial) crime statistics collected in recent years. But diffuse social anxieties about such themes as law and order are rarely, if ever, simple responses to published statistics. Nor are they necessarily a reflection of personal or group experience. A survey of public opinion polls over a fifteen year period on law and order issues suggests that:

> Most peoples' involvement with the criminal law is not a matter of personal experience . . . Evidently, however, you don't have to have experienced the gunfire to be concerned about the battle . . . From Gallup polls over the last 15 years, the trend of increased public concern over law and order is unmistakable.[12]

The same article reveals some interesting variations. Serious concern about crimes of violence was already high in 1965, but has increased further since that date; concern about juvenile delinquency increased steadily from 1965 to 1977, but had fallen back by 1979; anxiety about rape increased considerably in the mid and late 1970s. Finally, public concern about drugtaking, and organised crime, peaked in 1969 (the former quite dramatically) but appears to have receded since.

A number of sociologists have argued that such social anxieties about particular kinds of crime, and about law and order in general, cannot be fully understood without reference to processes located in the wider economic, political and social context. In this respect it is useful to examine the notion of the 'moral panic', and some recent work on the thesis that the 1970s saw Britain drifting gradually into a 'law and order society'.

Stanley Cohen describes a 'moral panic' in the following terms:

> Societies appear to be subject, every now and then, to periods of moral panic. A condition, episode, person or group of persons emerges to become defined as a threat to societal values and interests; its nature is presented in a stylized and stereotypical fashion by the mass media; the moral barricades are manned by editors, bishops, politicians and other right-thinking people; socially accredited experts pronounce their diagnoses and solutions; ways of coping are evolved or (more often) resorted to; the condition then disappears, submerges or deteriorates and becomes more visible . . . sometimes the panic passes over and is forgotten, except in folklore and collective memory; at other times it has more serious and long-lasting repercussions and might produce such changes as those in legal and social policy or even in the way the society conceives itself.[13]

Although Cohen's book involves a detailed case study of the social reaction to the Mods and Rockers in 1964, he clearly sees the applicability of such an analysis to groups such as the Hells Angels, Skinheads, Hippies, drug abusers, student militants, political demonstrators, football hooligans, and vandals. It is also clear that although such panics can be examined in the 1960s as more or less discrete social phenomena, most commonly they shared a concern over the behaviour of *youth*. In this period also, a key role in the generation of moral panics is given to local 'right-thinking people', often referred to as 'moral entrepreneurs', and ultimately, most crucially, to the mass media. Although the novelty implicit in such ideas was initially seductive, there was always a danger that the necessary qualifications and limitations would be neglected. Cohen himself has since admitted that his 'attempt to suggest why moral panics occur, not just "now and then" but at particular times and in particular forms, hardly gave much basis for further generalization'.[14] The importance of such studies is that they sensitise us to the processes and agencies which can contribute to widely held notions about 'lawlessness', 'disorder' and particular forms of deviant behaviour or dissent (the prevailing definition of behaviour into either of these categories can, of course, be crucial). Furthermore it is also suggested in such studies that those same processes *may* have *real* consequences for the forms of deviance in question. For example, one does not have to accept all the details of

Young's study of drug use to recognise the role of misperception, often disseminated by the mass media, in the formulation of policy and public attitudes towards drugs in Britain in the period 1965-1971.[15] It is also pertinent that although the late 1960s and very early 1970s exhibited all the features of a 'moral panic' about drug use and addiction, that particular cluster of anxieties seems to have subsided since, in spite of the fact that the number of *registered addicts* has shown substantial increases during the late 1970s to a figure well in excess of that at the height of the 'moral panic'. The point need hardly be made that there is no simple relationship between 'public anxiety' about such issues and the 'official' indicators of the size and nature of 'the problem'.

A good deal has been written since the original applications of the 'moral panic' idea in attempting to look at the agency attributed a pivotal position in their promotion — the mass media.[16] A common theme in such work is that in spite of important differences both within and between different news sources, the media appear to operate in an ideological capacity, shaping and reflecting a consensual view of the society. For some that 'consensual view' bears the heavy imprint of the 'primary definers' — accredited representatives of major social institutions[17] so that such agencies are able to establish an initial definition of a topic which will set the agenda for all subsequent discussion; and 'The media thus tend . . . to reproduce symbolically the existing structure of power in society's institutional order'.[18]

Some critics are not convinced by this kind of interpretation of the nature and functions of media presentations. Anderson and Sharrock[19] argue that media presentations are amenable to other equally plausible readings than the one suggested by the media scholars as an exclusive and consistent standpoint.[20] A further criticism is that '"The reader" does not make many appearances in the media literature as anything other than a passive dope'.[21] Unless we assume that readers and viewers are like empty receptacles into which media messages are poured, it is doubtful whether we can see the media as mechanistically producing and reproducing dominant ideologies among the public in relation to crime, the nature of society or anything else. An important point here is to establish whether, and why, certain groups in the population are receptive to particular interpretations of the nature of deviance and crime. As we show below, this is something that Hall et al.[22] attempt to do.

Neither of these criticisms appears to be one that completely silences. It still seems reasonable to suggest that the 'primary definers' such as the police and judiciary have a special relationship with the mass media. As a result the 'primary definers' and the media:

Are active in defining situations, in selecting targets, in

initiating 'campaigns', in structuring these campaigns, in selectively signifying their actions to the public at large, in legitimating their actions through the accounts of situations which they produce. They do not simply respond to 'moral panics'. They form part of the circle out of which 'moral panics' develop.[23]

The moral panic itself is seen as a mechanism by which an increase in the control exercised by the state can be seen as legitimate:

> To put it crudely, the 'moral panic' appears to us to be one of the principal forms of ideological consciousness by means of which a 'silent majority' is won over to the support of increasingly coercive measures on the part of the state, and lends its legitimacy to a 'more than usual' exercise of control.[24]

While these authors can discern a succession of separable moral panics concerning social and moral issues (especially 'youth' and 'permissiveness') during the early 1960s, they suggest that there has been a gradual change occurring since:

> In what we think of as the middle period, in the later 1960s, these panics follow faster on the heels of one another than earlier; and an increasingly amplified general 'threat to society' is imputed to them (drugs, hippies, the underground, pornography, long-haired students, layabouts, vandalism, football hooliganism).[25]

It is suggested that in the third stage, the moral panics have coalesced into a general panic about social order — a wide ranging, broadly based law and order campaign seen first in Britain in that produced by Mr. Heath's Shadow Cabinet before the 1970 election. Whereas in the first stage, the alert was initially sounded by local 'moral entrepreneurs', now the tendency to 'panic' is firmly entrenched in certain key institutions within the society:

> Post 1970, the law and order campaigners seem to have effecitvely sensitized the social control apparatuses and the media to the possibility of a general threat to the stability of the state. Minor forms of dissent seem to provide the basis of 'scapegoat' events for a jumpy and alerted control culture; and this progressively pushes the state apparatuses into a more or less permanent 'control' posture.[26]

But it is not being suggested that such periods of alarm are somehow the sole creation of the mass media, the 'primary definers' and other campaigners. It is the fact that there already exists widespread social anxiety among two major groupings which provides a fertile seedbed. From the standpoint of many in the non-commercial middle classes, the period of postwar affluence was tainted by an unbridled materialism and hedonism — characterised by the pundits as a new 'permissiveness'. This was deeply disturbing for those who had taken for granted the virtues of thrift, respectability and moral discipline. For many in the 'respectable' working class it was a period of dislocation and erosion for many 'traditional' working class neighbourhoods and life styles.[27] For middle aged and older members of both groups then, there was a sense of loss of the familiar landmarks, a feeling that 'fings aint what they used to be'. In such times of felt cultural dislocation, social anxiety comes to focus, not on its structural causes, but on visible symbols and symptoms of change, from Mods and Rockers through to Blacks and Asians.[28] For such groups the 'mugger' was a tailor-made folk devil:

> his form and shape accurately reflected the content of the fears and anxieties of those who first imagined, and then actually discovered him: young, black, bred in, or arising from the 'breakdown of social order' in the city. . . the very token of 'permissiveness', embodying in his every action and person, feelings and values that were the opposite of those decencies and restraints which make England what she is.[29]

It is not possible to do full justice here to the many complex and interwoven arguments presented in *Policing the Crisis*. Stanley Cohen, one of the more sympathetic commentators, writes:

> At too many points, it seems to me, their determination to find ideological closure leads them to a premature theoretical closure. The actual material selected as proof of the slide into the crisis (newspaper editorials, statements by MPs and police chiefs) does not always add up to something of such monumental proportions. The diffuse normative concern about delinquency is, I think more diffuse and less political than is suggested. And the assumption of a monolithic drift to repression gives little room for understanding why some objects are repressed more severely than others.[30]

But perhaps the central argument of the book, that a 'crisis of hegemony' (or 'exhaustion of consent') has been developing in Britain since the successful hegemony of the immediate postwar period, which has resulted in a growing reliance on its reserves of coercion of the part of the State, is an important one. While the succession of moral panics of the 1960s is seen as the first set of symptoms of 'the crisis' as experienced by sectors of the public, the 'law and order society' of the 1970s is experienced as a more general crisis or threat, in which a general exercise of more discipline, authority or coercion by the State can be seen as increasingly legitimate. Why has such a generalised concern with law and order arisen during the 1970s, a period when as we have shown, the official statistics of recorded crime show a fluctuating pattern, but an overall annual average rate of increase of about 5 per cent, which is half the more consistent trend experienced during the late 1950s and the 1960s? Taking these figures alone, we might find it easier to comprehend the embryonic law and order campaign of Mr Heath's Shadow Cabinet of 1970, than the full blown campaign of Mrs Thatcher's platform in 1979. Without necessarily accepting all of the arguments presented in *Policing the Crisis*, it can help us to pin-point some important changes in this period which might explain the prominence of the law and order issue.

Our first conclusion must be that certain forms of dramatic and threatening violence have appeared during the 1970s, and early 1980s: especially important to mention here are the bombing and other activities of the IRA. But as Chibnall has argued, 'The Violent Society' as a pre-eminent theme in law and order news had already been established before the bombing campaign in England, which can be dated from 1973.[31] Chibnall traces the development of concern about organised crime from the mid 1960s, alongside a number of dramatic events involving violence e.g. the Moors Murders, the activities of the Richardsons and the Krays. Rather later was the moral panic about political violence centred upon student demonstrations, the escalation of conflict in Northern Ireland, the Angry Brigade (1971) and violent picketing in 1972:

> The notion of 'The Violent Society' is seen to result from the convergence of a criminal violence theme, originating in the mid sixties, and a political violence theme which developed a few years later. The implications of the analysis are that interpretations generated in one domain of newspaper discourse (e.g. crime news) can easily be, and have been, transposed through linking concepts (e.g. the violent society) to other domains (e.g. political and industrial news).[32]

The notion of convergence into a 'Violent Society' or 'Law and Order Crisis' theme is one that is also explored by Hall and his colleagues[33] and Ian Taylor.[34] Once established, such themes become not only organising frameworks for media presentations, but also a *political resource* that can be used to legitimate the need for control, whether in the form of new laws on picketing, increases in police powers, or simply to win votes. Taylor quotes Mrs Thatcher in Birmingham in 1979 giving a good example of 'convergence':

> . . . in their muddled but different ways the vandals on the
> picket lines and the muggers in our street have got the same
> confused message — 'we want our demands met or else' and
> 'get out of way, give us your handbag or else. . .'[35]

So the first point is that the prevailing social imagery of the 'Permissive
Society' in the 1960s, with its associated moral panics, had been
replaced, with the help of the mechanism of convergence, by the theme
of 'The Violent Society' in the 1970s.

The second major change was that in the 1970s the police and the
judiciary had indeed come increasingly to the fore as 'primary definers'
on the law and order issue. A number of authors have noted the
'politicization' of the police during this period.[36] This process has
undoubtedly been accelerated by the development of political terrorism
during the 1970s, but police chiefs have also been forced into a more
openly political posture because of mounting concern and criticism
about the way in which police work has developed during this period.
The important point here however, is that the police have been
encouraged into such a posture by a number of challenges to their
definition of what exactly constitutes the 'law and order' issue. For
many the issue should also, or even mainly be concerned with issues
concerning the law and the institutions of law enforcement and
punishment. From yet another perspective, the 'problem' lies in
unemployment and the economic recession. For Ian Taylor however the
definition of these 'primary definers' has been paramount, with the
claim that in:

> the TV coverage of the 1979 General Election, every single
> program in which 'law and order' was discussed was framed
> primarily in terms of the perspective on crime raised by the
> Police Federation and by the Home Affairs Committee of the
> Conservative Party, and the only two groups who got to
> speak to the issue, other than politicians themselves, were
> policemen and two members of the Judiciary (Lord Denning
> and Melford Stevenson).[37]

The ascendancy of the 'New Right' philosophy of 'law and order' may,
of course be symptomatic of the disarray among those who might have
been opposing it, or of deeper developments in British politics and
society.

The third development which appears to have been gaining
momentum since the 'mugging panic' of the early 1970s is the
possibility of a 'convergence' being forged between the issues of race
and crime. A recent Home Office study of the relationship between race

and crime came to the following conclusions:

> the extent of total recorded indictable crime in any conurbation or police division is not related to the presence of ethnic minorities; that blacks were in the Metropolitan Police District (1975) arrested more frequently than whites; but that a large part of this excess can be statistically accounted for by the deprivations specific to the black, white and Asian population . . . Finally, it has been found that while victims' reports and arrest rates point to the conclusion that blacks are excessively involved in recorded street crime, the data also suggests that blacks are more liable to be picked up by the police (particularly 'suspected person' and other violent theft arrests).[38]

Susan Smith[39] compares the careful way in which such research is presented with the press release on the 1981 Metropolitan crime statistics issued by New Scotland Yard on 11 March, 1982. In particular she draws attention to a table presenting recorded offences of robbery and other violent theft, broken down by victims' perceptions of the colour of their assailant, and makes the following comments:

> This information, it will be recalled, pertains to a mere 3% of all recorded crime . . . Although more assailants were labelled 'coloured' than 'white' in 13 (out of 24) of the districts, without details of the population composition of these areas it is impossible to draw any valid conclusions as to whether 'coloureds' are over represented or not.[40]

Using the more complete data of the Home Office Study[41], she is able to dispel the notion that the majority of violent street crimes are committed by coloured people against whites.[42] What is most interesting however, is that out of the 14 tables, graphs and diagrams presented in the press release, the daily newspapers emphasised the one table with an apparent bearing on the issue of race and crime. She compares this with the comparative neglect by the media of the House of Commons report on racial attacks which revealed that Asians are 50 times, and blacks 36 times, more likely to be the victims of racist attacks than whites.[43] Whatever the reasons for this kind of selectivity in media presentation, it does have the consequence of defining the problem of law and order in a particular way — at the level of black street crime. Although there are obviously important issues surrounding the relationship between race and crime, we hope it is clear from our argument that there are other ways of looking at the problem of law and order. Such definitions have real consequences, for which the 'primary definers' and the mass media must bear considerable responsibility.

Penal crisis, pragmatism and political ideology

A final aspect to which we want to draw attention is the way in which the resurgence of the 'law and order' issue as a political rallying call perhaps owes as much to the way it embodies an *enduring response* to crime as to the manner in which it reflects the *currently perceived problem* of criminal behaviour. Specifically, we ask the question — to what extent do the penal policies associated with the call for 'law and order' at the present time represent an 'informed' response, soundly based on current penological wisdom, rather than a symbolic gesture in response to moral panic?

For most penological commentators the 1960s in Britain was a decade in which a major struggle was being waged in support of the so called 'rehabilitative ideal' — the notion that society's response to crime, especially to juveniles in trouble (and causing trouble) should be determined primarily by considerations of their individual welfare rather than punishment for anti-social behaviour. Indeed, this 'welfare approach' towards juvenile delinquents was officially accepted in Scotland, but in England and Wales very similar proposals by the Labour administration in the mid 1960s met with stiffer opposition, and only eventually reached the statute book in the much diluted form of the Children and Young Persons Act, 1969.

Amongst other signs of growing support for less punitive measures for offenders were the recommendations of the Wootton subcommittee of the Advisory Council on the Penal System (1966-70) on alternatives to custody,[44] many of which were incorporated into the 1972 Criminal Justice Act. At about this same period, during the second half of the 1960s, there emerged ominous signs of the penal dilemma that has dominated every government's response to the crime problem throughout the last 15 years — the literal incapacity of the prison system to accommodate all those required to be kept in custody, either awaiting trial, or as sentenced prisoners. By 1965, a decade of rising crime rates, with no substantial decrease in the police clear up rate and no major change in sentencing practice by the courts, had produced unprecedented demands on the prison system that were swiftly overtaking its available physical capacity. Whatever penal philosophy had been espoused by the Government of the day, it would have been necessary to seek alternatives to imprisonment for entirely *practical reasons*. It is widely agreed that the important package of new penal measures introduced by the 1967 Criminal Justice Act (including such radical innovations, for Britain, as parole and suspended sentences) was as much the result of dire practical necessity as of any more sophisticated penological philosophy or ideological preferences. The contradictions inherent in the penal system of the time were further highlighted by the events surrounding the Mountbatten Inquiry into Prison Security (1966), whose recommendations drastically changed the official emphasis of Prison Department policy from the traditional one of the 'treatment and training' of prisoners to security and 'humane containment'.[45] Not only was this a major policy change, but it carried with it financial consequences that severely curtailed other options for developing the prison system.

Penal policy in the 1970s continued to be constrained by what one leading criminologist has described as 'the crisis of penological resources'.[46] This referred not only to the chronic overcrowding in local prisons but to the lack of adequate resources for developing community alternatives to custody. A new development was the collapse of faith in the 'rehabilitative ideal', which had been severely challenged (particularly in the United States) by results of empirical research demonstrating the ineffectiveness of penal treatment and strongly criticised for its theoretical weaknesses and essential injustices.[47] This resulted in something of a 'penological vacuum' which not only fostered the existing tendency for penal policy to be determined by a combination of inertia and purely pragmatic responses to crises as and when they occurred,[48] but also led to a spectacular revival, especially in America, of retributive theories of punishment and the so called 'justice model' of corrections, whereby penal measures were determined by the offenders 'just deserts'.[49]

In Britain, where such theoretical concerns were less explicit, there were echoes of similar ancient attitudes to crime and punishment in the ideas of the 'New Right'. At the same time, space was left in the arena of penal politics for the influence of professional interest groups currently dissatisfied with the criminal justice system's response to the crime problem and concerned with their own role in the struggle to preserve law and order. For example, there was continued pressure from magistrates throughout the 1970s for the restoration of powers to juvenile courts to impose residential care orders and for the provision of additional secure units; there were also demands from the police to be given more resources (especially higher pay) for the fight against crime on the streets of the inner cities; more recently, there was the campaign by prison governors for some effective action by the government to reduce the prison population, by introducing such measures as 'one half remission' of sentence or 'automatic parole'.

As the resource crisis worsened during the latter half of the 1970s and as the succession of 'moral panics' showed no sign of abating, the General Election of 1979 provided a tailor-made platform for exploiting the many interwoven strands of the 'law and order' lobby. The police role in the pre-election campaign is well known, as is the way they were rewarded by the immediate implementation of their pay award, with a guaranteed scale of pay that has kept them well up the earnings ladder in the last few years. Many of the measures in the 1982 Criminal Justice Act can be seen as direct responses to the wishes of various interest groups, especially the magistracy and judiciary, who have been given more power to determine the nature and length of custodial sentences.

Fundamental dilemmas and contradictions still remain however. On the one hand, encouragement has been given to the expansion of non-custodial measures, shorter minimum sentences for detention centre and youth custody orders have been introduced, and the courts have been strongly urged to pass shorter sentences.* On the other hand, one of the first actions of the new Home Secretary Mr Whitelaw in the summer of 1979 was to announce the setting up of experimental detention centre regimes to enforce the 'short, sharp, shock' effect upon young offenders, especially the 'violent young thugs'. Concern also continued to be expressed in official circles about the need to protect the public from the allegedly 'dangerous' offenders.[52] These developments confirm the importance of a further element that characterises contemporary responses to the 'law and order' crisis in many Western European countries — the trend towards 'bifurcation', in public attitudes and official policy towards offenders, described as follows by Professor Tony Bottoms[53]:

> Put crudely, this bifurcation is between on the one hand, the so-called 'really serious offender' for whom very tough measures are typically advocated; and on the other hand, the 'ordinary' offender for whom, it is felt, we can afford to take a much more lenient line.

It seems fair to conclude that 'law and order' penal policy is primarily about responding to the dictates of favoured political ideologies of social control and the pressure from the interest groups of 'primary definers' as far as available resources allow. Popular attitudes towards crime and punishment in Britain are likely to remain more Draconian than the inclinations of most Governments in the foreseeable future, particularly if these attitudes are reinforced by the regular supply of 'moral panics' by the news media. Public images of this kind can only begin to be revised if those responsible for penal policy adopt a stance which can be fully justified on the grounds of existing knowledge.

---

*   There was some indication that this encouragement to reduce the length of prison sentences was having some effect in 1980[50], but the most recent information from the Prison Department suggests that this effect may be short lived.[51]

Among well established penological facts are:

- increased resources to the police are most unlikely to reduce the crime rate, and may quite feasibly produce an increase in what is recorded;[54]
- harsher sentences upon convicted offenders will have no effect in deterring them (or other potential offenders) from future crime, nor indeed will more 'rehabilitative' sentences achieve greater success in changing their behaviour patterns;[55]
- detaining offenders in prison for long periods, on the grounds of 'incapacitation', is a policy that will have only marginal effects on the general crime rate, *even if* the prison population were to be increased by three- or four-fold.[56]

The other unfortunate but highly relevant fact is that 'facts' such as those just listed are unlikely to carry much weight with a Government if they run counter to the policies dictated by ideology and interest groups. In the final analysis, the 'law and order' *response* has even less connection with researched evidence of this kind than the 'law and order' *portrayal of the problem* has with the picture painted by official statistics.

Conclusion

We suggest that the notion that Britain is experiencing a crisis of criminal behaviour needs serious qualification. While overall *recorded* crime rates have grown considerably over the last 25 years, it is important to look at alternative evidence on the matter, and to bear in mind considerable variations in particular kinds of offence. While violent street crime appears to be a matter of considerable public anxiety, this nevertheless represents a very small proportion of total recorded crime.

We have attempted to show how anxieties about law and order can be generated and sustained by complex social processes in which the mass media, the police, the judiciary, politicians and various other campaigners may play significant roles. Fear of crime is to a considerable extent based on what is read in the newspapers or seen on T.V. The idea of the moral panic highlights the way in which attention is focused upon particular issues: 'social security scroungers' rather than tax evaders, 'vandalism' rather than driving offences. We have also suggested that concern about law and order may be a symptom of anxiety and resentment about the consequences for everyday life of deep rooted social changes in British Society.

Concern about law and order also reflects the apparent failure of our law enforcement and criminal justice system to 'cope with the problem'. at the basic level of civic order, having enough prison cells, or ultimately in demonstrating the 'effectiveness' of what they are doing. One could argue on other grounds that the real crisis of law and order lies in the police, the prisons and ultimately in the lack of a coherent penal philosophy. The decline of the 'Rehabilitative Ideal' has left a space which can be readily occupied by a 'get tough' punishment centred penal policy. Although there is no evidence that taking tough measures against individual offenders is an effective method of crime prevention in either the short or the long term, it would appear to be popular with the electorate. According to a Marplan/Sun Study in 1978 six out of ten adults thought that tougher sentences would reduce crime, while only six per cent thought more social workers or probation officers would help. A Gallup poll in 1979 indicated that 75 per cent of respondents favoured a reintroduction of the death penalty.[57] With such public attitudes about diagnosis and remedy, it is easy to see how the law and order issue can work for the Right. It is difficult to see how, in current times, a policy directed towards fundamental social and economic conditions, as favoured by other political and academic groupings, could have quite the same popular appeal.

Notes

1. F.H. McClintock and N.H. Avison, *Crime in England and Wales* (Heinemann 1968) p.19.
2. Home Office, *Criminal Statistics: England and Wales 1980* Cmnd.8376, (HMSO 1981) p.23 para. 1.8.
3. Ibid. passim.
4. Ibid. p.28 para. 2.5.
5. R.F. Sparks, H.G. Genn and D.J. Dodd, *Surveying Victims: A Study of the Measurement of Criminal Victimization* (Wiley 1977).
6. Ibid. pp.152-153.
7. For a preliminary report see M. Hough and P. Mayhew, *The British Crime Survey: First Report* Home Office Research Study no.76 (HMSO 1983).
8. Home Office (1981) op. cit. para. 2-6.
9. See A. Bottomley and C. Coleman, *Understanding Crime Rates: Police and Public Roles in the Production of Official Statistics.* (Gower 1981) pp.95-101.
10. Home Office, *Report of the Commissioner of Police of the Metropolis for the year 1981* Cmnd.8569 (HMSO 1982).
11. For English examples see D.J. West and D.P. Farrington, *Who Becomes Delinquent* (Heinemann 1973) and W.A. Belson, *Juvenile Theft: the Causal Factors* (Harper and Row 1975).
12. 'The law and order vote' *New Society* 12 June 1980 p.220.
13. S. Cohen, *Folk Devils and Moral Panics: The Creation of the Mods and Rockers* (MacGibbon and Kee Ltd. 1972) p.9.
14. S. Cohen, *Folk Devils and Moral Panics* New Edition (Martin Robertson 1980) p.xxiii.
15. J. Young, *The Drugtakers* (Paladin 1971) ch.10.
16. See for example S. Cohen and J. Young, *The Manufacture of News: Deviance, Social Problems and the Mass Media* (Constable 1973), S. Chibnall, *Law-and-order News* (Tavistock 1977) and S. Hall et. al., *Policing The Crisis: Mugging, the State and Law and Order* (Macmillan 1978).
17. Hall, op. cit. p.58.
18. Ibid. p.58.
19. D. Anderson and W. Sharrock, 'Biasing the News: Technical Issues in "Media Studies"' *Sociology* 13, pp.367-385.
20. See the modified views of Cohen and Young on this aspect in S. Cohen and J. Young, *The Manufacture of News: Deviance, Social Problems and the Mass Media* Revised edition (Constable 1981).
21. Anderson and Sharrock, op.cit., p.374.

22. Hall op.cit.
23. Ibid. p.52.
24. Ibid. p.221.
25. Ibid. p.222.
26. Ibid. p.222.
27. Ibid. p.157-158.
28. Ibid. p.160.
29. Ibid. p.161-162.
30. Cohen (1980) op.cit., pp.xxiv-xxv.
31. Chibnall op.cit.
32. Ibid. p.75.
33. Hall op.cit., pp.222-223
34. I. Taylor, 'The Law and Order issue in the British general election and the Canadian federal election of 1979: crime, populism and the state' *Canadian Journal of Sociology* 5, pp.285-311.
35. I. Taylor, 'Crime waves in post-war Britain' *Contemporary Crises* 5, pp.43-62.
36. See for example Taylor (a) loc.cit. and R. Reiner, 'Fuzzy thoughts: the police and law-and-order politics' *Sociological Review* 28, pp.377-413.
37. Taylor (b) loc.cit., p.56.
38. P. Stevens and C.F. Willis, *Race, Crime and Arrests* Home Office Research Study No.58 (HMSO 1979), p.41-42.
39. S. Smith, *Race and Crime Statistics* Race Relations Fieldwork Background Paper No.4 (Board of Social Responsibility, London 1982).
40. Ibid. p.16.
41. Stevens and Willis, op.cit.
42. Smith op.cit., pp.16-17.
43. House of Commons, *Racial Attacks* HC 106. (HMSO 1982).
44. Home Office, *Non-Custodial and Semi-Custodial Penalties* Report of the Advisory Council on the Penal System. (HMSO 1970).
45. See R.D. King and R. Morgan, *The Future of the Prison System* (Gower 1980).
46. A.E. Bottoms, 'An introduction to "The Coming Crisis"' in Bottoms and Preston (eds.) *The Coming Penal Crisis* (Scottish Academic Press 1980).
47. See S.R. Brody, *The Effectiveness of Sentencing* Home Office Research Study No.35. (HMSO 1976).
48. See A. Williams, 'The future of corrections' in H. Jones (ed.) *Society Against Crime: Penal Theory Now* (Penguin Books 1981).

49. See A.Van Hirsch, *Doing Justice: The Choice of Punishments (Hill and Wang 1976), E.Van den Haag, Punishing Criminals* (Basic Books 1975), J.Q. Wilson, *Thinking about Crime* (Basic Books 1975) and A.K. Bottomley, *Criminology in Focus: Past Trends and Future Prospects* (Martin Robertson, 1979).

50. See Home Office (1981) op.cit. pp.136-138.

51. See Home Office, *Prison Statistics England and Wales 1981* Cmnd.8654 (HMSO 1982).

52. Scottish Council on Crime, *Crime and the Prevention of Crime* (HMSO 1975); Home Office/DHSS, *Report of the Committee on Mentally Abnormal Offenders* Cmnd.6244. (HMSO 1975); Home Office, *Sentences of Imprisonment: A Review of Maximum Penalties* Report of the Advisory Council on the Penal System, (HMSO 1978) and J. Floud and W. Young, *Dangerousness and Criminal Justice* (Heinemann 1981).

53. A.E. Bottoms, 'Reflections on the renaissance of dangerousness' *Howard Journal of Penology* 16, pp.70-96.

54. R.V.G. Clarke and M. Hough (eds.) *The Effectiveness of Policing* (Gower 1980).

55. Brody op.cit.

56. K. Pease and J. Wolfson, 'Incapacitation studies: a review and commentary' *Howard Journal of Penology* 18, pp.160-167; S.R. Brody and R. Tarling, *Taking Offenders out of Circulation* Home Office Research Study No.64. (HMSO 1980); P.B. Ainsworth and K. Pease, 'Incapacitation revisited' *Howard Journal of Penology* 20, pp.160-169.

57. *New Society* op.cit.

PART 2:

CONTEMPORARY PROBLEMS OF
LAW AND ORDER

4 The Policing Crisis

By J.L. Lambert

Introduction

This chapter sets out to trace the course of the current policing debate against the background of developments and trends in policing in the seventies. It examines two of the dominant themes in the debate. Firstly, the procedure for investigating complaints against the police. Secondly, the community role in ensuring that police forces are accountable for their actions and policies. It argues that a blueprint for policing in the future will only emerge after an investigation which is allowed to range freely over the whole area of policing matters. Official consideration of aspects of policing, such as police powers or police complaints, obscures the essential relationships between functions, powers and accountability and ensures that any changes made are *ad hoc* responses to particular problems, rather than being an expression of coherent policing policy.

The Background

The traditional formulation of the nature of the police role emphasises impartial enforcement of the law and accountability. The existence of local constabularies, democractically accountable to local police authorities, has been seen as a safeguard against a national, government controlled force and has helped to foster the idea that the police role somehow stands outside politics. The enforcement of the law is a duty owed ultimately to the law itself and the task of enforcement is carried out impartially and even-handedly. In this way, civil liberties are protected and society is reassured that the police are not its masters but its servants. This comfortable analysis has been increasingly under attack in recent years. Indeed, the last two years have seen a public debate about policing, the intensity of which is virtually unprecedented. A number of factors account for this. The most immediate cause of the debate was undoubtedly the riots which took place in the early summer of 1981. The setting up of the Scarman Inquiry into the Brixton disorders[1] received enormous publicity and culminated in a lengthy report[2] which recommended changes across the whole ambit of policing matters. The riots were also significant, however, in that they provided the catalyst by which longstanding and deep-seated causes of dissatisfaction were highlighted.

There has been a growing realisation that the traditional formulation of the nature of the police role masks its true nature. The policing function inevitably involves the formulation of policies, the setting of standards, the assessment of priorities and the utilisation of limited resources. The police do not simply enforce the law. They make policy about what law to enforce, how much to enforce it, when to enforce it and against whom to enforce it. Consequently, the policies they adopt are likely to be elaborate and, we might add, largely publicly unarticulated and beyond the reach of judicial review.[3] At the heart of the policing debate, therefore, lies the issue of the control of discretionary power.

The myth that the police are simply objective agents of the law has also been exposed by their unmistakeable movement into the political arena. Chief constables no longer keep a low profile: in the Press and on the television they express clear opinions on the conditions of the times and the police role in the governmental process. They lobby unashamedly for greater police powers while, at the same time, denying the need for greater accountability.[4] Also, police staff organisations have become political pressure groups as was made very evident by, for instance, the campaign waged by the Police Federation to persuade Parliament to vote in favour of the reintroduction of capital punishment.

There has also been, over the last two decades, a radical shift in the organisation and character of routine policing. In 1966, for example, the number of police forces in England and Wales was reduced from 117 to 49. Subsequent reorganisations have further reduced the number to 43. Consequently, we have fewer, larger police forces, all capable of responding reasonably efficiently across the range of operational functions. An incidental result of this policy, has been that chief constables now wield, and speak with, greater authority than ever before. Alongside this reduction in the number of forces, there has been increasing centralisation and reliance on centrally funded facilities like the Police National Computer.

But despite these trends, and the fact that we presently have more police officers than at any other time in the history of the police service it has been impossible to maintain a policy of preventive policing. To compensate for this, reliance has been increasingly placed on faster response times as a measurement of police efficiency and this new emphasis has been aided by increased mobility and more sophisticated communications systems. And so there developed the 'reactive' or 'fire brigade' style of policing so typical of the seventies. In the words of John Alderson, former Chief Constable of Devon and Cornwall, the 'technological cop' had arrived and for Alderson and many others, the inevitable worsening of police/public relationships began.[5] It was no longer possible to maintain the Dixon of Dock Green image — the idea of the policeman being merely a public-spirited citizen in uniform[6] — in the face of the fire-brigade style of policing. The modern policeman belongs to a highly organised service with an explicit hierarchy and an associated chain of command. His powers are far greater than those possessed by the ordinary citizen and these are augmented by his membership of a technologically advanced and disciplined force. The policeman, it is argued, therefore, has become remote from the public. This is a process which many fear will continue as long as police and public continue to meet, more often than not, in conditions of stress. The opportunities for strengthening police/public understanding have diminished. Recognition of this has led some forces to move to a pro-active style of communal policing,[7] which has at its heart the aim of putting the policeman back into the community he serves.[8]

Reactive policing and the adoption of 'hard' policing methods are closely connected and the creation of special squads of police to deal with emergencies has been especially attacked. The best-known of these squads is, of course, the Special Patrol Group of the Metropolitan Police Force, which was set up in 1965 to aid the local divisions and provide saturation policing in high crime areas. Since 1965, other forces have created their own groups, often named Tactical Support Groups or Force Support Units. Available evidence suggests that there are 27 such groups in existence in various parts of the country.[9] Their use in the policing of inner city areas has been seen by many as a cause for particular concern.[10] Throughout the seventies, the evidence that a widening gap was developing between the police and the ethnic communities mounted. Saturation policing in such areas, widespread and allegedly discriminatory use of the 'sus' laws and stop and search provisions, were constantly suggested as major causes of this alienation.

65

Indeed, when in 1980 the Home Affairs Committee of the House of Commons examined race relations in the United Kingdom, one of their central recommendations was the abolition of the 'sus' laws,[11] a step effected by the Criminal Attempts Act 1981.[12]

In Brixton, the SPG were used on four occasions between January 1978 and September 1980. Lord Scarman's conclusion was unequivocal: 'They provoked the hostility of young black people who felt that they were being hunted irrespective of their guilt or innocence. And their hostility infected older members of the community. . .'[13] The riots in Brixton began on April 10th 1980. 'Operation Swamp' began on April 6th and was scheduled to last until April 11th. It involved 112 officers (not from the SPG on this occasion). The Commander of the Operation's written instructions to his men ran as follows:

> The purpose of this operation is to flood identified areas . . . to detect burglars and robbers. The essence of the exercise, therefore, is to ensure that all officers remain on the streets and success will depend on a concentrated effort of stops based on powers of surveillance and suspicion proceeded by persistent and astute questioning.[14]

The success of such operations in law enforcement terms is a matter of conjecture — they may diminish street crime in the target area only at the expense of driving it elsewhere. The harm that they can do to police/public relationships, however, is now a matter of history.

The rift which appears to have developed between the police and the public in the seventies was not just a consequence of the style of policing adopted. The issue of what powers we give to the police is central to the current debate, though the link between function and powers is not always clearly made. The use of coercive powers highlights an enduring dilemma of policing in the United Kingdom, namely, that the police are expected to impose authority on, at the same time as being accountable to, the public. Abuse of power, in the form of wholesale corruption, can shake in a dramatic way public confidence in its police force, as the Metropolitan Police found to their cost in the aftermath of the revelations of corruption in the vice squad.[15] More insidious, however, is the damage that can be done by the arbitrary use of undesirably opaque powers. It is axiomatic that police forces need coercive powers in order to function efficiently. Thus, one major problem permeates the whole field of police powers: how to frame the law to give the police adequate powers to perform their duties, while at the same time ensuring that such powers do not allow arbitrary interference with individual freedom. That the law has not satisfactorily resolved this problem is partly attributable to the way that police powers have developed. Legislation has built upon common law foundations in a sporadic and piecemeal fashion. There is no code of police powers and the law can only be discovered by searching through the case-law and statutory provisions. The result has been confusion and complexity. The public is largely ignorant of the extent of police powers and the police themselves are compelled to operate within a framework of rules which is uncertain and ambiguous.

A classic example of the potential for misuse was provided by the now repealed 'sus' laws. Section 6 of the Vagrancy Act, 1824, gave a power to arrest 'every suspected person or reputed thief. . . loitering with intent to commit an arrestable offence.' The lack of specificity in the section was an invitation to the police to go on 'fishing' expeditions and throughout the seventies there was growing criticism of the use of this power. Stop and search provisions gave rise to similar controversy. For example, the famous section 66 power possessed by the Metropolitan Police[16] is one of the mainstays of their operational activities. In 1978, 50,000 suspects initially stopped under section 66 were then arrested as a result of that stop. However, stops were only successful in leading to arrests in 13% of cases. In 1978, therefore, some 48,000 people were stopped and searched under section 66 alone in the metropolis and in well over 80% of these cases the officer's suspicions were not confirmed by the search.[17]

The debate about who polices the police rumbled on throughout the seventies. In 1976, the passing of the Police Act, which created the Police Complaints Board and thereby introduced a modest independent element into the procedure for investigating complaints against the police, precipitated the retirement of Sir Robert Mark.[18] The obduracy with which the police resisted the Act was crystallised for many by Mark's opposition to it.[19] If a man who had acquired a reputation for rooting out corruption could be so opposed to the creation of the Police Complaints Board, what hope could there be of reconciling rank and file policeman to the new scheme? In the event, the Police Federation was won over to it by a promise from the Home Office that the 'double-jeopardy' rule would be applied in a rather novel way and by the concession that Federation members would have the right to sue malicious complainants in defamation.[20] Mark, of course, was not the only chief officer to oppose the new procedures. The feeling within the police service that there was no need for reform was widespread and chief constables, in particular, feared that civilian interference would undermine their authority over their men. The Police Complaints Board began its operations in 1977 against this background of hostility and very soon it became the subject of vigorous criticism.

The final trend which became apparent in the latter half of the seventies was the re-thinking by police authorities of their role and there were some notable public disputes between certain authorities and their chief constables. The Chairman of the South Yorkshire Police Authority went on record in 1977 as saying that the only function of the police authority was to rubber stamp decisions of the police. Relationships between the police and the authority became so strained that when the authority set up a Working Party to investigate the relationships between the police and the public in South Yorkshire, the chief constable refused to cooperate with it.[21] At about the same time, the chief constable of West Mercia was reported as saying that he was not prepared to be accountable to a local government committee for his actions.[22]

Perhaps the most publicised disagreement, however, was that which involved the Merseyside police authority. The chief constable refused to reveal to the authority the substance of the police inquiry into the death of Jimmy Kelly, who had died in police custody. This precipitated a row in which the chief constable told members of the authority to 'keep out of my Force's business.' In response, the authority set up a Working Party to examine the role and responsibilities of the police authority. In its Report, the authority reasserted the independence of police authorities and their ability to require chief constables to account for their actions.[23]

Chief constables, as one might expect, were opposed to any extension of police authorities' powers and even John Alderson, often regarded as the thinking man's policeman, denied under his system of communal policing the need for police authorities to play a more meaningful role in the policing of their areas. His police, he said, should contribute to 'the common good' and not be 'the servant or tool of the majority.'[24] Of course, not all police forces are subject to the police authority system in the sense outlined. The police authority for the Metropolitan Police Force is the Home Secretary and in the seventies there developed a strong lobby to subject the Metropolitan Police to the same police authority system that exists in the provinces, a lobby which was spearheaded by the Greater London Council.

The policing crisis, therefore, did not begin with Brixton and the Scarman Report. There was a serious and prolonged debate about policing which pre-dated Scarman. The particular significance of the Scarman inquiry is, however, that it provided the platform upon which pre-existing criticisms of the police could be brought to the attention of the public in a particularly dramatic and compelling way. All of the developments and trends in policing which have here been highlighted challenged the classic formulation of the police role set out earlier and reopened fundamental questions about the nature of policing and the relationship of the police with the public.

The policing debate, since Scarman, has concentrated on two predominant themes — the police complaints procedure and the general issue of accountability and it is to these that we must now turn.

The police complaints procedure

The subject of who polices the police was a recurrent one in the seventies. Indeed, this particular debate has a much longer history because the police complaints procedure was one of the factors that led to the appointment of the Royal Commission on the Police in 1959, whose terms of reference directed specific attention to it.[25]

The most persistent criticism of the present procedure is that investigation of all complaints is in the hands of the police themselves and that this either actually works against the complainant in that the complaint is not adequately investigated or, even though the complaint is properly investigated, there is little public confidence in the nature of the investigation. In other words, justice is not being seen to be done. There is now a widespread feeling that the 1976 Act does not contain a sufficiently convincing independent element. And as will become apparent, it is this problem which is proving to be the major stumbling block to satisfactory progress on this matter.

There is some evidence to suggest that complaints of assault are investigated less thoroughly than complaints of other criminal offences. This was a finding of a study undertaken by the Home Office Research Unit in March 1982,[26] and is implicit in the Police Complaints Board's proposal that allegations of assault should be investigated in a special way.[27] However, one of the most unsatisfactory aspects of the treatment of complaints alleging serious criminal offences was the operation of the 'double jeopardy' rule. Section 11 of the 1976 Act provides that where a member of a police force has been acquitted or convicted of a criminal offence, he shall not be liable to be charged with any offence against discipline which is in substance the same offence of which he has been convicted or acquitted. That is a concept of double jeopardy which is clear and reasonable. However, as part of the price extracted by the Police Federation for its acceptance of the Act, the Home Secretary issued a circular to the effect that where it had been decided by the Director of Public Prosecutions that criminal proceedings should not be taken, there should normally be no disciplinary charge if the evidence required to substantiate the disciplinary charge was the same as that required to substantiate the criminal charge.[28] In practice, therefore, double jeopardy very often meant no jeopardy, because the Police Complaints Board regarded itself as bound by the circular. In December 1982, however, on an application for judicial review against the Board, the Divisional Court ruled that the Board had unlawfully fettered its discretion by regarding the circular as binding and that the double jeopardy rule has no application to cases where officers have not undergone criminal proceedings.[29] This significant decision, although it almost certainly caused consternation in the Home Office and Police Complaints Board, is a clear indication to the Board that it is fully entitled to recommend that disciplinary proceedings be brought in such cases.

Another criticism of the scheme is that is is geared to complaints made against individual officers and does not cater for a complainant who is more concerned to raise the issue of, for example, the policy incorporated into a Force's standing orders or the levels of patrols in particular areas. Consequently, the role of the Police Complaints Board is restricted to disciplinary matters and the Board has little chance of acting positively to satisfy complainants or reassure the public generally. Related to this, is the fact that the decision to record a complaint as a section 49 complaint is entirely a matter for the appropriate deputy chief constable. In other words, the role of the Board and the fate of a complaint is dependent on decisions made by deputy chief constables. It may be possible, for instance, to view a complaint about routine stop checks on motorists in two ways — either as a complaint about the conduct of individual officers or as a complaint about force policy. If, in the deputy chief constable's opinion it falls into the latter category, there is, under the Act, no complaint.

Finally, it has been argued that the system is excessively formal. Once a complaint has been recorded as a complaint, and assuming it is not subsequently withdrawn, it is subjected to a formal investigation followed by reference to the Board. The very formality can itself act as a deterrent to complainants and when the complaint is a minor one, it is arguably unnecessary to subject it to such a cumbersome procedure. In essence, then, the system lacks a convincing independent element. It is over formal and rigid. It is wasteful of the time of the police, the DPP and the Board. And there is insufficient discussion of policy matters arising from complaints.

In 1980, the Board recognised the mounting criticism of the procedures and suggested that they were particularly directed to cases where unexplained serious injury is sustained by individuals in police custody.[30] They recommended that such complaints should be dealt with by a specialist squad of investigating officers, seconded for a two or three year period and answerable to an independent lawyer.[31] Following this recommendation, the Home Office set up a Working Party under the chairmanship of Lord Plowden[32] to consider the Board's proposal.[33] It concluded that the recommended change was 'impracticable and unnecessary'.[34] What it suggested was greater use of officers from outside forces and the granting of extra, but unspecified powers to the Police Complaints Board.[35]

Shortly after the publication of this Report, the riots occured and the Scarman inquiry was set up. Before Lord Scarman's Report was published, however, the Home Secretary announced a further Working Party under the chairmanship of Lord Belstead.[36] In November, 1981, Scarman reported. He concluded that if public confidence in the complaints procedure is to be achieved, any solution falling short of a system of independent investigation for all complaints is unlikely to be successful.[37] As an alternative, however, Scarman proposed a series of more limited measures including independent supervision of investigations and some form of local conciliation procedure.[38] The Belstead Working Party reported early in 1982.[39] In general terms, it endorsed the Plowden Report, but its proposals were subsequently disowned by both the Police Federation and the Superintendents' Association.

Throughout this time, the newspapers made very interesting reading. In October 1981, the chief constable of Lancashire was reported as commenting that the only way to allay public disquiet about the procedure was to have independent investigation,[40] a view shortly after supported by James Anderton and Peter Imbert.[41] In the same month, Alf Dubs MP introduced into the House of Commons a Bill to set up an independent police complaints procedure under which a police ombudsman would carry out investigations with his own staff.[42] Sir Cyril Phillips, the new chairman of the Police Complaints Board, estimated the cost of an independent system of investigation for complaints of serious injury at around £10 million per annum.[43] At the very end of 1981, the Police Federation released a statement in favour of independent investigation, a dramatic *volte face* which was, however, hedged around with a number of important and probably unacceptable qualifications.[44] Early in 1982, the Shadow Home Secretary appeared to commit a future Labour government to independent investigation of all complaints against the police.[45] And in March 1982, the Home Office stated its view that an independent investigatory force would require around 800 men and cost £10 million per annum.[46]

In the meantime, the whole issue of police complaints was under investigation by the influential Home Affairs Committee of the House of Commons. It reported in May 1982[47] and argued that the best solution to the problem was represented by the Royal Commission on Criminal Procedure's recommendation that a system of regional Crown Prosecutors should be set up in England and Wales. These prosecutors should be given responsibility for the investigation of complaints against the police. Unfortunately, the Report does not delineate sufficiently clearly the role of the prosecutor in the complaints procedure except to say that he should oversee the investigations carried out by the police and would have power to interview witnesses himself.[48] In the short-term, however, and until such a system is established, the Committee recommended immediate changes, among which are:

1. a rewording of the double jeopardy rule to restore the position to that set out in the 1976 Act;[49]
2. the establishment of regional complaints offices headed by independent assessors who would assume responsibility for the investigation of complaints alleging serious criminal offences;
3. the introduction of a conciliation process for complaints not involving criminal offences.[50]

The Committee did not recommend independent investigation because it was not convinced that an independent organisation would do a better job than the police.[51]

While the Committee was deliberating, the Home Secretary announced that he was prepared to be guided by it. By the autumn of 1982, therefore, there were no less than five sets of official proposals on the table and it is significant that four of the five completely rejected independent investigation. When the Police and Criminal Evidence Bill was published shortly afterwards, it confirmed that the Home Office intended to settle for modest changes in the procedures based largely on the Plowden/Belstead recommendations, namely, greater use of officers from outside forces, the appointment of an independent assessor to supervise the investigation of serious complaints (the chairman or deputy chairman of the Police Complaints Board) and informal resolution of minor complaints.[52] The Home Office has thus settled for the soft option of introducing changes, the effect of which will be mainly cosmetic, because they do not tackle the fundamental issue — that the police investigate themselves. The opposition to independent investigation has been based not so much on the principle, but on the practical difficulties of implementing such a procedure — practical difficulties which may have been overrated.

What the Home Office should be moving towards is a system of police ombudsmen established on a regional basis who would have their own staff consisting of lawyers, investigators and conciliation officers. The ombudsman would be responsible for investigating all complaints made against the police and deciding the appropriate manner for dealing with them. After the investigation of complaints alleging criminal offences, a report of the investigation should be sent to the Director of Public Prosecutions, unless the ombudsman is satisfied that no question arises of a criminal offence having been committed. Where the complaint alleges a disciplinary matter, after the investigation, the report should be sent to the deputy chief constable with an appropriate direction. A conciliation process should be available for complaints of a minor nature. Staffing such a scheme would, of course, be difficult but not insuperable provided that sufficient time is allowed for recruitment and training before the scheme becomes operational. It might initially be necessary to use a combination of police and lay investigators, though the use of seconded police officers would be a short term exigency. Such a scheme has the support of the Commission for Local Administration and the qualified support of the Association of Metropolitan Authorities.[53] All it needs to make it work is commitment from the government and from the police themselves.

Accountability

It is reasonably clear that there are not going to be major changes in the institutional arrangements for securing the accountability of the police in the near future, even though the accountability issue has figured prominently in the current debate.

The growing tension between police authorities and chief constables has already been mentioned. The problem really derives from the Police Act, 1964. That Act was passed as a result of the recommendations of the Royal Commission on the Police, which reported in 1962.[54] The Royal Commission recognised that 'the problem of controlling the police is the problem of controlling chief constables.'[55] However, having recognised the problem, the Commission did not go on to resolve it. Indeed, the 1964 Act is formulated in a rather curious way. Under it, police authorities have the duty to maintain an adequate and efficient police force for their areas,[56] but operational control of the force is in the hands of the chief constable.[57] In the exercise of this operational control, the chief constable is independent of central and local government and to a large degree, of the courts. In constitutional terms, no one possesses the authority to direct the chief constable to follow particular operational policies and he is not required to justify his operational decisions to anyone. The completeness of the chief constable's operational control is underlined by the fact that he alone is responsible for all appointments and promotions below assistant chief constable and is the disciplinary authority for these ranks.[58]

It is inevitable, therefore, that local police authorities operate within confined limits. The authority, for instance, has no power to give instructions to the chief officer regarding the use of the police, though it does have the right to call for a report from him on any matter connected with the policing of the area.[59] However, when this right to call for reports is examined, it is found that the information which a chief constable is required to provide is confined to that which the police authority needs to enable it to discharge its functions.[60] As a result, although police authorities are entitled to ask questions about any matter connected with the policing of the area, some matters related to the policing of the area are impliedly held to be no business of the authority and that decision is in the hands of the chief constable. The result of this is that the chief constable is empowered to decide what the functions of the police authority are. In March, 1982, for example, Mr Anderton, chief constable of Greater Manchester, refused to answer questions addressed to him by his police authority on the attendance of the police at a factory engaged in an industrial dispute with its employees. Mr Anderton was reported as saying that he would not answer questions about the disposition of his force as, under the 1964 Act, the information was not needed to discharge the functions of the police authority. He complained about the 'political overtones' to the questions which he regarded as 'irregular' and 'thoroughly unreasonable'.[61] The resolution of such disputes is in part provided for by the 1964 Act, because under section 11 the Home Secretary can give a ruling on the admissibility of the question. Not surprisingly, this procedure is rarely resorted to. In this case it was not, and the questions remained unanswered.

The ability to ask questions, therefore, does little to diminish the operational autonomy of chief constables and, in practice, the respective roles of police authority and chief constable will depend upon the relationships forged between individual authorities and their chief officers.[62] In this connection, it is useful to refer to a survey of the 41 police authorities outside London conducted jointly in 1976 by the Association of Metropolitan Authorities and the Association of County Councils. It revealed that in a significant number of cases, the chief constable did not report regularly to his police authority on the policing of the area[63] and that in the majority of cases, police authorities only infrequently used their ability to call for reports on specific policing issues.[64]

All of this does tend to bear out the criticism that traditionally, police authorities have concerned themselves with financial matters to the exclusion of nearly everything else. In other words, they have been unable or unwilling in the past to use their statutory powers, limited though they are, to the full.[65] Even the presentation by the chief constable of his annual report to the authority is not always seen as an opportunity to make him account for the way in which the area is policed. Although he is obliged by statute to present an annual report to his authority, he is not required to consult with the authority over its contents, or refer it to the members in draft. The style of presentation and, more importantly, the contents of the report are entirely matters for the chief constable. The result of this is that some reports are much more informative than others and it is not unknown for annual reports to omit to mention important developments in policing in the area or important statistics.

An understanding of the constitutional position of the chief constable, therefore, is crucial to an understanding of the current accountability debate. His statutory duty to direct and control his force means that he alone is responsible for the orders and policies which result from that duty and the performance of the policing function will depend largely on his views and attitudes. In England and Wales, this extensive autonomy of the chief constable is especially important because most prosecuting decisions are made by the police.

The discretion to prosecute is, of course, only one aspect of the enormous discretionary power vested in the police. The significance of prosecution discretion, however, is two fold. First, selective law enforcement inevitably shades into law-making as by their prosecution policies, the police, and in particular, chief constables, decide which laws to enforce and on what occasions. Secondly, prosecution discretion is largely unchallengeable. The courts have made it clear that the power to review prosecution decisions is likely to be reserved for exceptional cases.[66] It is no part of the police authorities' duty to oversee prosecution policies and the impact of central bodies upon chief constables' discretion is apparently limited.[67] There is at the moment, therefore, no effective institutional apparatus to secure accountability or even uniformity in prosecution decisions.

To summarise then, a chief constable's general decisions regarding the deployment of his force are entirely a matter for him. He is not accountable for those decisions in any meaningful way. Decisions about deployment, however, will have a crucial effect upon what offences are prosecuted and for their prosecution policies, the police are equally unaccountable. In the light of this, it should come as no surprise that chief constables jealously guard their position against any encroachments by police authorities and that there are no immediate plans either to increase the powers of police authorities or diminish the powers of chief constables will undoubtedly give them considerable satisfaction.

Perhaps the most obvious method of reconciling the competing demands of independence and control would be the establishment of an independent prosecuting service. Removal from the police of their prosecution discretion would diminish their power and have other consequential benefits for instance, achieving a degree of uniformity in prosecution decisions. The Royal Commission on Criminal Procedure[68] recommended the establishment of regional, independent Crown Prosecutors.[69] Unfortunately, however, under the Commission's proposals, the Crown Prosecutor's involvement would not commence until *after* the decision to prosecute has been taken by the police and thus the prosecutor's ability to *control* the prosecution decision will be substantially reduced. It should also be noted that the recommended system is unlikely to be introduced for some considerable time.[70]

What then, of the role of the community in securing greater accountability? In the aftermath of Scarman, much has been said of increased liaison between the police and the public. In the autumn of 1982, the Home Secretary issued a circular, directed to police authorities and chief constables, advising the setting up of consultative committees.[71] In the circular, it is said that local communities have the right to wide-ranging discussions with police authorities and chief constables on policing policy. However, it also makes very clear that the deployment of officers, the method and timing of operations and the stage at which these are discussed by the consultative committees, are matters for the chief constable and his senior officers. It is the Home Office's intention to give this scheme statutory authority.[72]

Some local councils and police authorities have taken their own initiatives in this area. For instance, Northumbria Police Authority has made efforts to set up a sub-committee to work with the chief constable to try to improve supervision of police stations by senior officers.[73] Greater Manchester County Council has appointed a Community Liaison Officer, at a senior level, reporting to the Police Authority and the Policy Committee of the County Council.[74] Merseyside Police Authority has appointed a sub-committee to monitor complaints against the police.[75] These developments, together with the consultative councils operating at district and parish level, can perform a useful function in bringing police and community closer together but they can only operate effectively and, in particular, can only hope to exercise a controlling function, in the context of an expanded role for the police authorities.

One way forward, which would not involve radical change, would be to place police authorities and chief constables on a more equal footing. This need not necessarily require diminishing the operational powers of chief constables. A network of police/community liaison committees could report regularly to the police authorities which themselves could be given enhanced powers to seek reports from their chief constables across the whole range of operational matters and a statutory right to be regularly consulted on general policing policy for their areas. These apparently modest changes in practice would have a significant effect as they would considerably strengthen the position of police authorities. As has been said, the extent to which operational matters are discussed by the police authority is entirely a matter for the chief constable. If such a system was buttressed by an independent prosecuting service, police accountability would no longer be a slogan.

Conclusions

The police are going through a difficult and transitional phase and their relationship with society is no longer as readily definable as perhaps it used to be.

The Police and Criminal Evidence Bill contained the basis of governmental strategy for dealing with the policing crisis — considerably expanded coercive powers, minor changs in the procedures for investigating complaints against the police and modest innovation in police/community liaison.

The policing debate, however, will continue because the recommended changes are *ad hoc* responses to what are perceived to be current policing problems. There has been little or no attempt at an official level to take a long-term view of the changes that might be necessary in policing in England and Wales. The last fifty years have seen three Royal Commissions dealing with the police. The first was mainly concerned with police powers.[76] The second, with structure and organisation.[77] The most recent, with pre-trial criminal procedure.[78] By their terms of reference, all three have been confined. The Royal Commission on Criminal Procedure, for example, suggested wide-ranging reforms in the law relating to police powers[79] and the prosecution of offences. As has already been stated, the adoption of a system of independent crown prosecutors has important implications for police accountability. In narrow terms, the commission was aware of that,[80] but it nowhere assesses the impact of its recommendations upon the general arrangements for securing police accountability. On police powers, it argued that law enforcement procedures should be open, fair and workable,[81] but it did not consider what functions society wishes the police to perform and how police powers and the conditions of their exercise are related to the performance of these functions.

In any consideration of policing, the first question to be asked must be, what role do we want the police to perform in society? The answer given to that question has implications for everything else. If the main role is seen as law enforcement, then the police must be organised and equipped, both physically and in terms of the powers they possess, to enable them efficiently to enforce the law. If, on the other hand, the main role is seen as preventing crime and preserving the peace, this equally has implications for police organisation and powers. The preventive role, for instance, will depend on securing the active cooperation of the community and community involvement in policing must inevitably raise questions about community involvement in monitoring and controlling police activities. The most likely answer to the question, however, is that we wish the police to do all of these things. But are we content to allow affairs to continue with perhaps minor modifications, in the way that they have done hitherto? Or is there now a need for a radical review of functions, powers, recruitment, training and accountability? A further point is that the police have taken on a number of roles beyond crime prevention, peacekeeping and law enforcement. In particular, they have entered upon a significant helping and referral role. As a disciplined, organised body, operating with good communications 24 hours a day, the police have proved useful as general providers of assistance — dealing with domestic disputes, lost and found property, missing persons, information giving, the chronically alcoholic and so on. It has been estimated that up to half the time of the police is spent on activities largely unconnected with the prevention and detection of crime. This vast area of police activity must be taken into account when examining the nature of the policing function. Law enforcement, as such, may well be hindered and complicated by the fact that so much police effort is expended on non law enforcement activities. Preventive policing, on the other hand, may well be assisted by this helping and referral role.

It must also be remembered that the effectiveness of the police is largely determined by external factors — the nature of the laws they are enforcing and the preparedness of the public to instigate police activities. It is regarded by many as axiomatic that if the public lacks confidence in and respect for its police, then police efficiency is directly and adversely affected.

Clear, understandable and acceptable policing policies; precise, minimum coercive powers; real opportunities for community liaison and consultation with the police; independent investigation of complaints against the police and an independent prosecuting service — all of these should help to build public confidence and contribute to more effective policing.

The essential interrelationship of these issues, however, will not be considered at an official level if we continue to institute investigations, whether at the level of Royal Commission or Departmental Working Party, which by their terms of reference are forbidden to explore the wider issues. The kind of inquiry needed would be expensive in terms of time and resources, but until it takes place fundamental questions about policing are not going to be satisfactorily answered.

Notes

1. Lord Scarman was appointed on 14 April 1981 to hold a local inquiry under section 32 of the Police Act by the Home Secretary. The terms of reference were 'to inquire urgently into the serious disorder in Brixton on 10-12 April 1981 and to report, with the power to make recommendations.'

2. The Report was published in November 1981 (Cmnd. 8427).

3. The courts have consistently taken the view that policing policy and the control of prosecution discretion will be the subject of review only in exceptional cases. See *R v Metropolitan Police Commissioner ex p. Blackburn* [1968] 2 Q.B. 118 and *R v Metropolitan Police Commissioner ex p. Blackburn (No. 3)* [1973] Q.B. 241, in which Lord Denning MR said '. . . in the carrying out of their duty of enforcing the law, the police have a discretion with which the courts will not interfere' (p. 254).For a more recent example, see *R v Chief Constable of Devon and Cornwall ex p. CEGB* [1981] 3 All E.R. 826.

4. The best example is provided by the famous 'shopping list' of powers submitted by Sir David McNee, former Metropolitan Police Commissioner to the Royal Commission on Criminal Procedure (Cmnd. 8092). See, *Written Evidence of the Commissioner of Police of the Metropolis.*

5. See e.g. the text of a lecture delivered by John Alderson entitled 'From Resources to Ideas' to the Ditchley Conference on Preventive Policing, March 1977.

6. 'The principle remains that a policeman in the view of the common law, is only a person paid to perform as a matter of duty acts which if he were so minded he might have done voluntarily.' *Royal Commission on Police Powers and Procedure*, (Cmnd. 3297) (1927) para. 15.

7. Both the terminology and the policy are most closely associated with J.C. Alderson. His own force adopted the communal policing concept in the mid-seventies. He explains and develops his ideas in his book *Policing Freedom* (MacDonald and Evans 1979).

8. The chief constable of Humberside, for example, refers in his Annual Report for 1981 to 'the move towards community policing' being developed throughout the year. See also the comments of Mr Radley, deputy assistant commissioner, Metropolitan Police, reported in *The Times*, 15.12.81.

9. Details of these Groups are included in 'Policing the Eighties' *State Research Bulletin* (vol. 3) No.19, September 1980.

10. See e.g. Rollo, 'The Special Patrol Group' in P. Hain (ed),

Policing the Police, Vol. 2, (Calder, 1979) pps.153-208.

11. Race Relations and the 'Sus' Law, *Second Report from the Home Affairs Committee,* Session 1979-80, H.C. 559 (1980).

12. See S.8. Note, however, that it was thought necessary in view of the abolition of 'sus' to create a new offence of interfering with vehicles, See S.9.

13. Report of the Scarman Inquiry into the Brixton Disorders, op.cit. para. 4.22.

14. The instructions are quoted in the Scarman Report, ibid., at para. 4.39.

15. Sir Robert Mark provides an account of his efforts to eradicate corruption in his autobiography, *In the Office of Constable* (Collins 1978). An interesting and detailed account of the nature and scale of the corruption is provided by B. Cox et. al. in *The Fall of Scotland Yard* (Penguin, 1979).

16. Section 66 of the Metropolitan Police Act 1839 provides a power to stop and search any person or vehicle reasonably suspected of conveying stolen property or property unlawfully obtained. Similar provisions operate, by virtue of local legislation, in many other parts of the country.

17. These statistics are taken from the Report of the Royal Commission on Criminal Procedure, Law and Procedure Volume 1, Appendix 3, Cmnd. 8092-1.

18. See *In the Office of Constable*, op.cit. chap.11.

19. Sir Robert Mark described the Police Complaints Board as 'a fatuous if costly, irrelevancy.' See *In the Office of Constable*, p.284.

20. The operation of the double-jeopardy rule is discussed in the Fourth Report from Home Affairs Committee, Session 1981-82 on Police Complaints Procedures, H.C. 98-1 at paras. 12-15. See also, Home Office Circular No. 32/1980.

21. See 'Working Together' A Report on Relationships between the Police and the Public in South Yorkshire, South Yorkshire County Council, March 1977.

22. *Worcester Evening News* 12.12.9. Reported in *State Research Bulletin* (vol. 4) No. 23, May 1981.

23. *Role and Responsibilities of the Police Authority*, Merseyside Police Authority.

24. See J.C. Alderson, *Policing Freedom*.

25. The terms of reference of the Commission were *inter alia*, 'to consider the relationship of the police with the public and the means of ensuring that complaints by the public against the police are effectively dealt with.' The majority of the Commission did not think there was a need for completely

independent investigating machinery and s.49 of the Police Act, 1964 follows the majority recommendations of the Commission. Section 49 was, however, criticised in the House of Commons during the passage of the Bill. See e.g. H.C. Deb (5s) vol. 691, cols. 812-830.

26. *Ethnic Minorities and Complaints against the Police*, Home Office Research and Planning Unit, Paper 5.
27. Police Complaints Board, *Triennial Review Report*, (Cmnd. 7966) (HMSO 1980) para. 69.
28. See Home Office Circular No. 32/1980.
29. See *R v Police Complaints Board ex p. Madden* [1983] Crim. L.R. 263.
30. Triennial Review Report, op.cit. para. 62.
31. Ibid., para. 74.
32. At that time, Chairman of the Police Complaints Board.
33. Report of a Working Party on the establishment of an independent element in the investigation of complaints against the police, (hereinafter, the Plowden Report)(Cmnd. 8193) (HMSO 1981). In addition to the chairman, the Working Party comprised three representatives of the association of Chief Police Officers, two representatives of the Superintendents' Association, two representatives of the Police Federation, one HM Inspector of Constabulary, the Director of Public Prosecutions, a representative of the Police Complaints Board and a representative of the Home Office.
34. Plowden Report, op.cit. at para. 20.
35. Ibid.
36. Under Secretary of State at the Home Office. See H.C. Deb. 30th July, 1981, c.467-8.
37. Scarman Report, op.cit. para. 7.21.
38. Ibid., paras. 7.24-7.26.
39. Its recommendations are discussed by the Home Affairs Committee, Fourth Report, op.cit. paras. 30, 31.
40. *The Times*, 12.10.81.
41. Chief constables of Greater Manchester and Thames Valley respectively. See *The Times*, 9.11.81.
42. Mr Dubs' Police Complaints (Reform) Bill was introduced into the House of Commons on 27.10.81.
43. See *The Times* 27.10.81.
44. See *The Times* 9.11.81. The Police Federation demanded that a Bill of Civil Rights be written into any new legislation which would give a police officer against whom a complaint is made the protection of the Judges' Rules, the right to appear before an independent tribunal with full legal representation and the right

of appeal to a Crown Court. However, independent investigation should only apply to complaints of a disciplinary nature. Complaints alleging criminal offences should be investigated by the police. See *The Times*, 10.12.81.

45. See *The Times*, 20.1.82.
46. See *The Times*, 11.3.82.
47. Fourth Report, Session 1981-82, H.C. 98-1.
48. Ibid., paras. 37-43.
49. See now *R v Police Complaints Board ex p. Madden*, op.cit.
50. Home Affairs Committee, Fourth Report op.cit., paras 15, 57-8, 63.4.
51. Ibid., para. 55.
52. See particularly clause 66.
53. Home Affairs Committee, Fourth Report, op.cit., paras. 34, 35.
54. Report of the Royal Commission on the Police, Cmnd. 1728 (1962).
55. Ibid. at p.34.
56. Police Act, 1964, s.4(1).
57. Ibid. ss, 5(1), 6(1).
58. Ibid. s. 7(2).
59. Ibid. s. 12.
60. Ibid.
61. *The Times*, 13.3.82.
62. Note also that the police authority controls the expenditure of the force (Police Act s.8), 50 per cent of which is met from local authority funds and 50 per cent from central government (the local 50 per cent attracts an element of rate support grant). This power of financial control can undoubtedly be used as a lever in appropriate circumstances.
63. Survey of all police authorities outside London on matters of practice by the Joint Working Party of the Association of County Councils and the Association of Metropolitan Authorities. The chief constable did not report regularly on the policing of the areas in 10/41 cases.
64. It did not happen at all in 7/41 cases and was a frequent occurrence in only 10/41 cases.
65. For instance, the Police Act, 1964, imposes a duty on police authorities to keep themselves informed about the handling of complaints in their areas. That power could be used to ask for details about the pattern of police complaints, the nature of the complaints and whether particular police stations are more involved than others. For most police authorities, however, their only exposure to this part of their role is when the statistics on police complaints are presented to them by the chief constable in

his Annual Report and the method and form of presentation is entirely a matter for him.

66. Op.cit. n.4.
67. This was a finding of the Royal Commission on Criminal Procedure op.cit. See, particularly, the discussion at paras. 6-42-6.47.
68. Ibid.
69. Ibid. chap. 7.
70. In its Fourth Report, the Home Affairs Committee recognised that such a major change is unlikely to take place within the next five years. See para. 43.
71. For the text of the circular see H.C. Deb. Vol. 25, col. 281.
72. See the Police and Criminal Evidence Bill, clause 67.
73. *The Times*, 21.6.81.
74. The independent Tribunal set up by the Greater Manchester County Council into the Moss-Side disturbances recommended such an appointment.
75. *The Times*, 14.9.81.
76. Royal Commission on Police Powers and Procedure op.cit. Its terms of reference were '. . . to consider the general powers and duties of police in England and Wales, in the investigation of crimes and offences. . .'.
77. Royal Commission on the Police, op.cit. Its terms of reference were 'to review the constitutional position of the police. . . the arrangements for their control and administration and in particular to consider: (1) the constitution and functions of local police authorities; (2) the status and accountability of members of police forces. . .'.
78. Op.cit. n.4. Its terms of reference were: '. . . to examine. . . whether changes are needed in England and Wales in (i) the powers and duties of the police in respect of the investigation of offences and the rights and duties of suspect and accused persons, including the means by which these are secured; (ii) the process of and responsibility for the prosecution of criminal offences; and (iii) such other features of criminal procedure as relate to the above. . .'.
79. Ibid. See the summary of recommendations at paras. 5.1-5.18.
80. Ibid. See particularly the discussion at paras. 6.48-6.60.
81. Ibid. at para 2.18.

5 'Community Policing'; A Sceptical Appraisal

By P.A.J. Waddington

Introduction

Since the inner city disturbances of 1981 the concept of 'community policing' has dominated public discussion of policing policy. Indeed, it has been siezed upon by all political parties as a panacea for solving the crisis of public confidence in the police.[1] It profoundly influenced the recommendations of the Scarman Inquiry.[2] Police forces throughout the country have been eager to show that they are implementing such ideas in their areas.[3]

The largely uncritical acceptance with which this notion has been welcomed is itself a danger. Any proposal, however attractive, should be subjected to careful and sceptical scrutiny. In seeking to do this, I shall assume that advocates of 'community policing' mean what they say: that they are not advocating it as either a public relations 'cover' for 'soft' policing, acceptable to liberal opinion, or as an attempt to subvert oppositional groups — the velvet glove of class oppression.[4]

Since the major exponent of 'community policing' is the former Chief Constable of Devon and Cornwall, it is important to underline that this appraisal will be concerned with the *concept*, not its implementation in his or any other force.[5] It may be that many positive initiatives are taken in the name of 'community policing', but are not always derived from nor necessarily consistent with that notion.[6]

However, the practical implications of 'community policing' will concern us in one respect. Since this notion has been widely seen as being most clearly applicable to the policing of inner city areas of high ethnic minority concentration, critical attention will focus particularly on its applicability in this context.

'Community policing': an outline of the concept

The concept of 'community policing' is most systematically articulated by John Alderson in his book *Policing Freedom*[7] and it is to the argument presented therein that I shall address this critique. In it he begins by drawing attention to the first duty of the police, which is the maintenance of the 'Queen's Peace', not the enforcement of law. The police must use their discretion to enforce the law in such a manner as to maintain public tranquility and prevent crime.[8]

However, the police alone cannot maintain social order through external regulation. Order is overwhelmingly maintained by the community itself, through instilling acceptance of communal values and standards of proper conduct.[9] Effective maintenance of order must always be through the consent of the community, for this is the prime influence. The police officer must be a part of that community, a 'citizen in uniform', not an alien force, otherwise the potential for tyranny inherent in policing would quickly be realised.[10]

Policing by consent, he continues, has been the tradition of the British police. However, strains have arisen because of increasing industrialisation, urbanisation, bureaucratisation and cultural pluralism. These factors have destroyed the moral consensus, and undermined the communal basis of social life.[11]

The police response has been to rely on mobility, specialisation, and technology, which has distanced them from those they serve. The emphasis has shifted from preventative to reactive policing: rather than trying to prevent trouble by their presence, they await the occurrence of trouble and seek to respond quickly to it. As social problems grow, this dependence on reacting to trouble produces an emphasis on the means of repression, by officers whose only contact with the public is conflictual, which further alienates the police and the policed.[12]

The alternative, in Alderson's view, is to reawaken the tradition of policing by consent and maintain the 'Queen's Peace' through preventing crime. However, this cannot be achieved by reaffirming a moral consensus. In a multicultural society the police must accept and be acceptable to *local* community values.[13] They must also influence that community to reinforce those influences which promote the maintenance of order and the prevention of crime.[14]

The proposed vanguard for this initiative must be the local

permanent beat officer,[15] who through his routine presence can nurture non-conflictual relationships with members of the community, promote positive, and counter negative, influences. He embodies the principle that the police work on behalf of the community and are not an alien presence. He must be sensitive to and accept the community's definition of his role, and influence it through being an exemplar of the 'good citizen'.[16]

Through this means, it is argued, cultural differences will be respected and individual freedoms guaranteed. The community will define what is tolerable and not be oppressed by the enforcement of alien values through repressive means. Maintaining order and preventing crime will be a collaborative enterprise.

An example of 'Durkheimian Romanticism'?

What scant critical attention the concept of 'community policing' has received, has been to label it 'Durkheimian',[17] as though this were criticism enough. Whilst the theory does undoubtedly rest on Durkheimian assumptions, Alderson, at least, does not rely upon a notion of a single moral consensus uniting the whole society. He quite explicitly acknowledges cultural pluralism, what sociologists, even non-Durkheimians, would describe as 'sub-cultures'. He shares the necessary sociological assumption that the norms and values of each sub-culture largely determine the actions of its members. Social order, then, is largely determined, at the sub-cultural level of the local community, by these norms and values which the police must accept and seek to influence.

A more serious objection is not that the concept is 'Durkheimian', but that it is fundamentally *romantic*. As Howes says[18] of senior police officers, including Alderson, attending a conference in 1975:

> In both (urban and rural areas) it is often difficult to discover evidence, even in older age groups, of any residual allegience to 'the community' as either a meaningful concept or a physical configuration. Yet the police . . . emphasised the need for a specific community role, of community leadership and heightened community involvement, as if a prime objective of contemporary policing was to recapture and revive what Peter Laslett has called 'the world we have lost'. Surely an expensive and demanding exercise in vain pursuit of an 'ideal type' which, rather like the notion of 'original sin', has gradually retreated to the periphery of everyday evidence and values?[19]

Alderson does not pretend that a moral consensus can be regained at the societal level, whilst regretting the passing of such an era. What he does believe, is that the formerly harmonious relationship between the police and policed can be resurrected at the local level.

His conception of policing rests upon harking back to a romantic idyll of harmony and tranquility — 'the world we have lost'. But when and where was this idyll to be found? Police historians[20] generally agree that the police were introduced and employed during the 19th century to suppress 'the dangerous classes'. In doing this the police neither sought nor obtained the consent of those they policed.[21] Even relatively recently, it is reported that in some traditional working class districts the police were unwelcome and resented.[22]

Nor, in the past, were the police any less isolated than they are now. As representatives of the law, they found the expectations that ordinary citizens had of them, whether on or off duty, onerous. They, therefore, kept themselves apart.[23] Indeed, the modern policeman, living in his own house amongst non-police officers, is in this respect less isolated than generations of his predecessors who lived in segregated police housing 'colonies'.

If harmonious relations were not characteristic of urban policing in the past, perhaps they were to be found in the village — the paradigmatic 'community'. However, according to Cain's comparative study of rural and urban policing[24] it was not the supposed homogeneity of communal values in the village which allowed the local constable to benefit from the support of those he served. According to her account, it is, in fact, clear that the constable did not police with the unanimous consent of the village. What he actually benefited from was the smaller scale of the village which meant that his 'beat' would normally encompass the full social spectrum, from the most respectable of the 'respectable classes' to the roughest of the 'disreputables'. Knowing his place, the constable would impose 'respectable' values on the disreputable members of the village and receive support from 'respectable' villagers for so doing.

Paradoxically, then, it is the rural policeman who polices a *heterogeneous* population and is readily able to obtain support from the dominant classes for his actions. By contrast, it is the urban policeman who, according to Cain's account, encounters a homogeneous community, for, in the larger scale of the city, his whole beat may be contained within a single class or ethnic boundary. Unfortunately, if it is a culture he neither understands nor perceives as legitimate, he confronts it as a hostile outsider. At the same time, he finds himself isolated from the support of the 'ordinary, decent people' on whose behalf he sees himself policing. Thus, although the city often comprises an array of sub-cultures, the individual policeman's experience tends to be contained within just one such group. Far from being a source of harmony, homogeneity of this kind can be a source of conflict.

However, whilst it is a romantic delusion to believe that 'community policing' will, in fact, resurrect 'the world we have lost' — because it is doubtful whether we ever possessed it — this does not mean it is undesirable to create this 'world' anew. That the concept is descriptively flawed does not mean it is prescriptively inappropriate. However, I contend that it is inappropriate.

Policing by consent — whose consent?

Central to Alderson's argument is the belief that the police must act with the consent of the policed. In a multi-cultural society this means with the consent of the local community.

The prime objection to this view is that if society is comprised of a number of local communities each possessed of a distinctive culture which the police must accept, this would necessarily entail fragmentation of policing policy along community boundaries. Conduct acceptable in one community may be unacceptable in another. Enforcement of the law could literally depend on which side of the street the act was committed. This is precisely the kind of arbitrariness in the exercise of police discretion of which many liberal criminologists have rightly complained:

> . . . in one area of the city, pinching bottoms constitutes the criminal offence of indecent assault for which the offender will be likely to be arrested and prosecuted, whereas in another area such conduct is consistently overlooked. To justify these different approaches on the basis that in one neighbourhood the dominant culture is Scots-Protestant and the other is Italian-Catholic gives rise to the legitimate complaint that the police are not enforcing the law equally.[25]

Such practices, Grosman continues, are 'inconsistent with any theory of the rule of law'.[26] Yet, Alderson proposes to elevate what is often seen as an abuse of police discretion to a principle of policing policy.

Alderson's argument would appear to rest on the unwarranted assumption that in a multi-cultural society, all the constituent sub-cultures are equally good. It is perfectly conceiveable, and often observed, that sub-cultures maintain orderly behaviour without that behaviour being desirable. For example, if Hall et. al.'s description[27] of the West Indian immigrant 'colony' as a sub-culture tolerant of illegal drinking, gambling, prostitution, small-time racketeering and petty crime is true, is it a sub-culture that society as a whole would wish the police also to tolerate?

Of course, so-called 'victimless offences', especially those involving alcohol and morality, do not occasion much concern amongst liberals, even though such offences may sometimes be distinctly harmful. However, the concept of 'community policing' does not propose to disregard them because they are minor social evils, but because the community tolerates such behaviour. If so, the police must also ignore far more disagreeable offences when committed within communities that are tolerant of these. In some districts racialist abuse, vandalism and assault may not only be tolerated but actively encouraged. To take 'community policing' seriously would oblige the police to ignore racial harassment, just as they are invited to ignore the petty crime of the black ghetto.

Even if there were no moral objection to accepting communal values, there would remain pragmatic ones, for it is assumed by advocates of 'community policing' that such values are homogeneous at the local level. However, as Hall et. al. reveal,[28] even the 'colony' is divided between the 'hustlers' and the 'respectable, church-going West Indians'. Brown, himself an advocate of 'community policing', recognises that the latter section of the Handsworth community were the most outspoken in favour of the police cracking down on the former, whom they felt brought discredit to West Indians as a whole.[29]

This raises the problem of not only which communal values the police should abide by, but also what is to count as a 'community'. If 'the community' is identified by shared norms and values, the distinctive sub-culture of the young Rastafarians would certainly qualify.[30] Therefore, the police would be obliged to respect their self-proclaimed habit of smoking 'ganja' whatever the surrounding community of 'respectable' West Indians thought. This would simply highlight the problem of a fragmented policing policy. Moreover, if skinheads could claim that they too share distinctive sub-cultural values, they must also be treated with equivalent tolerance.

Furthermore, as communities change, the values of some may conflict with the values of others. Lambert reports[31] that the Birmingham Police tacitly tolerated prostitution and allied offences in the 'red light' area of Varna Road. However, the Asian immigrants who began settling in that area in considerable numbers during the mid-1960s were outraged by the existence of brothels, their women being accosted, drunken men making a nuisance and the other accompaniments of this 'victimless offence'. Accordingly, they pressed the police to suppress prostitution and its associated manifestations. 'Community policing' offers no guidance as to which set of competing communal values the police should respond to in conditions such as these, because it is uncritically founded upon the assumption of communal consensus.

Added to these uncertainties is the distinct danger that a policy of 'community policing' would become the reality of 'ghetto-isation'. A tolerance for lawlessness in one area, which was not tolerated elsewhere, would soon leave the residents of that district isolated and imprisoned. Such, it has been reported,[32] has been the fate of Liverpool 8 since the riots of 1981. Because that district is no longer so strictly policed (presumably for fear of adverse public reaction) outsiders no longer venture into or through it and residents, appalled at what is happening, cannot move for no one will purchase their homes. It has long been a source of complaint in the USA that the police tolerate intra-racial violence amongst ghetto blacks, which then flourishes unchecked.[33] Again, however, advocates of 'community policing' seek to transform what is seen elsewhere as a form of racialism into a principle of policing policy.

In short, if advocates of 'community policing' mean what they say about policing by consent, then it is a prescription for arbitrariness and uncertainty. It must violate the 'rule of law' and holds distinct dangers for any community whose values tolerate a greater level of lawlessness than that tolerated elsewhere.

Two meanings of 'order'

At the risk of some incoherence in their argument, advocates of 'community policing' do not envisage the police passively accepting communal values, but seeking to influence them by reinforcing those aspects of the community which promote order. This is to be achieved by initiating various forms of community action in liaison with other interested groups. Through this means the police will fulfil their first duty, to maintain order by preventative action.

The flaw in this argument lies in conflating two meanings of the term 'order'. The first, from which the argument proceeds, points to the seamless web of reciprocal expectations that lubricates everyday social interaction. It is a sociological truism that social order results from people's acceptance of standards of proper conduct. However, it is a terminological confusion to believe, as advocates of 'community policing' apparently do, that the police have a duty to maintain 'order' in this sense. If they did, they would have the right, indeed the duty, to require parents, say, to adopt more effective methods of disciplining their children, if they believed that certain child-rearing practices were likely to lead to delinquency.

That the police do not have this duty, nor indeed the right, testifies to the narrower conception of 'order' that they are charged with maintaining. The police task is to intervene when disruption of social order is or threatens to become intolerable. They have no duty actively to promote harmony and tranquility, merely to prevent disharmony and tumult.

Nor is it either appropriate or desirable that the police should assume this wider responsibility. It is not appropriate because they are not the most strategically placed social agency to perform this task. They play *a* part in the maintenance of the wider social order, but *everyone* has a duty to participate in this. Educators, for example, could make a much more convincing case that their's is the central role, for it is they who are given responsibility for instilling the values that guide conduct.

It is not desirable that the police should take the initiative in these matters, because in doing so they pose a threat to civil liberties. Harmony and tranquility are to be valued, but if pursued with single-mindedness may result in suffocating conformity. Individual civil liberties must also be safeguarded, even if they present some threat of disturbance to the fabric of social order.

Indeed, from this point of view there is much to be said for the 'reactive' style of policing, to which 'community policing' is posed as an alternative. If the police await complaints from the public before intervening, as they overwhelmingly do,[34] then it is left to the public to determine what is and is not 'intolerable'. If the police assume wider responsibilities for promoting harmony, it will be they who define what is tolerable. It is a sad irony that a doctrine designed to avoid tyranny, would if it were taken seriously, promote it. It would certainly seem to satisfy one of Chapman's criteria of the police state — 'penetration'.[35] This is the 'encroachment of the police apparat, under one pretext or another, on the general police powers of other institutions — licensing, social security, the professions, education, the media. . .',[36] indeed all the things 'community policing' prescribes.

A more agreeable style of policing?

In the public mind 'community policing' means none of these things, it is synonymous with the restoration of the 'bobby on the beat'. This figure, being less remote than the police officer flashing past in his patrol car, is the spearhead of 'community policing', because he will be able to resurrect close, personal relations with the members of the community through his non-conflictual contact with them.

The issue here is not whether permanent beat officers, who have been an integral part of police operations for well over ten years, perform a valuable role, but whether they are the model for the police force of the future. To believe that returning more officers to foot patrol duties will improve police-community relations is a romantic delusion. When the police patrolled mainly on foot, before the introduction of mobile patrols on a wide scale, they did not enjoy particularly close personal relationships, nor have much non-conflictual contact, with members of the community, especially in the inner-city areas where 'community policing' is offered as a solution to poor community relations.

According to Cain,[37] the urban beat policeman had few 'peace-keeping' duties and adopted a definition of 'real police work' as involving mainly the arrest of those engaged in serious crime. Denied much opportunity for this, officers harassed and arrested the more vulnerable sections of society, such as the homeless and the intoxicated. Relations between the police and young white delinquents in the 1950s and 60s were no better, to judge from contemporary delinquency studies,[38] than they are now between the police and young black delinquents. Reading the delinquency studies of that period, one could easily be forgiven for believing that the allegations of police harassment and brutality made then were actually the contemporary complaints made by young blacks now. The foot patrols did not know many individual members of the communities they policed, for there are simply too many for them to know on a personal basis.[39]

Despite the fact that things were not much better in the past, it is widely claimed that the public want policemen back on the beat. However, public 'wants' are not undifferentiated: in an emergency the public usually demands a swift response from the police. For example, Maguire found[40] that victims of burglary immediately turned to the police expecting an equally immediate response, which they normally received. Where there were complaints, these included not responding quickly enough, even though victims realised that there was little, if any, chance of catching the offender. Within any given level of resource allocation these demands are contradictory, since beat officers will always be slower to respond to an incident than mobile patrols.

Indeed, 'reactive' or 'fire brigade' policing has been subjected to undeserved criticism. In purely law enforcement terms, a prompt response to a complaint from a member of the public by the police is more likely to lead to an arrest. The reason is less dramatic than the popular image of the search, chase and arrest. The public are far more likely to witness offenders committing offences, simply because they are more populous than are the police. By being able to rapidly respond to public compalints, therefore, the police are more likely to catch the offender committing the offence. Often, it is victims and witnesses who detain the offender or identify them so as to lead to an immediate arrest. Maguire found that the detection rate for burglary increased from less than thirty per cent to almost forty per cent when the offence was discovered shortly after its commission and reported immediately.[41]

It is also often alleged that 'reactive' policing is 'hard' policing, in which police and public have only conflictual contact. However, the majority of calls received by the police are for non-law enforcement assistance. This fact has led Punch and Naylor to describe the police as the 'secret social service',[42] for it is the only 'fully mobile, 24 hour emergency service'.[43] It is, moreover, a service which is most extensively used by those in the deprived, high-crime areas whose residents are thought to be most alienated from the police.[44]

In short, it is difficult to disagree with Reiss,[45] who remarked about a similar debate in the USA:

> Some people. . . may claim that, in the past, when police were organised around foot patrols, they were far more effective in dealing with crime. However, such an attitude may rest in nostalgia rather than fact. There is good reason to believe that the foot patrolman responded primarily to citizen mobilisations, he was relatively ineffective in dealing with crimes without citizen cooperation, he rarely discovered crimes in progress, and his capacity to prevent any crime was extremely limited by his restricted mobility, especially after the advent of the automobile.[46]

Rejecting the tradition of British policing

By emphasising 'reactive' policing, and in their enthusiasm for technology, police policy-makers are accused by advocates of 'community policing' of discarding the tradition of British policing of which this country is rightly proud. The essential component of this tradition is the common law conception of the office of constable as one of the local citizenry. This conception is threatened with replacement by that of the 'professional' police officer — detached, isolated and anonymous. This appeal to tradition is not only unconvincing, it is misconceived, since, if anything, the traditional role of the police supports the 'professional', not the 'community policing' conception of the constable.

The concept of the police officer as a 'citizen in uniform', so often employed by advocates of 'community policing', is a legal notion of limited sociological and historical significance. It draws attention to the fact that, in law, the police have few powers not possessed by the ordinary citizen[47] and are not immune to legal action by virtue of their office. Indeed, a police officer is legally responsible, as an individual, for the actions he takes in fulfilment of his duty. As advocates of 'community policing' rightly observe, this is part of the common law heritage contained in the ancient office of constable. In pre-industrial England, the constable was a member of the local community, appointed for a limited period in rotation, and responsible to the Justices of the Peace.

What this picture of unbroken continuity ignores, however, are two important facts. It ignores the inefficiency, corruption and disrepute into which, by the early 19th century, that office had been brought. It was the collapse of this system of policing under the strains imposed by industrialisation and urbanisation which necessitated the introduction of the modern, professional police force. It also ignores the significant break with the past that was contained in those reforms of policing.

According to Miller,[48] whilst retaining their traditional legal position as 'a citizen, locally appointed under the Crown', the New Police were a distinct departure from tradition. Certainly in London — the model of British policing — officers were not members of the community which they policed. There was a policy of recruiting men from outside London if possible and certainly from outside the district they were to police, in order to minimise the possibilities for corruption and local involvement. For the same reason, married men were preferred and a strict code of quasi-military discipline, governing both private and professional life, applied. Constables were attired in quasi-military uniform which was meant to set them apart from ordinary citizens. They were expected to behave with detachment, impartiality, impersonal authority and restrained force. They did not always do so, but this was the foundation of their traditional image, much later to be described as making the police almost a sacred social institution.[49] In other words, far from being that of the integrated member of the community, responsive to particular local values and norms, the tradition of British policing is one of detached professionalism.

The New York police, which share the same common law tradition, did develop along the path of the police officer being a 'community constable'. Locally recruited, responsive to the values of his ethnic community, locally and democratically accountable to elected representatives, not in uniform so as to demonstrate that he was as much a citizen as those he policed, the early New York police officer was almost the model 'community policeman'. He was also corrupt. The reasons for corruption are greater than those relevant to his role as a 'community constable', but the fact that police officers were integrated into their local communities had something to do with it, argues Miller.[50] His prime duty was to his local ethnic community, in whose service he would be expected to ignore breaches of the law and harass the latest wave of immigrants without much regard for legality.

If this study in comparative history is any guide for the future, the model the police should pursue is their true tradition of detached professionalism.

Conclusion

'Community policing' is a romantic delusion, not for the 'world we have lost', but for one we never had. It harks back to a harmonious idyll, where the police were everyone's friend. It was never thus, and it is unlikely that it ever will be.

The police were introduced in their modern form to contain the growing violence that accompanied urbanisation. They retain today the same essential role as monopolists of legitimate force in civil society. Their authority to intervene in almost any emergency rests upon their capacity to resort, if necessary, to legitimate coercion. In a society which is simultaneously posing greater strains upon the police to deal with conflict in its manifold forms, whilst rightly demanding higher standards of competence and professional integrity, the legitimacy of police authority is a most sensitive issue. To respond to this situation by the futile search for social harmony, would be to avoid the questions that must be confronted. What is required is not less, but more professionalism, especially in the management of conflict.

The problems which most acutely confront the police are those of policing the inner-cities. Here, most of all, what is required is impartial, impersonal authority and restrained use of force. In these areas the police may indeed be seen as a visible irritant. It is even more essential, therefore, that they be seen as representatives of the law, above considerations of class and race. Whatever the deprivations and disadvantages suffered by those in the inner-cities, the police must take the situation as they find it. It would be contrary to the rule of the law, and to the long-term detriment of the police themselves, if they were to adopt a policy of tolerating greater lawlessness in some areas than in others.

The solution to the problems of policing the inner-cities will not be found in policing alone and least of all in 'community policing'. To focus upon policing is to distract attention from the deprivations and disadvantages suffered by residents of the inner-cities, the response to which brings so many young people, both black and white, into conflict with the police.[51] As Terence Morris wrote in his sadly prophetic foreword to Lambert's study of policing the inner-city of Birmingham[52] dated August 1968:

> (Rejecting those who reject them is the natural response of young blacks) and the reapers in the field will not be the local councillors, the writers of letters to the local newspapers, the

authors of racialist broadsheets, but the agents of order out there on the streets. It will not be of their sowing, but it will be the police who will bare the brunt of what may come.[53]

* I am grateful to Mr P.S. Schofield, Lecturer in Law at the University of Reading, for having read the original script and for a number of invaluable suggestions.

Notes

1. P.A.J. Waddington, 'Are Our Politicians Chasing an Illusion?', *Police*, 15 (3), 24-26.
2. *'The Brixton Disorders 10-12 April, 1981'*, Report of an Inquiry by the Rt. Hon. the Lord Scarman (Cmnd. 8427), (HMSO, 1981).
3. See, for example, the *Report of the Commissioner of Police for the Metropolis for the Year 1982*, HMSO, 1983.
4. M. Brogden, *The Police: Autonomy and Consent* (Academic, 1982, pp.214-19); L. Bridges, 'Keeping the Lid On' and L. Kushnick, 'Parameters of British and North American Racism', both in *Race and Class*, 1981/2, vol. 23 (2/3), pp.182-4, and pp.197-8, respectively.
5. J. Brown, *Policing by Multi-Racial Consent* (Bedford Square Press, 1982); and C. Moore and J. Brown, *Community Versus Crime* (Bedford Square Press, 1981).
6. Ibid. See also, P.A.J. Waddington, 'Beware the Community Trap', *Police*, 1983, vol. 15 (7), pp.32-4.
7. J. Alderson, *Policing Freedom* (MacDonald and Evans, 1979).
8. Ibid., ch.3. See also, J. Alderson, 'The Case for Community Policing', in D. Cowell, T. Jones and J. Young (eds.), *Policing the Riots* (Junction Books, 1982), p.139.
9. Ibid., pp.35-6.
10. Ibid., ch.3.
11. Ibid., ch.24 and 25.
12. Ibid. pp.41-2.
13. Ibid., pp.46-8, and ch. 26.
14. Ibid., pp.46-8.
15. Otherwise known as 'Community Constable', 'Home Beat Officer', 'Resident Beat Officer', 'Area Beat Officer'.
16. Ibid., p.176 and p.179.
17. See, for example, S. Holdaway's review of D. Watts Pope and N.L. Weiner (eds.), *Modern Policing* (Croom Helm, 1981) in *Sociology*, 16 (3), pp.464-5.
18. G. Howes 'Introduction', in J. Brown and G. Howes (eds.), *The Police and the Community* (Saxon House, 1975).
19. Ibid., p.5.
20. See, for example: C. Reith, *A New Study of Police History* (Oliver and Boyd, 1956); T. Critchley, *The Conquest of Violence* (Constable, 1970); J.J. Tobias, *Crime and Police in England, 1700-1900* (Gill and Macmillan, 1979); K. Chesney, *The Victorian Underworld* (Penguin, 1968).
21. Indeed Alderson admits as much, ibid., 'Introduction'.

22. B. Whittaker, *The Police* (Eyre and Spottiswoode, 1964), pp.54-5. See also ch. 2 in this volume.
23. M. Banton, *The Policeman in the Community* (Tavistock, 1964, ch.7); M. Cain, *Society and the Policeman's Role* (Routledge, 1973).
24. Ibid. ch.4.
25. B.A. Grosman, 'The Discretionary Enforcement of Law', in S.F. Sylvester and E. Sargarin (eds.), *Politics and Crime* (Preager, 1972), p.72.
26. Ibid., p.73.
27. S. Hall, et. al., *Policing the Crisis* (Macmillan, 1978).
28. Ibid., pp.348-62.
29. Op. cit., ch.3.
30. E. Cashmore and B. Troyna (eds.), *Black Youth in Crisis* (Allen and Unwin, 1982), ch.1 and 2.
31. J.L. Lambert, *Crime, Police and Race Relations* (OUP, 1970).
32. N. Lyndon, 'Inside the Ghetto', *Sunday Times*, 4 July 1982, p.17.
33. See, for example, J.H. Skolnick, 'The Police and the Urban Ghetto', in A. Niederhoffer and A.S. Blumberg (eds.), *The Ambivalent Force* 2nd edn., (Dryden, 1976).
34. A.J. Reiss, *The Police and the Public* (Yale University, 1971); R. Mawby, *Policing the City* (Saxon House, 1979); E. Cumming, I. Cumming and L. Edell, 'Policeman as Philosopher, Guide and Friend', *Social Problems*, 1965, vol. 12 (3), pp.276-86.
35. B. Chapman, *Police State* (Pall Mall, 1970).
36. Ibid., p.118.
37. Cain, op. cit., ch.3.
38. T. Morris, *The Criminal Area* (Routledge, 1957), ch. 10; and D. Downes, *The Delinquent Solution* (Routledge, 1966), ch. 7.
39. Cain, op. cit., ch. 4.
40. M. Maguire (in collaboration with T. Bennett), *Burglary in a Dwelling* (Heinemann, 1982).
41. Ibid., ch. 5.
42. M. Punch and T. Naylor, 'The Police: a Social Service', *New Society*, 1973, vol. 24 (554), pp.358-61; M. Punch 'The Secret Social Service', in S. Holdaway (ed.) *The British Police* (Edward Arnold, 1979).
43. Punch and Naylor, ibid., p.358.
44. Reiss, op. cit., pp.15-17.
45. Ibid.
46. Ibid., p.97.
47. Even this observation is of dubious accuracy, since the police officer's power to arrest on suspicion that an offence has been

committed is qualitatively greater than that enjoyed by the citizen. (P.S. Schofield, personal communication).

48.   W.R. Miller, *Cops and Bobbies: Police Authority in New York and London, 1830-1870* (University of Chicago Press, 1977).
49.   Banton, op. cit., ch. 7.
50.   Op. cit., ch. 1.
51.   Lambert, op. cit., ch. 1-4.
52.   Ibid.
53.   Ibid., p.9.

6 Law and Order in Multi-Racial Inner City Areas — The Issues after Scarman

By John Rex

Introduction

The events which occurred in Brixton, Southall, Toxteth and other places in the summer of 1981 posed the question as it had not been posed for a very long time of the role of the police in society. This has been largely overlooked because of widespread misunderstanding in political quarters as to what the enquiry conducted by Lord Scarman was about.[1] His report is commonly thought to have been a report on race relations and it is true that issues were confused by the fact that, once he had been appointed, there was a clamour for an enquiry into the so-called 'social' causes. Scarman, however, was a Judge and his true competence was limited strictly to legal and police matters. Clearly no one man without sociological training could in the time available possibly have produced a satisfactory account of the social causes and what was included in the report on these questions was pretty well the received and often dubious wisdom of the main departments concerned with race relations matters.

This interpretation of Scarman seems the more justified because of what has happened or not happened subsequently. Had the riots been due to social causes like unemployment, poor schooling and lack of social facilities they clearly would have recurred because in all these areas things have actually got worse since 1981. What has received more consideration is the effectiveness of policing and there have been changes there both in the direction of greater effectiveness in police control of the areas and in greater sensitivity to community responses, whether or not these changes were in accordance with Scarman's specific recommendations. Temporarily at least the police have been held back from doing their job in ways which in 1981 provoked riot. What still has to be demonstrated is that the changes initiated are sufficiently strong and permanent to produce a lasting law and order situation which is regarded as legitimate by the communities concerned.

Models of policing

Before we look at Scarman's findings or his recommendations we should perhaps stop and ask ourselves what exactly we expect of police in modern urban society. Are they to be thought of as a strictly non-political force whose task it is to protect life and property and at the same time to guarantee the rights of individuals to pursue political interests in a normal way? Are they, on the other hand, to be thought of as representing the interests of one section of society and using 'legitimate' physical coercion against certain other groups defined in terms of class or age or race. Or, finally, do we in fact accept to some extent that we live in a police state in which the police are not ultimately subject to political authority, and in which they, rather than the politicians, decide what kind of law and order shall be enforced?

Clearly there are certain understandings which have been worked out between police, politicians and public about the limits of police intervention in industrial conflicts, in political demonstrations and, more generally, in community affairs. In industrial conflicts we think of it as the duty of the police to allow legal picketing but to intervene if either side appears to be breaking the rules of the game. Obviously this does not prevent the police from sometimes being charged with bias, but the important thing is simply that this is a recognised area of debate. Again, so far as marches and street demonstrations are concerned, our understanding is that where such activities do not have a clearly illegal aim, they should be permitted and that it is the duty of the police to facilitate them. We prefer it to be left to elected politicians to say what kinds of demonstration are and which are not illegal and we try to limit police discretion as much as possible. Finally, in homogeneous communities, and particularly in working class communities the 'heaviness' of policing, that is the extent to which laws limiting social practices are enforced, may be limited by the degree of public consent. Thus, for example, the police may wink at violations of the law relating to drink and gambling and law and order will not break down because the community sets its own limits to what is and what is not permissible.

An alternative to this liberal model of the role of police in a democratic society is the model of their role in a class state. Such a model is of course never suggested as an ideal. Even if it were a guide to policy it would actually be disguised in terms of the liberal model. It is, however, the model which critics often use to explain actual police behaviour. The police are seen as central to the repressive state apparatuses which are concerned with maintaining the rule of the dominant class and suppressing opposition to it.

In my own view what has happened in Britain with the rise of working class political power and the emergence of the Welfare State is that the second model has become less applicable than it once was and that the existence of such power means that the police are forced to work within the framework of the first so far as the working classes are concerned. This is something which one may expect to see for fairly long periods, though, of course, a radical move of politics to the right and the decline of working class power might well be expected to see the revival of the role of police as agents of a class state.[2] What is more important, however, from the point of view of this chapter is that, although a liberal pattern of policing may have prevailed so far as the working classes are concerned something far more akin to the repressive class state model may have operated in the policing of immigrant areas. While most White people in Britain feel that they can ultimately rely on the police to defend them, for many young Blacks they seem an alien force or an occupying army. In a word — in fact in the word most widely used today by young Blacks — they represent Babylon.

But just as our government is unlikely to admit to setting up repressive apparatuses to act against the working classes, so it will not publicly admit to setting them up against racial minorities. There may, of course, be a measure of hypocrisy about this and the more so in the case of racial minorities than in the case of the working classes, but even the mere protestation of high moral ideals makes some difference to a society and the police may well find that there is little support in public discourse for overt oppression of Black people. The problem then is whether they still act illegitimately, that is to say, without public support.

In fact there is a fundamental contradiction in our society between our ideological professions and our actual practice. The result of this is the emergence of illegitimate political forces which follow through the practice without being burdened by ideological professions. More than this they may actually challenge formal ideologies and develop their own alternative ones. Thus while British governments have vacillated between high-sounding ideological professions and *de facto* acceptance of discrimination and oppression in racial matters, extreme right wing groups have arisen which do not hesitate and are quite open about encouraging racial attacks. As they put it, using a racist phrase, they are prepared to call a spade a spade.

The question which we have to ask is how the police relate to groups of this kind. Do they allow them a place within the liberal consensus, facilitating their political activities along with those of, say, trade unions or peace demonstrators? More than this, and worse than this from a liberal point of view, do they themselves use their control of legitimate violence to further the racialist policies of the extreme right? Are the police in fact an independent racialist force in their own right?

To ask these questions is not to assert any particular answer to them. In fact aspects of police organisation and behaviour can be found which fit the liberal model, the class model and the police state model both in relation to the policing of the working classes and in relation to the policing of racial minorities. Our task in the first place must be to use these models as ideal types to interpret social reality, and we should certainly resist any attempts by the police public relations apparatus to deny us the right to ask such questions. Beyond this, however, there is a further task. Since there are those in the police as well as outside who allow their behaviour to be influenced by all three models we also have to ask which model will prevail or what kind of resultant of conflicting pressures will emerge.[3]

There has in fact been little in the way of objective evidence on what happens in the policing of multi-racial inner city areas which would enable us to carry out either the interpretative task of seeing to what extent the different models of policing are operating or the more predictive one of suggesting what kind of resultant will emerge. On the one hand there are works like that of the journalist Derek Humphrey[4] and the publication of the Lambeth Council before the riots in Brixton,[5] which simply document Black minority complaints without really testing their validity. On the other there are the press releases of Scotland Yard suggesting high rates for particular crimes amongst Blacks which on the whole do not stand up to critical scrutiny.[6] More recently there has, it is true, been a more thoroughgoing study by the Policy Studies Institute[7] which is to be published after this chapter was written, but insofar as this was a study commissioned by the Commissioner of the Metropolitan Police, it may also be thought to have limitations.

In these circumstances the Scarman Enquiry does have considerable importance. It is, of course, not of itself an objective study. Perhaps the best way to define it is to say that it both sought to discover whether proper policing procedures were operating and at the same time to say what those proper policing procedures might be. If anything its ideological stance is that of the liberal policing model though it necessarily modifies this as it spells out its meaning in a specific context.

What is most important about the report, however, is that it is an attempt by government at the highest institutional level to gather and assess the evidence and reach policy conclusions. In what follows we will look at what Scarman found and the recommendations which he made.

The Scarman report

The fact that what Scarman actually said should actually be almost an object of research is a result of the fact that the Inquiry and the Report came quite widely to be viewed as a study in race relations. This was due to the fact that the Labour Opposition and the liberal members of all political parties partially misunderstood what was intended when the enquiry was announced. Thinking that it would be the kind of enquiry which would apportion guilt and that the focus would be on the criminal intentions of the young Blacks, they insisted upon an enquiry into 'the social causes'. What they overlooked was that the enquiry would also be one into policing methods and that this was Lord Scarman was particularly well equipped to do. Since, however, the demand for the social causes investigation was conceded and the task of doing it was assigned to Scarman what one has in the report is on the one hand a meticulously careful account of the events which occurred together with a set of important if arguable recommendations regarding police procedure; on the other, a set of propositions about the causes and remedies of race relations problems which were presumably put together by civil servants on the basis of reports received more or less at random which sometimes simply represent civil service wisdom and are sometimes fatuous and misleading.[8] What we can gain from the Scarman Report however is an important insight into what happened in Brixton and into the sociology of policing as it appears to someone as eminent as Lord Scarman.

The event which triggered the first phase of the rioting was, according to the police, an attempt by a policeman to rescue and give first aid to a bleeding man running from several others who had stabbed him. Strangely, there is no record of any attempt to arrest the man's attackers though that may indeed have occurred. But, even if we allow that the policeman concerned was motivated by the highest humanitarian aims and was not actually intent on arresting an injured man for being involved in an affray, what is clear is that the bystanders did not see it that way. They believed that the man concerned needed medical attention and did not believe that he would get it if this was left to the police. There was no way in which they could see that policeman as a protector and friend. Even what he was to represent as a humanitarian act was seen by the community as an attack.

The second incident was of a more routine kind. Marijuana is widely used in the West Indian community and the police use their powers to stop and search where there is reason to suspect possession of the drug. The widespread claim in the community is that they use such powers even when there is no reasonable ground for suspicion and that such stopping and searching is one of the main ways in which the community is 'harrassed'. It was not surprising then that when the police saw a taxi driver stuffing pound notes into his socks they claimed that they thought these were packets of marijuana and decided to search him. Equally it is not surprising that the crowd watching became angry and truculent and resisted the police search.

Beyond these triggering events, of course, all sorts of other decisions were made about the appropriate police action and at each stage decisions were made which escalated the conflict. Numerous criminal acts were committed by those who had originally only been onlookers as they took part in resistance to the police and each time they were dealt with police action against them produced more resistance. Very soon stones were being thrown, cars were being set on fire and shops were being looted. From an original set of simple police actions a situation which seemed to be approaching a local uprising or civil war seemed to be in progress. The officers commanding the police began to talk of military strategies and comparisons were made with Belfast.

The police would see the account of the Brixton events in the above paragraphs, even though it is based on Scarman, as profoundly biassed against the police. Many of them believe that, given the existence of a large criminal minority amongst those on the streets, the reactions of the public were not simply those of innocent outrage. Criminal gangs were using these events to undermine law and order and behind them were various groups of political agitators waiting for any chance to foment revolution. More moderately there are some who would say that, in the event, a policeman arresting a potentially dangerous criminal cannot be expected to act with the sort of nicety required by his liberal critics and that faced with the need for rapid decisions on the spot any sensible policemen would have done what was done and that in these circumstances riot was inevitable.

Such police reactions are understandable and there is no doubt an interpretation of the events which is distorted in that it assumes that the members of the public who became engaged in the disturbances were all political innocents doing nothing but going about on their lawful occasion and being meaninglessly assaulted by the police. But the police reactions also include strong veins of authoritarianism and racism and the questions which have to be asked relate to the ways in which their task of maintaining law and order can be effectively carried out without risking the danger of minor incidents escalating into riots. The point as Scarman saw it was not only to preserve law and order but how to do it without disturbing what he called 'public tranquillity'. It was with this in mind that he made his recommendations.[9]

The first set of recommendations related to recruitment and training. Means should be found of eliminating those who are racists at the moment of recruitment, the training which all police are given should be extended to six months and should include training in understanding the cultural background of ethnic minorities. Secondly Scarman calls for much more careful monitoring and supervision of young constables, for training Inspectors and Sergeants in this supervision as part of their managerial training and for making racially prejudiced and discriminatory behaviour to be made an offence under the Police Discipline Code punishable by dismissal.

Scarman does not call for the ending of hard policing methods and the use of the Special Patrol Group and their replacement by methods of so-called 'community policing'. He thinks that the hard policing methods must be kept in reserve by the police at all times. Nevertheless he does criticize the specific decisions which were taken in Brixton such as the organisation of Operation Swamp involving massive stopping and searching of large sections of the population. He also does recommend a number of specific measures of community policing based upon the notion that the officer on the beat should know and be known by those whom is he policing.

Under the heading of consultation with the local community, Scarman first of all abstains from making police accountable to police committees of local Councils, but argues for the setting up of 'consultation'. In the case of London what is recommended is not the setting up of new police committees of the Borough Councils or of the Greater London Council but consultation with the 'community', a term which is left ambiguous as possibly meaning the elected Councils but also referring to ethnic minority liaison.

Most of the above recommendations refer to changes in policing practice. There is also a set of recommendations about changes in the law. These include a careful watch on the development of the Criminal Attempts Act which was passed in 1981 with the abolition of the 'sus' laws, the rationalisation of the law on stop and search, a system of random checks by lay visitors to police stations to witness the interrogation of suspects and the reform of the police complaints procedure to allow for an independent element in the investigation of complaints.

Finally, there is the question of the handling of riots and events which might lead to riot. Scarman does not oppose the possession by the police of such equipment as water cannon, C.S. gas and plastic bullets, but says that they should only be used in the gravest emergencies where there is real apprehension of loss of life and then only if their use is authorised by the Chief Officer of Police himself.

In trying to estimate what difference the Scarman report has made to the multi-racial inner city areas, four things are to be noted. Firstly the recommendations themselves are very moderate. Secondly they have by no means been accepted by Government or by the Police Authorities. Thirdly some kind of changes are in train, which have some relation to Scarman although they do not necessarily and literally follow from his recommendations. Fourthly, the reaction of the police as a whole has been negative and that of the Police Federation positively hostile.

The problem of racism

Clearly the *sine qua non* of any change which would ensure that our system of policing the multi-racial inner city areas moved towards the liberal model is the rooting out of racism. Scarman's approach to this is to treat racism as a clearly identifiable condition in a potential recruit and racially prejudiced and discriminatory behaviour as a quite specific punishable offence. It must be said at once that this represents from a social science point of view a somewhat simplistic and dated approach to the problem. Racism is something which pertains not simply to the psychology of individuals but to the belief systems which operate in society. In this sense it is, as the Policy Studies Institute will argue, pervasive in the police. The problem is what, if anything, can be done about it.

The major development which has occurred is the adoption of a programme of what is called Human Awareness training at the Police College at Hendon. This is apparently a version of what is sometimes called Ethnic or Racial Awareness training which is widely used in the United States[10] and has also been used recently by Local Authorities in Britain.

There clearly are limitations on what is likely to be achieved at Hendon, but there are also serious limitations about the method itself. The Hendon syllabus was introduced at a time when a Lecturer at the college had just been dismissed for making public the racist quality of the essays produced by Hendon cadets and it can hardly be without significance that the title 'Human Awareness' was preferred to 'Racial and Ethnic Awareness'. There does seem to have been some reason to suppose that any outright challenge to racist thinking at Hendon was being avoided.

More generally, however, the use of Racial and Ethnic Awareness training itself may be criticised. It was developed first in the United

States after the Government had publicly committed itself to an overall programme of bringing Black Americans as equals into the mainstream of American life and it therefore had some legitimacy. It was also clear to those who took the courses that they would be rewarded for accepting its aims. These things are also partly true in some local authority areas in Britain where the authority has embarked on an Equal Opportunity policy. In fact the conditions of the success of the policy are (a) that the trainee should know that he is receiving a course in what is his employers committed policy and (b) that he knows that he will be rewarded for supporting that policy. If either of these conditions are not true then the training will at best have only a superficial effect as a training in ideal ethics removed from the everyday reality of life, but, at worst will be counter-productive. Both of these things are probably still true at Hendon.

It probably is the case that the senior officers who have introduced this training programme at Hendon do genuinely wish to change racial attitudes and there is a sense in which their understanding of racism and their aim to change it are more radical than Scarman. But the problem in institutionalising such a system remains that of first educating the educators. Those who have had contact with police inspectors[11] and have discussed race relations with them will know how difficult this is. Certainly the present generation of Inspectors not merely have archaic colonialist, racist and authoritarian attitudes, but have probably gained their promotion because they do. Toughmindedness is far more likely to lead to promotion than refined sensibility towards ethnic minorities.

It can also be argued that to set out to improve the attitudes of policemen is misguided. The likelihood is that they will include some good, some bad and some morally indifferent men. What one can do is to insist on codes of conduct as to how they should conduct themselves professionally. Not merely is this a matter of public servants not giving offence to the public, although that is important. Much more to the point in the policeman's case is the fact that if he behaves in a racialist way he cannot be professionally successful. The fact of the matter is that the Policy Studies Institute study still found in 1982 that racial abuse accompanied arrest very widely indeed. It is perfectly possible to control this if there is any will to do so, whether the police involved hold racist beliefs themselves or not.

The prevention of racial conflict in the Inner City clearly does depend upon a large scale education programme, nonetheless, and such a programme must include the police. What Scarman has done perhaps is to put the issue on the agenda and to give those few Senior Policemen who are converted to the cause of anti-racism a basis on which they can argue with their less enlightened colleagues. There is reason to suppose that the implementation of Section 71 of the 1976 Race

Relations Act[12] by Local Authorities has created some momentum in this direction in Local Government. The terrain is tougher in the police, but it is worth noting that a fight is being waged there too.

Probably the next most important set of proposals in the Scarman report is that which relates to accountability and community relations. On the first part of this little headway has been made. The police claim that if they were subject to Local Government we would have a political police and in operational situations they would have their hands tied behind their backs. Members of police committees on the other hand claim that a police force which is *not* accountable will be the most political of all. Statements by some Chief Constables recently certainly do suggest that this is true. One at least seems intent on enforcing if possible the narrow-minded morality of the so-called Moral Majority.

It is possible that some councils might emerge in the future who would seek to direct the police for political purposes and there can really be no guarantees that they would not, any more than there can be guarantees that police who are unaccountable will on their own. But no institutions can ever be guaranteed as perfect. It would surely be possible to envisage a situation in which a chief constable, while insisting on his own day-to-day operational control regularly discussed questions of policing policy with his police committee and, more than this, modified that policy in the light of discussion. What has actually emerged, however, is a situation in which the majority of chief constables seem to have simply asserted their independence and even the Home Secretary himself seems to lack the power and the authority to tell them what to do.

What Scarman recommended was a statutory duty to make arrangements, not for accountability, but for community liaison. The former concept requires recognition of an elected authority. The latter can be achieved through a hand-picked committee. Much effort was put by the Home Secretary himself into forming a liaison committee in Brixton and, given the disastrous break-up of an earlier committee, the police have been anxious to keep this one in being. But such committees suffer from a general problem. They can seem to work very amicably and to the satisfaction of the police yet at the same time to lose their connection with the community. One may well expect in a future riot that the liaison committee had been persuaded to approve the forms of policing which led to the riot. Little would then have been achieved.

Community liaison will work best, in fact, if at least there is a strong representation from the elected members of the local council as well as of a wide range of minority organisations. They will moreover need to discuss major issues of police policy even when the views of committee members are radically opposed to the police themselves. The choice is really between open argument in the committee chamber or violent confrontation in the streets.

What such committees ought to be discussing are the other recommendations of the Scarman Report, in which in most cases Scarman has suggested leaving great power in the hands of the police but argues that it should be used with discretion. The task of the Community Liaison Committee could be precisely the exercise of that discretion. There are many examples of 'hard policing' where the introduction of tougher methods has not been the result of some immediate operational exigency and where the policy issue involved could have been discussed with a Community Liaison Committee. Again, if it is true as the Policy Studies Institute report suggests that Black Youths are far more often stopped and searched than White Youths, then it would be appropriate for the Liaison Committee to ask why and, if unconvinced by the answers to require the police to revise their policy.

Finally one should notice the importance of an independent element in the complaints procedure. Most people in Brixton remember that after the riots a raid was carried out on certain homes under the pretext of looking for bomb-making equipment which involved quite needless damage to property. The redress obtained from the subsequent enquiry carried out by the police was minimal. In cases like this clearly there is a need not merely for an independent element in the complaints procedure. What was necessary was a wholly independent investigation.

Recently it has become apparent that many complainants who fail to get satisfaction under the complaints procedure may take civil court actions against the police. Some have gone directly to the courts. The police response to this is to say that because standards of proof are lower in the civil courts it might well be the case that even though damages may be awarded in the courts an action under the disciplinary procedures would fail. Those who make this point seek to emphasise the importance of justice to the police officer concerned. They seem to ignore the question of justice to the complainant. One might as well say that the standards of proof required for the defence in the disciplinary procedure are too low.

The Asian community

In focussing on the findings of the Scarman Report we have, of course, been dealing primarily with the problems of Brixton and with those of a West Indian descended community. A quite different range of problems, however, faces areas of Asian settlement like Southall, East London and parts of the West Midlands. There the complaint is not of police harrassment but rather of the failure of the police to protect the lives and property of Asian citizens when they have been attacked.

The sorts of experience which Asian citizens have had in places like Southall or Coventry recall the experiences of the Jews in the inter-war period. Houses have been daubed with racist graffiti; burning material has been pushed through letter boxes; shops and temples have been subject to arson attacks; individuals have been physically attacked and quite a number actually murdered. The failure of the police to protect the community against such attacks has led to demands for the setting up of vigilante groups amongst young Asians and to conflict between these groups and their potential attackers. There was a Home Office investigation of this topic and it was admitted that the problem existed. Nonetheless the Home Office refused to accept a recommendation of a largely Christian group that special Police Units should be set up to deal with this situation. It remains the case today that many Asians are gravely dissatisfied with the kind of protection which police offer them.

Coupled with the problem of racial attacks has been the problem of racist and Fascist marches into the immigrant areas. Although these have now abated somewhat there were a number of instances where groups known to have violently racist policies marched into immigrant areas carrying Union Jacks and apparently protected by the police. In the reverse situation where Asian marches (usually protesting against racial attacks) occurred the police responded to racial abuse by outsiders by merely separating those concerned from the march.

It was against this background that the riots in Southall occurred in the days which followed the July riots in Brixton. A group of skinheads using a pop concert as a base and a recruiting ground set out to attack Asian shops in Southall. Young Asians prepared to defend themselves and, seeing the police not as their protectors but as part of the enemy, confronted the police as well. Previously, of course, the largely white Anti-Nazi League had confronted the National Front in the area and one of their members, Blair Peach, had been killed by the police.

What happened in Southall was not studied by the Scarman tribunal which has therefore dealt with only part of the total problem. It should be remembered moreover that there is no neat distinction which can be made between the problems of the Asian and the West Indian communities. Asian youths complain of police harrassment and West Indians are subject to racial attack. The Scarman Report is therefore an incomplete report on the problems of policing inner-city minority areas. It needs to be extended to take account of the need to protect Black and Asian minority communities from attack. Liaison committees might well expect reports from the police on this matter and should be able to demand more effective protection.

Conclusion

In this discussion of the Scarman report and its recommendation what we have done is to assume that what is sought at present in Britain is a liberal type of policing, one, that is, which is not political in helping one group to pursue its interests at the expense of another, but which rather holds the ring so that individuals and groups in a free society have their lives and property defended and are free to live their lives in their own way. Given this goal, certain recommendations follow. Scarman may be said to have made the very minimal recommendations necessary. Those who want to see this type of society realised will want to see Scarman's recommendations implemented plus much more besides.

A quite different question, however, is the question of what is likely to happen as distinct from what anyone might want to happen. To judge this one has to look at the trends of opinion both within the police and within majority and minority communities. So far as the first of these is concerned there seems to be little ground for optimism.

The great weight of police opinion after the publication of the Scarman Report was against its implementation. Almost immediately the public was told that crime rates in places like Brixton were soaring and were out of control because of the new soft policing methods which Scarman required. Statistics were published by Scotland Yard purporting to show that certain types of crime popularly referred to as mugging were largely committed by Black people and there was systematic resistance to Scarman on issues like that of making racially prejudiced behaviour a disciplinary offence. Finally, the Police Federation has continued to campaign politically against the report with some of its officers making grossly offensive and racist speeches at fringe Conservative meetings.

Certainly, if one went by majority opinion only, one would expect that the police would continue to be a law unto themselves especially on racial matters and that, if their right to go their own way were challenged by a liberal Home Secretary, they would simply defy him. And that may well be the truth of the matter. It is, however, the case that we do now have a minority of relatively senior policemen who have taken on board the Scarman recommendations and more besides. It remains to be seen whether they have the wits and the skill to outmanoeuvre the more vocal reactionary majority.

For the present it does seem that organised racism amongst the White majority in Britain is in retreat. Significantly a motion at the Conservative Party Conference of 1983 which called for an end to all immigration, voluntary repatriation and the repeal of all race relations legislation was overwhelmingly defeated. It remains to be seen, however, whether this defeat in the public forum of the Conservative

Party does not merely result in a renaissance of various extreme neo-Nazi and racist groups as well as in the encouragement of racial attacks by minorities amongst the young White unemployed.

In the circumstances one would not expect that Black politics would move more towards moderation. Young West Indians who think about politics today are more and more concerned with the politics of resistance and it is a more important matter for them how they prepare to defend themselves on the streets against the police than how they vote or what kind of support they seek from political parties. If they relate to the British political system at all it is likely to be through the organisations of the Far Left. The stage seems set then for years of confrontation if not actually for a repetition of the riots. It may even by the case that there are those in the Black political leadership who do not want any change in policing policy because confrontation is what they most need to advance their kinds of political cause.

Obviously these developments will be accelerated or checked by the extent to which on other levels Britain succeeds in promoting equality of opportunity and racial integration. To that extent those who set up the Scarman enquiry were right to suggest that the enquiry should be extended to take on board other questions than those of policing. But the system of policing takes on a life of its own as a political fact and the future of race relations may well be dependent upon the kind of police force which we allow to exist. Even more seriously British society as such becomes endangered, if, as a result of their pursuit of independent policies in the race area, the police become independent of political control. That is why the Scarman issues are important not merely for the Blacks of Brixton but for all of us.

Notes

1. *The Brixton Disorders 10-12 April 1981.* Report of an inquiry by the Rt. Hon. the Lord Scarman (Cmnd. 8427)(London, HMSO, 1981).

2. The relationship which I envisage here between policing in a class society and policing in a society where there is countervailing class power parallels what I have written elsewhere about the working class in the Welfare State. See especially the opening chapter of J. Rex, and S. Tomlinson, *Colonial Immigrants in a British City* (Routledge and Kegan Paul, 1979).

3. The idea which I am advancing here is based upon my reading of Myrdal's famous appendix on 'Facts and Valuations in Sociology' which is republished in his *Value in Social Theory* (Routledge and Kegan Paul, 1958).

4. D. Humphry, *Police, Power and Black People* (Panther Books, 1982).

5. Lambeth, Borough of, *Final Report of the Working Party into Community/Police Relations in Lambeth* (1981).

6. These statistics were not published but given as a press release.

7. At the time of writing the report of the Policy Studies Institute which was commissioned by Sir Patrick MacNee of Scotland Yard and for which the research team was led by David Smith has not been published, but it has been extensively leaked. See the front page article in the *Guardian*, 29 October 1983.

8. My own research Unit was one body which gave evidence to the Scarman Report but there was no serious discussion of this evidence and could not be in the time. The whole set of arrangements here was quite different from that which was made after the 1967 riots in the United States where the Kerner Commission received and used large bodies of social science evidence.

9. Scarman report op.cit.

10. J. White, *White Awareness — a Handbook of Anti-Racism Training* (University of Oklahoma Press, 1978).

11. I write this with regret but after many visits to the Junior Command Course in Bramshill Police College.

12. This Section of the Act calls on, though it does not require, Local Authorities to promote Equal Opportunity Policies in Employment.

7   Strikes, Free Collective Bargaining and Public Order

By Andrew Cox

Perceptions of a developing crisis in labour relations

Academic and political perceptions of labour relations have changed remarkably since the 1950s. In 1952, an Oxford industrial relations expert could write of the 'withering away' of the strike as a trade union activity. Strikes existed at local levels but they were of short duration; large national and disruptive strikes had not been seen since 1933.[1] National arbitration and conciliation was replacing the strike due to industrial harmony in an era of economic growth. This perception was mirrored in social and political writings of the time. The period was characterised as an age of consent, faith in authority and legitimacy.[2] Political writers talked of Britain as an homogeneous society in which fundamental class conflicts had been superseded by a political and industrial consensus over the welfare state, economic growth and redistributive justice.[3]

Contrast this view with writings of the 1970s. In labour relations class conflict and industrial militancy are seen as the cause of Britain's precipitate decline. Social and political writers talk of 'The New Barons', 'The New Leviathan', 'Union Power' and a crisis of industrial relations.[4] This view maintains that Britain is 'strike prone', and this is the proximate cause of Britain's economic decline. Furthermore, public order is threatened by the new tactics of militant (communist inspired) trade unionism — wildcat strikes, mass picketing, flying and secondary pickets, the closed shop, the refusal to maintain essential services and clashes between strikers and the police. To restore industrial harmony and re-assert the primacy of Parliament and the rule of law it follows from this analysis that the trade unions must be controlled.

This view commands considerable popular support amongst the electorate and it is clearly the strategy favoured by the Conservative Government of Margaret Thatcher. Despite its electoral popularity, however, both this view and the earlier consensus view can be seen as partial analyses which are historically contingent. Neither of them fully explains what was happening in labour relations in the post-war period, nor explains fully the breakdown in industrial relations which has been manifest since the late 1960s. To understand more clearly what was happening in this period one must first look at the empirical evidence of strike activity. From this, it can be argued, that, while strikes may contribute to Britain's economic difficulties they are hardly appreciably worse anywhere else, nor do they constitute the fundamental threat to law and order which the media and right-wing political commentators portray them as.

Trends in British strikes: the empirical evidence

Strike statistics are at best a rough guide to what has been happening because they suffer from a number of serious limitations and distortions. Strike statistics take little account of the differences between strikes. A one-day stoppage in a small engineering factory is unlikely to have the same impact as a six month stoppage in British Leyland; yet they each appear as one strike in statistics. British strike statistics are also not strictly comparable with other countries. Britain has an elaborate system of data collection. The accuracy of statistics will depend a great deal on the method of collection. Britain relies on employer notification to the Department of Employment. Some countries rely solely on government officials or social security officers. Clearly then the sophistication of each country's data collection system will affect statistical series. Added to this, of course, there is evidence in some countries that governments and employers often try to conceal strikes from public attention. Furthermore, British statistics exclude certain strikes systematically. Political strikes do not appear and, to be counted at all, a strike must last for one full working day, involve at least 10 workers or result in the loss of over 100 working days. This implies that the number of strikes in Britain may be higher than is officially recorded.[5]

Bearing these caveats in mind what can we say about trends in strikes in Britain?

i) *There has been an increase in the number of strikes since 1945 compared with earlier periods.* This has not been an exponential growth. The average number of strikes since 1945 has been higher but it has tended, apart from one or two years, to remain between an average of 2,000 to 2,500 strikes per year, compared with an average below 1,000 in previous years. Remember of course that the size of the working population has also grown rapidly.

ii) *There has been a reduction in the number of workers involved and in the number of working days lost.* The average size of strikes involved 300 workers in 1900 and 1940-1950. This rose to 600 in the 1960s and was much higher in the early 1970s. But this rarely approached the levels experienced in the mass national stoppages between 1914 and 1930.[6] The annual average of working days lost has fallen dramatically. Up to 1933 the average was 15 million per annum. Since 1933 the annual average fell to 3 million until the return of large national stoppages in the 1970 period, when it rose to around 11 million.

iii) *Wildcat or Unofficial Strikes have dominated in all periods.* Over 90 per cent of strikes have not been officially sanctioned. Such statistics were only kept since 1960, but historical evidence supports this view. However, the periods when strikes have resulted in massive numbers of working days lost (1920s and 1971/72) have seen official strikes increasing.[7]

iv) *By international comparison Britain's strike rate is average and has not changed appreciably recently.* Generally Britain has a higher number of strikes (like Australia and Canada) than elsewhere. But the number of working days lost and workers involved is around the average. The duration of British strikes is relatively low by comparison with many other countries. Furthermore, even when Britain had a wave of strikes after 1968, this was an international phenomenon in which 'unofficial' strikes predominated; while in Britain the trend was towards more official strikes. Even in this period the increase in all indicators was only around the average. The percentage increase in all countries for the number of stoppages was proportionately higher than in the UK. Only the USA had a lower percentage increase. In terms of man days lost the UK had an increase lower than the average.[8]

What conclusions can we draw from this quantitative analysis? First, it is clear why some writers felt that industrial harmony had returned to Britain in the immediate post-war years. The number of working days lost and workers involved in strikes fell dramatically after 1933. This was due to the ending of national stoppages. On the other hand, little was made at the time of the fact that localised disputes were much higher and national stoppages were to return in shipbuilding and engineering (1953) and on the railways (1955). But does the return to national stoppages support the 'New Leviathan' thesis of Britain's decline? On the surface it does, but on closer analysis we can see that this explanation is at best partial. The 'New Leviathan' thesis rests its case almost exclusively on the fact that the number of strikes in Britain are 'unofficial'; that they are caused by militant shop-stewards (communist inspired mainly); that the number of strikes in Britain is higher than elsewhere; and, that they are disruptive of economic performance and a threat to public order. How much truth is there in this interpretation?

It is true that there has been a rise in the number of strikes recently. But, if strikes have always been largely 'unofficial' in Britain this alone cannot be the only, or the most potent, explanation of this trend. There must be other reasons why strikes have increased in number since 1945. Secondly, even in the period of the 1970s when public order was said to be breaking down the number of strikes did not rise remarkably compared with the whole of the post-war period. Only in one or two years (1969-1972 and 1979) was the increase remarkable and most of this increase can be explained by large official stoppages not unofficial action. It is official action (often in the public services) that has caused so much media and political attention, rather than unofficial action. However, this trend has not been maintained consistently and in comparison with the 1910-1920 period recent strike activity has been lower. What is remarkable, then, is the political and media attention to this action compared with the earlier period. Furthermore, internationally Britain's situation is not unique. Britain may be above average in terms of the number of strikes since 1945, but this has always been the case. Added to this Britain's record of increased strike activity after 1968 is no worse than in other countries. On this evidence Britain may have more strikes in number but is not 'strike prone' compared with other countries. Indeed, as Turner has argued, strikes in Britain are short and involve fewer workers on average compared with the longer stoppages in other countries. From this Turner argues that economic disruption from strikes is likely to be less in Britain than in countries where large national stoppages spread to other industries, seriously hampering industrial performance.[9]

Despite the refutation of the 'New Leviathan' thesis contained in these statistics, one cannot escape the conclusion that, compared with the period 1933-1967, industrial relations are in a state of turmoil not experienced since the 1910-1930 period. These changes are however qualitative rather than quantative. National stoppages lasting longer than the localised disputes of the immediate post-war period have returned and these have spread to new groups (doctors, teachers, health workers and air-traffic controllers) who have not normally been regarded as strike prone. The effects of strikes are now more apparent because they occur more often in essential services, where a new militancy and willingness to allow essential services to fail has been noticed. But, what is most apparent is not that there are strikes in the essential services (these occurred in transport and mining in earlier periods) but that strikes now appear to be directed *against the state.* In this way strikes come to take on a more clearly political image, because they seem to question the legitimacy of government decisions in a way that was not apparent when many of these strikes were against private employers.

Arguably the real problem here is not the practices of trade unions but the way in which the state has adopted different strategies to manage British capitalism. These have necessitated increased state intervention in the traditional voluntaristic labour relations process developed in Britain since the nineteenth century. When we understand that it is the state which is questioning the status quo, as it seeks to restructure labour relations in the interests of economic growth, in an era of economic decline, then it becomes clear that the industrial crisis is not due to the trade unions as such but the state's misguided interventions. This causes a perception of a political and economic crisis when in fact strike activity in Britain is not appreciably worse than elsewhere, and is hardly the fundamental cause of economic decline. Because the state finds it difficult to sustain its policies, politicians come to blame trade unions as the most immediate symbol of their failure. The press and media comes to accept this rationalisation of failure and the defensive activities of trade unions become the cause rather than the effect of economic decline.

The state and the politicisation of labour relations in post-war Britain

The British state has used four approaches historically to manage labour relations. These four approaches can be defined as *legal repression, legal restraint, voluntarism* and *corporatism. Legal repression* refers to the forceable use of the law to make trade union organisation illegal. This approach has not been used in Britain since the era of the Combination Acts (1799-1825).[10] *Legal restraint* refers to the use of the law to confine trade union actions within certain legally defined parameters, where the unions have certain legal rights as well as obligations (such an approach has been used historically in the USA). *Voluntarism* refers to a system in which the state keeps out of labour relations and tries to ensure that the legal system does not interfere with the free development of collective bargains arrived at between employers and workers. *Corporatism* refers to a state-labour relationship in which trade union leaders are incorporated into state decision-making and, in return for policy concessions and a commitment not to restrain trade union actions legally, the state expects the leadership to intervene on behalf of the state to control its own members in the interest of economic growth.

Prior to 1945, apart from the development of corporatist relationships in the two world wars, the traditional response of the state to labour relations in Britain was *voluntarism*. A premium was placed on avoiding the use of the law in resolving labour conflict. This was not always possible, because the judiciary often tried to restrain trade union activities. The most notable examples perhaps being the 1900 Taff Vale and 1909 Osborne decisions.[11] But, since the state was not directly involved in managing industrial conflict, even when there were waves of strike activity in the 1880-1890 and 1910-1920 periods, strikes were not a key political or electoral issue. The state recognised the right to strike but it relied on employers to discipline the workforce. Strikes were therefore caused mainly by inter-union disputes, wage conflicts in periods of depression and conflicts with employers over union recognition. Only when the state sought to incorporate trade unions during the first and second world wars and impose wage restraint upon them, or when the judiciary attempted to circumscribe union rights, could it be argued that the state was contributing directly to strike activity. Interestingly, however, corporatist arrangements led to a wave of militant shop-steward and unofficial strike activity in both wars. This action was directed against the state and official trade union leaders, who were seen as reducing traditional trade union free collective bargaining rights.

Since 1945 things have changed remarkably. The state has gradually reneged on *voluntarism* for two main reasons. The post-war settlement ensured that the state would take a much more active role in economic affairs and welfare provision and, as Britain's economic decline became apparent, this has forced the state to intervene to restructure labour relations. It is this attack on voluntarism, in the context of an economic crisis which forces governments to reduce living standards and question traditional labour practices, which is the true cause of increased post-war strike activity, not the growing militancy of workers. True, workers are prepared to strike more readily and in areas which were formerly strike-free, but this is due, first, to economic decline and state intervention which provides the environment for wage militancy. We can more fully comprehend this changed relationship if we look at the various strategies adopted by the state to manage labour relationships in the context of the relative decline of the British economy since 1945.

(i)   1945-1959: Keynesian voluntarism

After the war unions wanted to return to voluntarism as a reaction to the corporatist trends of the war. Trade unions wanted to end the state's use of compulsory arbitration and manpower planning, but they also wanted to maintain a continuing bi-partite relationship with government, now that it was to take a more interventionist stance in relation to full employment, growth and welfare provision. Even after 1951 Conservative Governments' accepted this broad Keynesian approach to voluntarism and, indeed, went out of their way to conciliate industrial disputes in the early 1950s. Since economic growth was remarkably high and material living standards rose quickly in the 1950s there was a general perception that industrial harmony had arrived in Britain and media and political discourse reflected this perception.

The underlying reality was however very different. The number of local 'unofficial' strikes rose to new levels. This led to local wage rates rising well above nationally agreed rates and above the level of productivity. This process is known as *wage drift*.[12] In the conditions of relative prosperity and full employment wage increases higher than manufacturers would ideally prefer could however be countenanced.

The state guaranteed full employment and encouraged national wage agreements but there were inherent problems here. The state had taken responsibility for a large number of industries in the essential services after 1945. It had become a large employer in its own right in transport, mining, power supply and service industries. Indeed the exponential growth of the tertiary sector after 1945, with more and more workers paid for by the state in welfare services (teachers, doctors, nurses, manual local authority workers, etc.) meant that labour relations could no longer be left to the private sector alone. The main reason for this was that although wage drift occurred in this period it was confined largely to the private sector; national agreements were more effectively maintained in the centralised bargaining system in operation in the public sector. Whenever the gap between national agreements and local wage drift grew disproportionately there would be a problem of relativities viz-a-viz the public and private sectors, generating national stoppages. In the early 1950s this problem was bought off by conciliation and the state conceding higher settlements in the public sector.[13]

Politicians began to realise the dilemma which the state faced by the end of the 1950s. It was gradually becoming apparent that Britain's economic growth was poor relative to other countries and that, in order to encourage economic growth, wages would have to be curbed so that profits could rise for re-investment.[14] It is this problem of relative low growth, and the government's response to it, which is crucial in understanding the gradual return of national stoppages in the late 1950s. The state began to redefine its role in labour relations and, while it did not intervene directly to control wages, after 1955 the state became much more active and started to politicise industrial relations. All of this was a trend against voluntarism and it generated national stoppages — on the railways (1955), in engineering and in shipbuilding (1956) and public transport (1957).[15]

Now that Britain's economic performance was in decline, and given the state's central role as employer after 1945, it was impossible for the state not to take a stance on labour relations. But what strategy should the government choose? All of the approaches which the state might choose in Britain are prey to contradictions. Furthermore, all of them (apart from voluntarism) politicise industrial relations, the state and the legal system.

(ii) *1960-1967: incipient corporatism*

By the end of the 1950s, while the strategies of *legal restraint* and *corporatism* were being debated in the Conservative party, Macmillan adopted instead the corporatist approach. This was not a fully state directed approach because it tried to win *voluntary* acceptance for wage restraint. To have been a fully fledged approach the state would have had to incorporate unions and impose compulsory arbitration of wage disputes. The government did not do this, and because the unions feared that they were being allowed to participate in discussions about economic planning in the NEDC simply in order that they would accept wage restraint, the approach merely led to union opposition and strikes. Macmillan would not impose pay norms compulsorily, except in 1961, and attempts to win voluntary restraint failed after concerted union strike action in shipbuilding and engineering (1962) and construction, railways and postal services (1963-64).[16]

Clearly the state was now politicising strikes as it attempted to intervene in labour relations. The Labour Government which retuned to office in 1964 merely served to reinforce these trends as its own corporatist strategy came into collision with Britain's declining economic performance and the voluntaristic defence of union rights, in a period of rising inflation and material expectations. Labour tried to strengthen the approach adopted by Macmillan. Economic planning was to be supported by new administrative structures (DEA, Ministry of Technology, IRC, a National Plan and Regional Planning). Trade union leaders were incorporated more effectively, with Frank Cousins of the TGWU becoming Minister of Technology. Wages and prices were to be controlled through a National Board for Prices and Incomes and a Royal Commission was created to look into trade union 'wildcat' strikes. This corporatist strategy was to be cemented by higher economic growth, higher social spending and more redistributive justice. It was a strategy which failed.[17]

The problem for Labour was the structural decline of British industry. The decline in Britain's share of world trade, and the beginnings of the end of the long post-war boom in Western capitalism, left Labour continually beset with sterling crises, generated by the decline in export competitiveness and a lack of confidence by international bankers and currency holders, who disliked Labour's expenditure commitments and interventions in industry. Labour responded to these sterling crises by using traditional deflationary measures of reducing expenditure and curtailing its planning exercises. This implied as well a policy of income restraint to shift resources out of consumption into export related industrial investment. This of course was a particular problem because it also coincided with a rising trend of inflation and material expectations. Gradually, Labour was forced to turn against its union allies. Initially it had been intended that incomes policy would be supported voluntarily, but this did not have the desired effect. While the unions might agree nationally to restraint, 'wage drift' through unofficial action ensured that the policy was broken. The seamen's strike of 1966 was a classic example of this dilemma. This strike more than any other symbolised the politicisation of labour relations by the government. Wilson accused communist wreckers of causing the strike and focused media and public attention on strikes to a degree unseen before. From this date Labour moved towards a statutory approach to incomes policy and a policy of further deflation and expenditure cuts.[18] Voluntarism had gone and was to be replaced by a six month freeze on wages, with severe restraint afterwards.

This was a new approach, the law was being used now to impose state incomes policies on workers. This approach quickly alienated workers and unions even though strikes fell for a while in 1966. The problem was that after the statutory freeze the problem of wage drift reappeared. Private sector workers could use 'unofficial' action to find productivity loopholes in the policy. Public sector workers could not and they had to rely on the TUC to win concessions from government for the low paid. In an inflationary period this approach was made doubly difficult to sustain by the government. Public sector workers felt that they were bearing the brunt of the freeze and they wanted an end to it. Even private sector workers felt that they might be able to win higher wage rates under free collective bargaining. It is not surprising therefore that rank and file trade unionists voted for anyone (whatever their politics) who argued for more aggressive wage tactics than official union leaders had accepted under Labour's freeze. This rising wage (as opposed to political) militancy was fuelled also by the further decline of the economy. After devaluation in 1967 harsh cuts in public expenditure were imposed and these hit low paid workers most. Increases in indirect taxation also contributed to the problem. This explains why wage militancy spread to workers in the public sector, who had traditionally refrained from striking. These workers were squeezed by expenditure cuts, higher taxation and incomes restraint and had little benefit of wage drift.[19] Strikes and unofficial action increased as a result — often against the cautious policy stance adopted by the official leadership.

(iii) *1968-1972: Legal restraint under Wilson and Heath*

Wilson realised that corporatist structures could not be made to work. Unofficial action undermined incomes policies and he was losing his traditional support from the trade unions. But pressure to reduce wages and control union actions was crucial if the government was to retain overseas confidence. This led Wilson and Barbara Castle to reject both *corporatism* and *voluntarism* and turn instead to *legal restraint*. It was this decision which brough 'wildcat' strikes more fully into the political spectrum, even though unofficial action has been the dominant and politically non-contentious tradition of union activity in Britain.

The result of this decision was that in 1969 Wilson and Castle produced *In Place of Strife*: a White Paper which promised legal restraint through the adoption of conciliation pauses in strikes, secret ballots and compulsory union registration. This was a politically and industrially naive act. The trade unions and their sponsored MPs in the Party were undividedly hostile because this was perceived as a direct attack on traditional trade union rights and privileges. The unions therefore defended the industrial status quo against both corporatist and legalistic changes. Labour however was in a 'cleft stick'. At the same time it had been agreed that statutory incomes policy should be ended. The consequence was a massive wave of strike activity as free collective bargaining was allowed again in 1968. What was new here, however, was that wage militancy had spread to new groups in the public sector — particularly amongst the low paid (manual workers, refuse collectors and white collar workers) — who did not have the benefit of wage drift and who were most adversely affected by expenditure cuts.[20] This can only be seen as a direct consequence of state policies to restructure labour relations in an era of relative economic decline.

Labour lost the 1970 election as a result but the Heath government which replaced it did not learn this lesson and also tried to intervene in industrial relations through the adoption of an even more strident strategy of *legal restraint*. Heath's 1971 Industrial Relations

Act included provisions to outlaw the closed shop, new legal categories of 'unfair industrial practices', a National Industrial Relations Court, new rules for union organisation to control unofficial action, a new Register of Trade Unions to ensure immunity from civil and criminal damages, legally binding contracts and secret strike ballots and conciliation pauses.[21] Unfortunately for Heath this strategy was ignorant of the history of voluntarism and industrial relations practice; it also was introduced at a time of rising trade union membership and declining economic performance. As a result it could not be implemented successfully and merely served to generate more strikes and further politicise industrial relations.

The TUC saw the Act as an attack on their historic privileges and they were generally united in their opposition to it. The result was a rise in official national stoppages which were directed against the law and the state. Furthermore, strikes took on a more violent and aggressive tone, with flying pickets and mass picketing being developed as tactics to break government and employer resolve. At one level it is clear that these tactics are a threat to the law and public order. But it is not the case that this action was due solely to an increased political militancy in the unions. Rather it was the government's policy which generated the conditions in which militancy could prosper. It was the state's attempt to reduce traditional union rights which explains much of the increase in strike action in this period. This explains the increase in large national official stoppages in the 1971-72 period. It does not however fully explain the rise in local, unofficial action.

To understand the general increase in strike activity and the willingness of formerly quiescent groups to strike and disrupt essential services (health workers, miners, teachers and postmen) we have to understand, not just the attack on trade unionism by Heath, but also the state's general economic policies in an era of rapidly rising inflation and declining economic performance. The state had become responsible for full employment and economic growth and because it is a large employer the state must take a view on public sector wage rates. At the same time the state is seen as the focus for union action to defend living standards and wage differentials. We saw that public sector workers had suffered most under wage restraint because they did not have the benefit of wage drift. The Heath approach to economic management exacerbated this problem; Heath reduced public expenditure in 1970-71 and sought to introduce a two-tier incomes policy. In the private sector free collective bargaining was allowed and these workers could use 'wage drift' to defend their living standards. But in the public sector 'wage drift' was not available to workers and living standards were being eroded by a government which adopted a covert incomes policy. It is hardly surprising that wage militancy rose and damaging strikes in mining, power supply, railways, postal services, teaching and the health service occurred. This is explained not due to Britain's strike proneness but by the state's actions in the era of worsening economic circumstances.

The return to corporatism: 1972-1979

Heath began to realise that *legal restraint* was exacerbating Britain's economic problems rather than resolving them. In the conditions of rising inflation, economic collapse (Rolls Royce, UCS, Alfred Herbert, British Leyland) and industrial conflict Heath returned to *corporatism*. A voluntary incomes policy was negotiated with the CBI and TUC and, in return, concessions in the form of increased social spending and participation in government policy-making were offered to the TUC. It was not surprising that the unions would not accept this package, given the attacks which the government was felt to have made on the trade unions. As a result Heath was forced to introduce a statutory incomes policy in 1972. A three month freeze was replaced by a legally-binding norm, with scope for free collective bargaining over the share of the norm to be given to workers, and a Pay Board and a Price Commission were reconstituted.[2]

This corporatist strategy had much the same fate as its predecessors in the 1960s. Corporatist structures are difficult enough to sustain given the unions' voluntarist history, but in the conditions of inflation, declining living standards and perceived state attacks on trade unionism, they are incapable of overcoming union antipathy. Furthermore, given that the incomes policy actually encouraged free collective bargaining within an overall norm, the conditions for unofficial action were increased. The number of strikes did not therefore fall appreciably in this period, although for a short while in 1973 the number of working days lost did fall dramatically. Working days lost were still, however, at an historically high level for the post-war period as a whole. The ultimate collapse of the strategy came with the 1973 miners work to rule and strike action, which led to the three day week, the February 1974 election and the return of a Labour Government. The miners strike was wholly to be expected given the politicisation of strikes by the state, the changed market position for coal after the oil price explosion and the impact of an incomes policy on traditional labour practices. Rather than explaining the miners strike in terms of political militancy, it is better explained in terms of understandable wage militancy, which takes on the form of a challenge to public order and the state because of the state's interventions into industrial relations since 1945. This gives the appearance of a challenge to the state; this is rarely conscious but more often the indirect consequence of the defence of traditional union privileges.

The Labour Government which replaced Heath had few options open to it. Legal restraint could not be adopted and this left Labour with a choice between *voluntarism* or *corporatism*. At first Labour tried to find a compromise approach between the two and was then forced inexorably into a fully corporatist strategy. This led to a bitter conflict between the trade unions and the state and the eventual collapse of the Labour Government in 1979. In opposition Labour had moved closer to co-operation between the party and the unions. In return for legislation to re-introduce the status quo in labour relations and some new legal rights and protections for workers the unions promised to use free collective bargaining in an orderly and sensible manner. But, while Labour fulfilled many of its promises to the unions in the 1974 Trade Union and Labour Relations Act, the 1976 Amendment Act and the 1975 Employment Protection Act, the unions, however, being decentralised and undisciplined, could not fulfil their part of the bargain. Once again, with the ending of incomes policies in 1974 wage militancy returned to the unions. This was not surprising given the large wage claim granted to the miners, rising inflation and the problem of wage drift.[23]

At first the Labour Government could do nothing to resist 20-30 per cent wage settlements in the public and private sectors. The government is not however a free agent in a capitalist economy. Britain was caught in a gathering economic storm of unprecedented proportions which the unions' actions were exacerbating. Not only was British industry uncompetitive and suffering from the effects of a three day week under Heath, but the whole western economy was suffering falling demand and rising inflation. British goods were increasingly priced out of export markets, inflation rose into the 20 per cent range between 1974-75 and sterling crises returned to limit the room for manouevre of the government. Labour needed to win trade union support for wage restraint to reduce the public sector borrowing requirement and maintain international confidence, but to achieve this it had to grant even more social and economic concessions to the unions than would be possible if it was to obtain financial support from the IMF and retain business confidence.

Gradually the government came to adopt a more corporatist strategy. In return for further incorporation of union leaders into policy-making, the government sought to buy time through voluntary incomes restraint to weather the economic crisis facing the West. But, while voluntary restraint was accepted between 1975 and 1976, the strategy could not be sustained. This was an era of rising inflation, the erosion of differentials due to the operation of flat rate increases under incomes policy, and increasing burdens on low-paid workers in the public sector. Public sector workers were particularly hard hit because of inflation, increasing direct taxation and the public expenditure cuts consequent upon the IMF loan granted in 1975/76. Furthermore, they did not have the benefit of productivity bargaining or 'wage drift' to increase their wage rates outside the incomes policy. The incomes policy therefore merely served to bottle up demands for wage increases in the future, and even in the private sector the operation of flat rate increases alienated skilled workers whose differentials and living standards were being affected adversely.

Furthermore, by 1977 it was clear that Labour was reneging on many of the broad political and economic promises made in 1974 (nationalisation, industrial democracy, a wealth tax and increased social expenditure) as it sought to sustain business confidence and sterling. This fueled political militancy in the unions. More importantly however was the return of wage militancy. Living standards were in decline, differentials were being eroded and the government seemed incapable of halting unemployment. Given these perceptions it is not surprising that the rank and file in the union, encouraged by politically militant activists, should come to question this second attempt at *corporatism* by Labour. Labour appeared to be bolstering capitalism at the expense of workers living standards, therefore the demand for a return to free collective bargaining in the interest of potential increases in living standards was understandable. By 1977 the government's demand for a 10 per cent pay norm had to be statutorily imposed because the unions would not accept this restraint voluntarily.[24] Strikes, nationally and officially, as well as unofficially and locally, began to increase. Once again, although the unions can be seen defending their traditional voluntarist rights as the state imposed its own solution on industrial relations, the problem appeared as political because the state now employs a large proportion of workers and an absolute majority of those who work in essential services — firemen, miners, power workers, health workers, refuse collectors, etc. Despite the fact that the attempt to impose the incomes policy led to a series of damaging strikes in the Winters of 1978 and 1979, it was not the case that these were caused by trade union political militancy. Rather they were caused by the reaction of trade unions to the intervention of the state in labour relations in an attempt to resolve severe economic difficulties. They were a consequence of Britain's economic decline not its fundament cause.

1979-1982: voluntarism and legal restraint

Although strike activity has declined since the Conservatives' return to office in 1979, the number of working days lost is still high by post-war standards and so is the number of workers involved. Only the number of strikes has declined, and this is still high relative to other countries. This implies that, while it might be argued that the Conservative Government has found a solution to strikes, this is a highly dubious contention. The true cause of declining strike activity is not Conservative industrial relations policy but the general economic policy of the government in the context of the world recession. As in the 1930s, the level of strike activity seems to decline in periods when jobs rather than incomes become the main concern of workers. While government anti-inflation policy has had some success since 1979, and reduced wage militancy, it is the remarkable drop in private sector strikes which has caused a relative decline in strike activity as a whole. This is hardly surprising given that private manufacturing industry has borne the brunt of government monetary and exchange rate policy. With jobs more important than wages the willingness of workers to indulge in wage militancy has declined. The abject failure of the TUC's Day of Action in May 1980 is testament to the fact that strikes in Britain are normally over wages rather than political issues. This is further evidence that political militancy is not the major cause of strike activity.

It is true however that, while strikes have continued in the public sector since 1979, the resolve of the government to maintain its pay policy for this sector, and cleverly buy off strategic workers — power workers and miners — with higher settlements than the norm, has contributed to the decline of national stoppages threatening essential services. This of course has not been true of the health services or the railways, but the government's approach has been resolute and appears to have defeated these wage disputes. There is a more subtle reason for this. We saw that there are a number of strategies available to the state to manage industrial relations. The least politically contentious of these is *voluntarism*, and it was towards this approach that the Thatcher Government moved initially after 1979. The benefit of this approach is that it gives the appearance of free collective bargaining at a time when government economic policy was so deflationary that unemployment was induced to reduce wage militancy.

In general however, while the unions railed against these policies and the 1980 Employment Act as an attack on their historic rights and a return to *legal restraint*, in practice the approach adopted by James Prior, at the Department of Employment, was to limit the role of the law and to resist his more right-wing colleagues' desires to restrain the unions further. This surely contributed to reducing strike activity. The introduction in December 1980 of quasi-legal Codes of Practice for picketing and closed shops was further testament to Prior's desire to maintain social and political peace by minimising the role of the state in labour relations.[25] Prior's firm belief was that the state could not legislate to create 'good' industrial relations because this had to be achieved voluntarily. Prior was however replaced by Norman Tebbit in September 1981. This was a clear sign of the Prime Minister's desire to move towards more *legal restraint* in industrial relations. Tebbit however did not move as vigorously as might have been expected, although there is little doubt that he went further in the 1982 Employment Act than Prior would have done. The 1982 Act has increased the amount of compensation payable to victims of the closed shop, introduced compulsory ballots after the two year period for existing closed shops, outlawed union only contracts, granted more rights for employers to sack workers in strikes, and, most importantly, trade unions will in future be liable for civil damages as corporate bodies rather than individual workers alone.[26] While these changes are a clear move towards a *legal restraint* strategy there is little doubt that they do not go as far as many of the Conservative backbench and Cabinet ideally prefer. The four main demands from this group which have not been met are the complete ending of the closed shop, compulsory secret ballots, legally binding contracts and a change in union funding to force workers to 'contract in' to the political levy rather than to 'contract out'.

In conclusion then one can argue that the Thatcher approach has oscillated between *voluntarism* and *legal restraint*, although ideologically many in the government would like a firmer commitment to legal restraint. It is to be hoped that this never arrives. While superficially it might appear that the return to minimal legal restraint is responsible for declining strike activity, on closer analysis this is doubtful. First there is evidence that employers and trade unions have ignored the 1980 Employment Act as Prior cleverly intended they should. Both this Act, and the 1982 Act, rely on employers to use the law to attack trade unions. This most employers are simply not prepared to do. Furthermore, given the mass picketing in public sector strikes in 1981/82, it does not seem that the police are particularly willing to take any more firm a line with strikers under the new legislation than they did in the past. If strikes have declined it must therefore be explained by the effects of the recession being worked out in a largely voluntarist system. This is further evidence that strikes are most fundamentally caused by wage rather than political militancy. Given the fear of job losses, the ordinary worker is unprepared to strike. But, the drift towards legalistic policies by the government recently may well be storing up antipathy amongst trade unionists for the future. This means that Prior's approach, based upon the assumption that industrial relation cannot be reformed by the law but only voluntarily, is probably correct. Changes in the law will only work if the willingness to strike has declined. What Norman Tebbit and his colleagues seem to ignore is that as soon as the main instrument of strike breaking — the recession — ends, then workers will return to wage militancy as inflation rises once more. If this coincides with severe legal restrictions on trade union activity then it is likely that Britain will repeat the experience of the early 1970s under Edward Heath when law and order appeared to be breaking down. What this chapter has attempted to show is that while a questioning of law and order may occur it is as much a symbol of the State's interventions into previously voluntaristic labour practices, rather than due solely to political militancy on the part of workers.

Notes

1.   A. Flanders, *Trade Unions* (Hutchinson, 1968), pp.166-7.
2.   Seymour, Lipset, *Political Man* (Heinemann 1969).
3.   D. Butler and D. Stokes, *Political Change in Britain* (Penguin, 1974), pp.193-208.
4.   In this genre see: S. Milligan, *The New Barons* (Temple Smith, 1976); and P. Johnson, 'Labour and the New Leviathan', *New Statesman* 11th February 1979.
5.   For further details of the problems with strike statistics see: R. Hyman, *Strikes* (Fontana, 1975), p.25ff.
6.   Ibid., pp.26-27.
7.   M. P. Jackson, Industrial Relations (Croom Helm, 1977), pp.192-3.
8.   Ibid., pp.195-6; and, E.W. Evans and S.W. Creigh, *Strike Activity in the U.K.* (Economics Association, Occasional Paper, 1979), pp.4-5.
9.   H.A. Turner, *Is Britain Really Strike Prone?* (Cambridge University Press, Occasional Papers No. 20, Department of Applied Economics, University of Cambridge, 1969), pp.27-45.
10.   D.F. MacDonald, *The State and the Trade Unions* (Macmillan, 1960), pp.17-23.
11.   B. Hooberman, *An Introduction to British Trade Unions* (Penguin, 1974), pp.9-10.
12.   'Introduction' in, E.W. Evans and S.W. Creigh (eds.), *Industrial Conflict in Britain* (Cass, 1979), pp.11-12.
13.   C. Crouch, *The Politics of Industrial Relations* (Fontana, 1979), p.30.
14.   L. Panitch, *Social Democracy and Industrial Militancy* (Cambridge University Press, 1976), pp.
15.   Crouch, op.cit., pp.35-42.
16.   M. Shanks, *Planning and Politics* (Allen and Unwin, 1978), chapter 1.
17.   Crouch, op.cit., pp.49-57.
18.   Ibid.
19.   Evans and Creigh, op.cit., pp.12-14.
20.   P. Jenkins, *The Battle of Ten Downing Street* (Knight, 1969).
21.   Crouch, op.cit., pp.73-83.
22.   A. Cox, 'Le mouvement syndical britannique et la recession economique des annees soixante-dix' in G. Couffignal (ed.), *Les Syndicats Europeens et la Crise* (University of Grenoble Press, 1981), pp.84-6.
24.   Ibid., pp.86-8.
25.   P. Jenkins, 'The Law, Trade Unions and the Constitution',

The Guardian 24th June 1981, p.13.

26. 'The Employment Act 1982', *Employment News* (Department of Employment Newspapers, HMSO, November 1982), pp.2-3.

PART 3:

LAW AND ORDER IN POLITICAL FOCUS

8 A Settled Polity: The Conservative View of Law and Order

By Arthur Aughey and Philip Norton

Introduction

Journalists observing Conservative Party Conferences have often recorded the consistent, strident appeals emanating from the floor for more 'law and order'. Too often such calls have been dismissed as a crude response to crime and disorder from those with privileges to defend. This may be part of it, but however crude the appeal the message is a sophisticated one.

The Conservative idea of law and order appears clouded in a confusion of political language. While arguing for a more disciplined society, Conservatives oppose 'too much' legislation, a crowded statute book and a 'hyperactive' Parliament. In other words, what is not being equated is political order with more 'law'. Obviously, something else is meant by 'law and order' in the Conservative scheme of things. To put it finely, the Conservative idea of the legal order is one, rather, of balance. It is concerned with adjusting the claims of, one, political discipline and, two, free social activity within an overall view of a settled polity.

'Ordered Liberty'

Historically, Conservatives have found philosophical comfort in the belief that there was a harmony between the legal order and the social order in England, between the *pays legal* and the *pays réel.* This being taken for granted, Conservatism has devoted itself to questions of emphasis and balance within a settled polity. Or, to put it more plainly, it has sought to weigh, in terms of changing circumstances, the claims of political discipline or authority of the state with the claims of a free society or the liberties of Englishmen. Conservatism has recognised the need for authoritative rules and institutions commanding the obedience of the nation but also the existence of a realm of activity in which the individual or group is free from coercion by the state. It has distinguished between the obligatory rules of the political community which, though limited and precise, need perpetual reinforcement and support; and the regulatory features of governmental administration which must be constantly scrutinised to avoid the infringement of choice and the curtailment of independence. The Conservative idea of law and order views the true life of the state as the harmonious balance between freedom and discipline, where the traditional rights of groups and individuals find legal protection and where the legal order and its provisions are buttressed by dutiful obedience. But it is more than a pure idea. It is held to have been the experience of English history.

Expressing this delicate political and legal relationship as the wisdom of English public life, Conservatism reveals its own spiritual home in the idea of a settled polity. Lord Butler, surveying the modern history of English Conservatism, thought he could do no better in attempting to encapsulate the spirit of politics than by restating a 'vital expression of Burke's much used by Baldwin'. He believed that at the heart of the Conservative scheme of things was the idea of 'ordered liberty', an idea bound up with the protection of the 'Rule of Law and the Supremacy of Parliament'.[1] However curious and delphic Lord Butler's elaboration of this idea it is nonetheless attractive to the Conservative mind. It has a nice harmonious ring to it and suggests a well-balanced synthesis of dangerously abstract opposites. Moreover, it has a congenial solidity. Not for Conservatives the speculative exploration of abstract ideas to their absolute conclusions but instead the realisation of concrete liberties within the form of the state; a preference, as Burke had it, for the real liberties of Englishmen to the pretended rights of man. Order is represented by the sovereign state and the rules of legal association which it maintains. Liberty is found in the right of individuals to do whatever is not expressly forbidden by the law. And the rule of law is the universal code of practice that ensures that everyone is equal before the law and that everyone is under the law.

The English legal order takes on the appearance of authoritatively articulated common moral ideas and in these society can recognise its own inherent reason. The authority of such rules is held to be all the greater because, to use a Burkean phrase, it is in conformity with human nature. Not human nature in the abstract, but the best nature of the English people as it reveals itself in a settled and practical manner of living. The law thus reflects what Disraeli termed the 'character' of the nation. Significantly, law is not seen as an imposition or command laid down from above, restraining a naturally free people. 'It is perceived instead as a formalisation in authoritative language of already existing sentiment. In the words of Nevil Johnson, Conservatives are disposed to see the law as more or less 'codified social practice'.[2] However, the values that it expresses are established but not created by the law, so the power of the law to correct sentiment, habit and prejudice is limited. Changes in public opinion are best left to evolutionary social forces. To try to enforce them by law is to bring the very law itself into disrepute.

Again, the disposition is to seek some form of balance, in this case a balance between, on the one hand, enlightened moral leadership (of which Conservatives would be highly suspicious) or what is more congenial, political prudence (something appropriate in the circumstances); and on the other, deep-seated social prejudice, so deep to be assumed to be 'natural' or customary expectation. Some recent examples may suffice to illustrate this particular disposition. For instance, despite continued Conservative Party support for the principles of the Race Relations Act and agreement with the goals of equal opportunity for women, there has always been a deep scepticism about the appropriateness of legislation for the attainment of such ends. One cannot change by legislation alone the dispositions of a people and there is a limit to the ability of a nation to assimilate or accommodate such pressures. In other words, it may be prudent to support the sentiment of such legislation yet, at the same time, oppose the logic of the means. The logic of the means is the ceaseless pursuit of the rights embodied in such statutes. As Paul Johnson argues it 'can only end in producing a conflict of rights'. For if 'each one of us sought to exact the rights explicit or residual in our laws, on every occasion and to the maximum of our powers, society would collapse and public policy would become impossible'.[3] Conservative thinkers assume that there exists a 'natural' body of sentiments and values, deeply-rooted and slow to change, that are not susceptible to mechanical re-ordering and command. These constitute the character of a society, the national spirit. To tamper lightly is to meddle seriously in the settled features of the polity. In this case, to create a 'litigational society', a restless and ceaseless pursuit of ideal abstractions, corrodes the civil restraints essential to satisfactory public and private life.

The basis of this idea of the legal order is an idealised view of common civility, or individually internalised social norms. Burke admitted as much when he argued that 'Manners are of more importance than laws. Upon them, in a great measure, the law depends'.[4] Churchill repeated it rhetorically in his post-war cry of 'Trust the People', and it has been at the heart of Conservative populism ever since. This concept of common civility has been most persuasively and articulately developed in the writings of Michael Oakeshott. In his book *On Human Conduct*, Oakeshott has explored the features of 'civil association' which is 'a moral and not a prudent condition'.[5] People know how to behave appropriately because they are part of a moral order, not because they react to commands from the state. Social discipline — the relationship of common civility — inheres in a traditional manner of living. In other words and to use a Conservative cliché, law should cut along the grain of established behaviour and not against it. Civility can be cultivated but not implanted. To attempt to wipe clean the social slate and to create a new citizen — in the manner of Rousseau's legislator or a Marxist popular dictatorship — Conservatives take to be a disastrous presumption. To rely upon legislative pronouncement and direction alone to 'educate' or to 'reform' attitudes distances legal values from popular sentiment, thus undermining social discipline and loosening the bonds of civility. The harmonious union of state and civil society degenerates into a relationship of coercion and resentment. This was one of the most incisive and critical observations Burke made of the possible course of the French Revolution. Though Burke would have put the necessity for self-restraint down to religion, modern Conservatism has had to look for a more secular explanation, such as patriotism. However this may be, the Conservative reading of English political history and the confusion of it with their own political ideal happily assumes this common civility to be an unquestionable support to government and the foundation of public order.

From the idea of civility flows the Conservative understanding of justice. As a 'moral condition', there exists a sense of what is right, what is wrong, what is appropriate and what is inappropriate behaviour. The provisions of the law express the spirit of this public morality even if the law is not concerned with the whole of morality. Everyone of sound mind and body is understood to be a responsible agent acting within a tradition of behaviour which guarantees his liberties and subscribing to its rules which ensures the orderly enjoyment of those liberties. Because everyone is thus formally equal before the law, the law must be applied equally to all without discrimination. This formal rule of law may be modified with general agreement on the basis of 'equity' in certain circumstances, but these exceptions must in no way be arbitrary. Justice, then, lies in the expectation of citizens that they will be treated fairly according to the common rules of conduct in a society or the 'demands of the general moral conscience'.[6] As Barker concludes in a fashion congenial to the

Conservative idea of ordered liberty:

> law is related to ethics in the sense that it seeks to secure the set of external conditions necessary for moral action, or the general framework of external order in which the moral conscience can act and determine itself most easily and most freely.[7]

As in all else in the Conservative idea, balance is of the utmost importance and in practice some redressing of the balance between too much order misapplied and too much freedom uncivilly pursued may be needed. Justice is fair play as it is commonly understood. But this justice is not 'social justice'.

Generally, Conservatism has treated the call for social justice as inadmissable, as no more than a demand for special treatment or for certain satisfactions just because they are felt to be needed or deserved. In other words, social justice is a call to be provided for rather than a just claim to be able to provide for oneself within universally applied rules. The Conservative suspicion is that advocates of social justice are not really concerned about justice at all, but about something very different. Behind the appeal to social justice Conservatives see lurking the spectre of egalitarianism, and egalitarianism is the death of justice because it is the denial of freedom and choice. A most recent attempt to treat of the idea of social justice in a Conservative fashion has been Roger Scruton's *The Meaning of Conservatism*. The idea of social justice is unconservative (and, by implication, unpolitical) because it creates a 'fiction that really all wealth, and perhaps all advantage, belongs to a single owner (the state), who (in some way inexplicable to man) has the duty to secure its distribution'. This engenders the cardinal sin, mentioned above, that allows the state to dominate society — indeed encourages political action in an unlimited scope to fashion society according to a 'fiction'. Scruton sums up the outcome of such activity in a way similar to our own formulation. He asserts that 'the adoption of the ethic of 'social justice' in the practice of government will already cause an unnatural strain in the social bond (the bond which is founded in friendly relations between citizen and citizen, and between citizen and state)'. The critic may counter that all it does is to shatter the illusion of the Conservative ideal and open up the preserves of privilege and wealth to the egalitarian dynamic of modern society.

Contemporary dilemmas

Assuming the mantle of the party of 'law and order' has proved a congenial, and electorally rewarding, task for the Conservative Party. In the decade of the 1970s, Conservatives were united in their execration of the Labour Government for its perceived failure to maintain the rule of law and to combat an ever-increasing crime rate. 'The Labour Government', declared one party document, 'has failed to provide any indication of a firm commitment to maintain law and order. Its own actions over, most conspicuously, the Clay Cross Affair have contributed directly to weakening respect for the law'.[8] Liberty could exist only in those societies in which there was respect for, and compliance with, the rule of law. The Labour Party, declared Sir Ian Gilmour, was no longer a reliable defender of freedom.[9] In the unwelcome luxury of Opposition such attacks fell easily from Conservative lips. When returned to Government the party faced a dilemma, both intellectual and practical, in seeking to rectify the faults which it had been so keen to identify.

During the period of the Labour Government from 1974 to 1979, Conservatives had been agreed upon the wickedness of the Government in pursuing policies which had created a rift between the *pays legal* and the *pays réel*. The legal order was perceived as being no longer consonant with the will of the nation. Equality under the law was seen as threatened by legislation which bestowed unique privileges upon the trade unions (such as the Trade Union and Labour Relations Act and the, in the event emasculated, Dock Work Regulation Bill) and by attempts to idemnify those who had broken the law (the Clay Cross Councillors). The supremacy of Parliament was threatened by the power wielded by the trade unions: this was manifested in the 1976 Budget when Chancellor Denis Healey made tax cuts conditional upon acceptance of wage restraint by the Trades Union Congress.[10] The overall perception of the Government's activity was summed up by Gilmour: 'The rule of law was broken', he wrote, 'and the rules of Parliament were by-passed when they proved inconvenient.'[11] A Government which abused constitutional norms — the rules of the game — created a bad example for other to follow. There was a sporting analogy relevant to this perception: misbehaviour on the football field encouraged bad behaviour on the terraces.

The problem for Conservatives was to determine how to respond to the challenge posed by these developments. For most Conservatives, it was sufficient to press for the return of a Conservative Government intent upon restoring the principles which reflected the consciousness of the nation and which were necessary for the maintenance of a settled polity; but one which was not committed to some grand design for reform, be it constitutional, social or economic. Pursuit of some visionary goal, be it social equality or a free market economy, involves pursuit of the unattainable, a pursuit that would entail the severance of the harmonious relationships which have evolved within society. It would be replacing one evil with another. Instead, a Government committed to well-established constitutional norms, and seen to be committed, and reversing the Labour challenges to the rule of law, was to be preferred. Respect for the rule of law was to be observed by regenerating respect for the courts and the police and by bringing trade unions back under the same legal umbrella as the ordinary citizen; though such change being carried out carefully, deliberately and within the bounds of what is practical (hence a failure to move quickly to abolish the closed shop in industry). The increase in crime was to be dealt with by resorting to traditional Conservative remedies: strengthening the police force and stiffer penalties for serious crimes. However, not all Conservatives were to be content with such a limited and largely defensive response to what they saw as a serious Socialist threat.

The traditional Conservative response was to be pitted against what may be termed a Radical Conservative response and a Neo-liberal one. The Radical Conservative response posited that the return of a Conservative Government by itself was insufficient to preserve the delicate balances within the constitution. Those balances, argued Lord Hailsham, were being eroded, allowing Government — any Government — to impinge upon the liberties of the individual. The constitution could no longer be taken for granted. What was needed, according to Lord Hailsham and like-minded supporters, was no less than a 'new constitution', one with entrenched clauses, and having as its objective to 'institutionalise the theory of limited government'.[12] The aim was not to create some new visionary constitutional structure and relationship, but rather to restore those that were presumed previously to have existed. In an important sense, it was not just radical, it was also reactionary.

The Neo-Liberal approach, which has achieved prominence in the party since Mrs Thatcher's elevation to the party leadership in 1975, seeks a specific goal: the realisation of a free market economy. Britain's economic failures were attributed to state collectivism, not to any failure on the part of market capitalism. Previous Conservative Governments had pursued courses which constituted compromises with the invidious Socialist advance: the famed 'ratchet' effect identified by Sir Keith Joseph. The time had come to abandon the 'Middle Way'. What was sought was a free enterprise society, one in which individuals were left to define their own destinies. The interplay of individuals that went to make up society would be rich and complex, largely beyond complete intellectual comprehension. Such a perception generates a new vision of order and the place of law in society. The interplay of individuals in a free market society would produce a spontaneous order, one not fashioned by conscious design. Similarly, the market economy would produce liberty, the individual being left to fashion his own life free of the dictates of government or morality embodied in law. Law was to provide but a skeletal framework within which the free market could operate. The free market would generate a self-regulating and self-organising society, a society characterised by Hayek as one of 'Cosmos'. Though Conservative free-market advocates claimed a continuity with past principles and spoke in terms of working 'with the grain of human nature',[13] the society they envisaged was at variance with the hierachy, custom, morality and predictability associated with the traditional Conservative approach.[14]

Such debate within the party, in the event, proved to be academic. Though support for a constitutional reformulation, in particular for an entrenched Bill of Rights, found favour among a number of jurists and prominent Conservatives, the return to the Woolsack of its most prominent advocate and the return of a Conservative Government took much of the wind out of the sails of the Radical Conservative approach. A Bill of Rights is an unlikely prospect and is now not at the forefront of constitutional debate.[15] Though employing the rhetoric of neo-liberalism, the Conservative Government of Mrs Thatcher has not abandoned state subsidies nor has it made any comprehensive attempt to roll back the frontiers of law which impinge upon individual liberty (in some cases, the reverse: for example, the imposition of the compulsory wearing of car seat-belts); indeed, it has not completely abandoned what amounts (in the public sector) to a form of incomes policy. Economic and political pressures, not least from within its own ranks, have denied it the opportunity to try to mould the ideal society which free marketers espouse. In any event, it is unlikely that leading members of the Government would have found it congenial to have made a comprehensive attempt to achieve such a society. Though a neo-liberal by intellectual persuasion, Mrs Thatcher remains a combative Tory at heart.[16] Though giving some evidence of having recognised the problem, Mrs Thatcher is unlikely to be able to free herself completely of her Tory antecedents and of the morality inherent in her Tory upbringing.[17] Neo-liberalism remains a guide to Government economic policy, not a prescription for the change in society, envisaged by unConservative economic liberals free of the shackles of Government responsibility.

The traditional Conservative response has remained the dominant response. All the debate may have served to do is to mask the party's response to the more tangible and electorally more important problem of the rising rate of crime. The traditional response of heavier penalties for offenders has often been an ace in the Conservative pack. But in responding to a rising crime rate and sporadic outbreaks of serious public disorder, the Conservative Government has found itself faced with another dilemma, a dilemma inherent in its basic tenets and its attitudes towards punishment.

To the Conservative, the concept of punishment is related to liberty within an established order. Each individual is conceived to be a free and responsible agent and so aware of the nature of his actions and their repercussions. When the law is consciously broken, what is deemed to have occurred is a moral outrage and that constitutes a virtual denial of the civil order to which the individual belongs. It is the individual who is responsible. To blame society or environmental conditions or anything other than the individual is to condone rather than to condemn, so creating a vacuum where no real and valid criteria of judgement can exist. Government policy may be designed to change particular aspects of social organisation, but justice demands that the law must punish acts according to the conscience of the community because of what it is. Its judgement must not flounder on the abstract possibilities of what society might be like. To maintain civility, the law must protect those who act civilly from those who do not. The purpose of punishment is not to create reformed characters from guilty men but to preserve order through force. It is not the transformation of society with which the force of law is directly concerned.

Conservatives, then, stress the need to uphold the law, to punish those who transgress its provisions and to defend the citizen from those who seek to commit unlawful and hence anti-social acts. The emphasis is upon punishment, upon the rights of the victim, upon the guilt of the law-breaker and not of society. When there is public disorder, it is perceived as the fault not of some general decline but rather of some wayward minority, a minority that — whatever the purported reasons for its actions — must be punished. Such a response was inherent in the Conservative response to the inner-city disturbances in the summer of 1981 and was to find expression in the report on the disturbances by Lord Scarman:

> The social conditions in Brixton, do not provide an excuse for disorder. They cannot justify attacks on the police in the streets, arson and riot. All those who in the course of the disorders in Brixton and elsewhere engaged in violence against the police were guilty of grave criminal offences which society, if it is to survive, cannot condone. Sympathy for, and understanding of, the plight of young black people . . . are no reason for releasing young people from the responsibilities for public order which they share with the rest of us — and with the police.[18]

To paraphrase Disraeli, when your house is on fire only a fool would concern himself with the origin of the flames. The wise man sends for the fire brigade.

Inherent in this Conservative approach is a problem. The emphasis upon the organic nature of society is insufficient to explain deep-rooted problems. To stress social and environmental factors in seeking the genesis of riots and disorder is not only to condone but to attribute fault to society itself. Whereas the Conservative can accept that individuals or small groups within society may be wayward and prepared to attack (literally) the society in which they live, to discern the cause of disorders as a widespread and terminal cancer is to kick away the very prop upon which Conservatism is founded. Given this, Conservatives have difficulty in going beyond the individual in discerning the root of criminal behaviour. There is the occasional hint of recognising some link between disorder and economic and social conditions (for example, in despatching Environment Secretary Michael Heseltine to be ministerial supremo for Liverpool)[19] but such recognition is often half-hearted and not accorded priority (Mr Heseltine, for example, not being given the money he asked for to restructure Liverpool's inner city), often perhaps indulged in to assuage doubts and deflect criticism while the natural balances within society re-establish themselves. Conservatives take comfort in the fact that Britain has survived without too much difficulty previous periods of rising crime rates and periods of disorder, none of which — seen through the nostalgic mists of Conservative history — has undermined significantly the society of which the Conservative Party is the living exponent.

Given this, Conservatives are capable of emphasising the need to punish the wrongdoer and come in to office usually on a programme of stiffer penalties and a strengthened police force — as was the case in 1979 — but have difficulty in going beyond that. If there is public disorder, if there is a spiralling crime rate, the prescription is largely more of the same. To concede the importance of economic factors in seeking the explanation for rising crime rates would be to condone the wrongdoings of the individual, to criticise or limit the police would be to threaten those who constitute the 'thin blue line' between law and lawlessness. There is an instinctive support for those who are vested with upholding the law. At a time when there have been important allegations of corruption in certain police forces (notably the Metropolitan and City of London forces) and problems of ensuring police accountability to Police Authorities, the Government has not been oblivious of nor totally idle in responding to such criticisms, but it has been far more concerned to strengthen the police force to enable it to respond to criminal acts.

The Conservative response of more of the same is inherent in the 1983 Police and Criminal Evidence Bill. Its provisions extend police powers of search and seizure as well as seeking to foster greater links between the police and local communities. Much emphasis is placed by

Conservatives upon the community itself dealing with the problem of crime.[20] If the criminal cannot be reformed, he can at least be deterred: deterred by a vigilant community, deterred by the patrolling policeman and deterred by the courts through a policy of deterrent sentencing. Increasing the powers available to the courts in sentencing those convicted of serious crimes has been a feature of this Conservative Government as of previous Conservative Governments.[21] Implementing such reforms, or more especially promising them, is electorally popular. But if such reforms fail to have the desired effect, Conservatives have difficulty in knowing where to turn next. Even a policy of more of the same generates demands on resources which can no longer be fully met.

This, then, is the dilemma faced by the current administration. It is capable of sustaining an intellectual debate within its ranks as to how the legal order should correspond to the moral consciousness of the nation. It is capable of responding to disorder and a rise in crime rates by advocating and implementing a strengthened police force and stiffer penalties for serious offences. But its problem lies at what may be termed the intermediate level. Its measures reflect an instinctive Conservative response to crime and public disorder. *If* such measures fail to meet the problem, the party has difficulty, a difficulty inherent in its perception of the problem, in knowing where next to turn. For the Conservative Party, the party of 'law and order', it is a perplexing conundrum.

Notes

1. Lord Butler, *The Conservatives* (Allen & Unwin, 1977), p.15.
2. N. Johnson, 'Constitutional Reform: Some Dilemmas for a Conservative Philosophy', in Z. Layton-Henry (ed.), *Conservative Party Politics* (Macmillan, 1980), p.132.
3. P. Johnson, *A Tory Philosophy of Law* (Conservative Political Centre, 1979).
4. Quoted in I. Gilmour, *Inside Right* (Hutchinson, 1977), p.41.
5. M.Oakeshott, *On Human Conduct* (Oxford University Press, 1975).
6. E. Barker, *Principles of Social and Political Theory* (Oxford University Press, 1951), p.119.
7. Ibid.
8. *The Campaign Guide 1977* (Conservative Research Department, 1977), p.441.
9. Gilmour, op.cit., p.198.
10. See *The Times,* 8 April 1976.
11. Gilmour, op.cit., p.197.
12. Lord Hailsham, *The Dilemma of Democracy* (Collins, 1978), p.226.
13. See, for example, *The Conservative Manifesto 1979,* p.7, and N. Lawson, *The New Conservatism* (Centre for Policy Studies, 1980).
14. See P. Norton and A. Aughey, *Conservatives and Conservatism* (Temple Smith, 1981), chapter 2.
15. See P. Norton, *The Constitution in Flux* (Martin Robertson, 1982), ch.13.
16. See Norton and Aughey, op.cit., ch.2.
17. For an identification of the conflict between Tory morality and free market amorality, see A. Gamble, 'The Free Economy and the Strong State', *Socialist Register* 1979.
18. *The Brixton Disorders: 10-12 April 1981.* Report of an Inquiry by the Rt. Hon. Lord Scarman (Cmnd. 8427) (HMSO, 1980).
19. There is also some recognition of this problem in the party's *Campaign Guide 1977,* op.cit., p.441: The Labour Government's 'general economic and social policies have also exacerbated the problem through, for example, generating very high levels of unemployment amongst young people in decaying inner cities'.
20. See especially J. Wheeler, J.P., M.P., *Who Prevents Crime?* (Conservative Political Centre, 1980).
21. As, for example, with the passage of the 1982 Criminal Justice Act.

9   Law, Order and the Labour Party

By Howard Elcock

Dilemmas

Socialist penology rests on the premise that crime is the product of social and economic inequality and deprivation as well as of individual psychology. Poverty, deprivation, ignorance and inequality are the ingredients from which criminals are manufactured. Hence, to reduce crime the Government must eliminate these causes from society by resuming the attack on Beveridge's five giants: Want, Squalor, Ignorance, enforced Idleness and Disease.[1] Success would in turn eliminate or at least reduce crime.

However, Labour Governments have faced three major obstacles to their policies. First, there is a common public belief that crime is the consequence of individual black-heartedness — a belief parallel with the British view that poverty is the consequence of individual greed or fecklessness which marks us out as different from our European neighbours who seem readier to acknowledge the social causes of poverty.[2] In consequence, demands for retributive punishment both as a deterrent to other prospective offenders and as the appropriate consequence of wrongdoing are as rife as attacks on social security scroungers.

Second, dealing with the social causes of crime is very expensive. It is cheaper, easier and more productive of apparent (if not real) action to deal with the symptoms of social problems than it is to attack them at their roots. Barbara Wootton has cautioned that 'it is easier to set up a clinic than pull down a slum'.[3] Crisis management is appealing to politicians who like to see evidence of dramatic attacks on social problems. It is also cheaper than taking measures to reduce deprivation and thus reduce the causes of crime.[4]

Third, retributive attitudes widespread in our society become inflamed when a well-publicised crime or a sudden rise in reported instances of a particular offence generate a 'moral panic' which in turn intensifies demands for severe punishment and more vigorous pursuit of offenders by the police.[5] 'Moral panics' increase public and political support for the agencies of social control, in turn bringing benefits to the police and other agencies.

For all these reasons, law and order is a classic illustration of the policy dilemma of 'speaking truth to power'.[6] Firmly held, strongly expressed public beliefs and attitudes about the prevention, detection and punishment of crime conflict both with our developing knowledge about which measures are most likely to reduce crime and with the social priorities which need to be adopted to eliminate its causes. Public agitation for the return of the rope and the birch distract attention from strategies for the treatment of offenders as well as demands for increased expenditure on schools, houses and social services. Both the latter are more effective than punishing offenders in preventing crime but they are commonly denounced as the policies of left-wing 'do-gooders'. Politicians soliciting votes are in their turn tempted to pander to public prejudices, however ignorant, rather than standing firm in supporting effective remedies for crime.

Crime and punishment

This problem can be illustrated in the context of three besetting problems confronting the Home Office, local authorities and other agencies responsible for the preservation of law and order. The first is sentencing policy and the treatment of offenders, which can be determined in accordance with one or more of three principles: retribution, utility and remedying the social causes of crime. Retribution demands that punishment ought to be in some sense equal and opposite to the offence; that society must ensure that the consequences of the offender's misdeeds are fully visited upon him or her. When we say 'it serves you right', we are accepting that punishment is and should be appropriate to the crime committed.[7] Desert also contains the idea of equity — that like cases should be treated alike and unlike cases differently.[8] We expect consistency from the courts in handing down sentences because we believe that if this week the penalty for parking on double yellow lines is a £10 fine, it would be unjust next week to hang somebody for the same offence.

Neither retribution nor equity are necessarily appropriate criteria for determining sentences under the second criterion, that of utility: however, equity contributes to the increase of individual or collective welfare by ensuring both that the law is clear so that we can avoid unwittingly breaking it and that sentences will not fluctuate widely between cases. Above all, the principle of utility requires that the treatment of offenders shall be determined by whether such treatment increases total welfare. Welfare may be increased both by improving the behaviour of individuals or the conditions under which they live and by increasing collective welfare, for example by making everyone feel more secure from attack or robbery. Thus deterrent sentences are acceptable under this criterion only if they do indeed deter; otherwise the diswelfare suffered by convicts is not outweighed by the increase in welfare brought by a reduction in crime. Equally, reformative or curative treatments must work. Utility can also be increased by requiring criminals to compensate their victims or by providing such compensation from the public purse so that the diswelfare suffered by the victims is reduced. Even retributive punishment could be utilitarian if it contributes to the sum of welfare. J.S. Mill wrote that 'It is universally considered just that each person should obtain (whether good or evil) that which he deserves; and unjust that he should obtain a good or be made to undergo an evil which he does not deserve'.[9] However, if a society were not to value desert, then retribution would lose its utilitarian value.

Both retributive and utilitarian theories of punishment or treatment make one central assumption, however: that the offender is to be regarded as responsible for his or her actions and must therefore accept their consequences as well as mending his or her ways — if necessary being helped to do so. Responsibility may not be complete, however; Blackstone argued that in at least some cases 'the want or defect of will' would exclude any action except treatment from consideration.[10] We accept pleas of diminished responsibility or mental illness in mitigation of the most serious offences but in this case offenders are required to accept treatment appropriate to the condition which caused them to offend — this may be Borstal or other training, detention in a mental hospital or a course of medical treatment.

The third principle for assessing punishment or treatment argues that crime is caused not just by individual illness or error but rather by defects in society. On this view, the responsibility for offences must at the very least be regarded as shared between criminals and the society which has deprived them of the resources needed for their proper development but the policy implications of doing this are both radical and expensive. Barbara Wootton has argued that 'By tracing the springs of anti-social behaviour to the individual rather than his social environment we are, after all, only following the path of least resistance; for difficult as it is to cope with the mishaps of individual men and women, the institutions in which they enchain themselves are even more obdurate still'.[11] However, if those institutions are to be attacked, inner cities must be rehabilitated and more resources provided for schools, youth services, intermediate treatment and other social services in the expectation that in consequence, crime rates will go down. Such an analysis underlay Lord Scarman's analysis of the causes of the Brixton disorders of the summer of 1981 because he argued that the riots were in part the result of heavy youth unemployment in Brixton and other inner-city areas. If unemployment is to be reduced and rioting thus eliminated, industry must be persuaded to locate in inner city areas to provide employment or public sector jobs must be made available in those areas.[12] Either course of action demands substantial expenditure, either in providing services and an attractive environment for potential employers, or for public sector developments in the inner cities.

The Labour Party's policies on crime and punishment are predicated upon a combination of the second and third principles to the virtual exclusion of retribution. Utilitarian measures include a better scheme for compensating the victims of crime both from state funds and by restitution of damage by offenders where that is possible. There will also be more effective treatment for offenders including better conditions for prisoners and prison staff. Further measures would include crime prevention 'as part of our action programme for run down estates', better support and technical services for the police to increase detection rates, so increasing the deterrent power of likely detection and measures to ensure that most non-violent offenders receive non-custodial sentences or treatment rather than being sent to prison. The special problems of female prisoners, particularly those with young children, are to be given attention.[13] Retribution has no place among these policies.

Prison overcrowding: the limited power of ministers

One of these policies — the reduction of the prison population by eliminating custodial sentences where they are inappropriate and reducing them where a prison sentence is necessary — has been a long-standing objective of penal reformers and the more progressive Home Secretaries but its achievement has proved to be formidably difficult. During his last period at the Home Office, Roy Jenkins said that a prison population of 42,000 would be unacceptable in a civilised society but in recent years it has stayed obstinately at around 45,000. It is well established that prison does not cure criminals: more than four out of every five released convicts return to prison — a failure rate that would be unacceptable in most other fields of public policy. Ian Taylor has written that

> Institutions which function to contain over 45,000 largely minor working class offenders in overcrowded custodial regimes, with reconviction rates of over 80 per cent, are not the institutions of social defence described in recent Labour Party booklets.[14]

Not only are prisoners kept in squalid, dehumanising conditions in a decaying prison estate, parts of which are literally falling down; the country also faces a substantial bill for accommodating, clothing and feeding prisoners many of whom should not be in prison at all. In 1979-80 the average cost of one prisoner was £7,000 a year but high security prisoners cost the nation more than twice that amount. Furthermore, new prisons are not only expensive; they are also unwanted neighbours.

The Labour Party proposes to take several measures to reduce the prison population. Maximum sentences for non-violent offences will be reduced, custodial sentences for petty offences will be abolished and more non-custodial alternatives to prison will be provided if a Labour Government is returned to office. Some Socialist critics of the prison system also urge democratisation of the criminal justice system in order to reduce the prison population as well as preventing prisoners being ill-treated or kept in inhumane conditions.[15] The national prisoners' group PROP has demanded the opening of prison administration to public scrutiny, the abolition of censorship of prisoners' correspondence, independent hearings for offences against prison discipline and education provided by LEA's rather than the Prison Education service, as well as a massive and lasting reduction in the prison population.[16] Not all these reforms are official Labour Party policy but many of them would command widespread support in the Labour Movement.

Attempts to reduce the prison population have so far foundered on the attitude of the Courts. During his term as Home Secretary William Whitelaw repeatedly appealed to judges to reduce the length of the prison sentences they handed down or to use non-custodial alternatives in order to reduce the load on the prison system. His appeals went largely unheard although they were supported by senior judges. In April 1980 the Lord Chief Justice called on the courts to bear in mind that overcrowding in many of the penal establishments in this country is such that a prison sentence, however short, is a very unpleasant experience indeed for the inmates. This plea plus (probably more significantly) an industrial dispute in the prison service, brought about a reduction in the prison population to below 40,000 in January 1981, with no discernible detriment to society's safety or tranquility but by April it had risen to 43,000.[17] Like the criminals they sentence, the Courts are incorrigible recidivists. The judges also indicated to successive Home Secretaries that if the parole system was extended to allow prisoners to be released on parole after serving a smaller proportion of their sentences, the judges would increase sentences to ensure that criminals had to spend the same amount of time in prison before becoming eligible for parole. The independence of the judiciary has long been regarded as a constitutional safeguard against tyranny but the unwillingness of the judges to accept Ministerial guidance on sentencing policy has both imposed degrading conditions on prisoners and compelled the taxpayer to meet substantial costs for imprisonment which in utilitarian terms achieves little or nothing. The 1983 Queen's Speech suggests that the second Thatcher Administration has given up the attempt to persuade the judges to co-operate with Government to reduce the prison population because Ministers now propose to deal with the prison system's problems by employing more warders and building two new prisons a year.[18]

It must be admitted that a Labour Home Secretary would find it just as difficult as his predecessor to change judicial behaviour in ways that would reduce the prison population. Ministers are far from being all-powerful and the restraints of the constitution make it impossible to reduce sentences except by legislation to reduce maximum sentences or remove the courts' power to impose custodial sentences for some offences. In this case, appropriate non-custodial alternatives must be provided. The 1983 Labour Manifesto did contain proposals to reduce maximum sentences for non-violent offenders and went on, 'we will stop putting petty offenders into prison. We will expand non-custodial alternatives and examine new penalties involving reparation and restitution to the victim.' Finally, a maximum period in custody for prisoners on remand was proposed.[19] The last proposal is of doubtful benefit since judges take account of long periods in custody on remand when handing down sentence. Quicker trials may therefore lead to longer sentences as judges compensate for the shorter period spent on remand. The most hopeful policy is the development of non-custodial alternatives to prison but again the courts must be persuaded or compelled to use them once they are established. Roy Hattersley has suggested that providing more courts, easing the conditions for granting bail and providing more resources for the police so that investigations can be speeded up, would reduce time spent on remand.[20] These proposals can be implemented by Government and Parliament and are not as open to frustration or obstruction by the judiciary as some of the other proposals in the Labour manifesto.

Another practice that increases the burden placed on the prison system is the tendency for moral panics to cause judges to hand down exemplary sentences for particular offences which are currently the subject of such a panic. For example, in 1972 mugging attracted wide publicity, causing much public anxiety. In consequence, Birmingham Crown Court sentenced a 16 year old mugger to 20 years' detention. The then Lord Chief Justice, Lord Widgery, commented that the protection of the public from similar incidents is a factor which has to be in the forefront of the sentencing exercise. The clear implication of this statement was that the 20 year sentence would deter others but a study by two members of the Home Office Research Unit showed that in Birmingham itself as well as Manchester and Liverpool, the mugging rate increased shortly after the sentence had been handed down and given extensive publicity.[21] The considerable cost imposed on the state by the sentence was thus wasted from the point of view of preventing recurrences of the offence. What did reduce the incidence of mugging later, however, was the taking of measures by the police to combat it, including prevention campaigns and special patrols. This leads directly to the third main area about which there is widespread concern: the efficiency and accountability of the police.

Police efficiency and accountability

The study of mugging suggested that the most effective deterrent to crime is the belief that if you offend you will be caught. What happens to the criminal after apprehension is, from the point of view of deterrence, of relatively little significance. However, apparently rising crime rates and falling clear-up rates have reduced the effectiveness of the expectation that crime will be detected as well as causing increasing anxiety to be expressed about the efficiency of the police. These anxieties are based on two main grounds. First, increasing crime rates and falling clear-up rates suggest that the police are losing their battle with criminals. The Metropolitan Police clear-up rate was only 17 per cent in 1981-2. However, the statistics concerned are notoriously unreliable (see above, ch.3). Only victim surveys give an accurate indication of the actual amount of crime committed, which remains largely stable. In contrast, both the rate of reported crime and the incidences of particular offences vary for reasons which bear no relationship to the actual amount of crime committed. For instance, general car ownership has not only brought new crimes to the statistics; it has also brought many middle class people into adversarial contact with the police for the first time.[22] If the police improve their relationship with the public, this can paradoxically produce an apparent crime wave as people become more willing to report incidents to the police. These reasons for the increase in reported crime bear no relation to the total amount of crime actually committed.

Similar arguments can be introduced when discussing falling detection rates. A falling clear-up rate may, for example, be caused by increasing numbers of minor offences which do not warrant the expenditure of much police time and resources to clear up. The Labour manifesto promised better technical support and information services for the police to improve detection rates. However, at local level, such proposals can face stiff opposition because of the expenditure involved. In any case, giving the police more resources is unlikely to reduce crime, although Chief Constables frequently support their bids for increased resources by referring to the supposed public danger implied by apparently increasing crime. However, more police equipment will not reduce crime — indeed, the reverse is the case on the basis of the last twenty years' experience. Changed policing methods might be more successful but do not necessarily demand more resources. The manifesto commitment to give the police more technical and other resources ought therefore to be urgently reconsidered by the Labour Party.

A second debate about police efficiency relates to the need to maintain the consent of the public to policing and secure their support when needed. The police have limited resources and are largely unarmed. They are dependent on information from the public as well as, occasionally, support in defending themselves or making arrests. The police must therefore retain public support and confidence and it seems that such support and confidence has been declining in recent years, for several reasons. The first was the development of fire brigade policing in the early nineteen-sixties. Then the coincidence of a shortage of manpower and the arrival of new equipment, notably personal radios and small cars, caused most police forces to reorganise their beat work into unit beat policing based largely on panda cars. In consequence, the bobby on the beat, on foot or bicycle, virtually disappeared in many areas to be replaced by an occasional car patrol passing through. The result was that personal contact between police officers and members of the public rapidly declined. In addition, local police forces were amalgamated into super-forces during this period, so that the senior officers became remote from the communities they were employed to serve. Both local knowledge and local contacts were thus sacrificed on the altar of efficiency in the use of both human and mechanical resources. Increasingly too, policeman and women lived in groups of police houses rather than in single houses surrounded by lay people. The criteria for judging success in police work also changed. Response times when incidents were reported were reduced but less contact with the public meant that less information was brought forward and fewer incidents reported.[23] As the police culture changed, beat constables who spent time talking to residents, shopkeepers or publicans on their beats tended to be suspected of idling or scrounging refreshments.[24] Finally, confrontations with demonstrators or workers picketing in industrial disputes involved the police in widely reported clashes in circumstances which made it appear that they were suppressing dissent or that they supported unthinkingly the Government and the established social order. In particular, suspicion increased in the Labour Party and the trade union movement that the real function of the police is to maintain the inferior and subordinate status of the working classes.

In detective work too, the police became increasingly remote from the rest of society. Criminal intelligence has become a matter of computers, filing systems and specialised intelligence officers rather than one of local knowledge and contacts. Another development which has alienated the public has been the creation of specialist squads, specially trained and organised for reactive policing. The most notorious example is the Special Patrol Group (SPG) of the Metropolitan Police, which is feared and hated by some groups such as demonstrators and coloured people.

At the same time as the police became professionalised and increasingly remote, other developments reduced public confidence in them. One was allegations of brutality towards suspects in police custody as well as abuse of power. The revelations of the conduct of Detective-Sergeant Challenor in fitting up innocent people for crimes which in some cases led to them serving substantial prison terms[25] in the early sixties was closely followed by the Sheffield Rhino Whip case involving mistreatment of suspects held in custody at police stations in that city. More recently, the deaths of Liddle Towers and Jimmy Kelly after being held in police custody have never been explained to the satisfaction of their families or MPs. The revelation that between 1970 and 1979, 274 people had died while in police custody provoked widespread concern although most of the deaths were clearly from natural causes and the police could not have been held in any way responsible for them.[26] These anxieties were exacerbated by the refusal of the police to countenance independent investigations of alleged ill-treatment as well as their resistance to proposals for independent investigation of complaints against the police. Similar fears were aroused by the refusal of the Home Secretary and the Metropolitan Police to permit a public enquiry into Blair Peach's death despite newspaper reports that SPG members were carrying unauthorised weapons and had been given a licence to ill-treat demonstrators. The fear and suspicion generated by these and other incidents further increased public and political anxieties about the police.

There have been occasions too when insensitive policing has damaged relations with local communities. Questioning and searching black youths in London streets alienated many of them. The 'Swamp 81' operation in which 943 people in black neighbourhoods were stopped and searched as part of a Metropolitan Police effort to reduce street crime, brought already bad relations between the Force and black communities to a new low. This set the scene for the Brixton riots in the summer of 1981. Lord Scarman, charged by the Government to enquire into the causes of the trouble, criticised police methods. He urged that contact between police and public be increased as a matter of urgency by a range of methods, including establishing local consultative councils at which senior officers could meet community leaders and residents to discuss grievances before they provoke violence.[27] A final cause for concern about the police is allegations of corruption, especially in London, for which officers are seldom brought to book. In particular, the failure of 'Operation Countryman' to identify more than a tiny handful of corrupt London officers has aroused widespread scepticism about the police's ability adequately to investigate their own members' misdeeds. *Quis custodiet ipsos custodies?*

The political response to these problems has been varied. The reintroduction of community policing to replace the reactive policies developed in the 1960s has been urged on forces following the success of John Alderson's policies in Devon and Cornwall,[28] although some Chief Constables remain openly sceptical. Several forces are establishing local consultative committes on the lines recommended by Lord Scarman.[29] He, however, recommended that the establishment of such committes ought to be made a statutory obligation on police authorities. His Lordship also urged more extensive education and training for police officers in order to increase officers' comprehension of the nature of the political and social issues in which their work involves them as well as increasing their awareness of the nature of the communities in which they must operate. Police training colleges are reviewing their syllabi and police studies courses are being developed at a number of Polytechnics and other institutions of higher education with the active encouragement and co-operation of local police forces.

Above all, however, recent years have produced increasing demands that the police be made more publicly accountable. First, there ought to be an independent process for the investigation of complaints against the police. This initially took the form of a proposal that the jurisdiction of the Parliamentary or Local Commissioners for Administration should be extended to include the police because until 1976 the police alone were charged with investigating complaints, unless they were referred to the Director of Public Prosecutions.

In 1976, a Police Complaints Board was created to provide an independent element in the investigation of complaints but its powers are limited to recommending disciplinary action under the Police Discipline Code. Furthermore, the members of the Board consider complaints individually and have no investigators at their disposal. In consequence, they do not form a collective view about the complaints coming before them and must rely on police information in making their decisions. It is perhaps not surprising, therefore, that only a very small proportion of complaints are upheld.

The Labour Party's proposals for restoring public confidence in the police include reducing the discretionary powers of the police, especially in the fields of search and arrest. If discretion is restricted, its abuse becomes less likely. The rights of suspects held in police custody would be clarified and strengthened. Labour proposes the establishment of a fully independent complaints system with its own investigators and intends to remove decisions about prosecutions from the hands of the police by creating an independent prosecution service akin to the Scottish Procurator-Fiscal. This will not only reduce the distress caused to those who are wrongfully prosecuted but also reduce the public funds wasted on the third of English criminal trials which are aborted before the case is submitted to the jury. This was recommended by the Royal Commission on Criminal Procedure and is now likely to be implemented by the Conservative Government, even if the legislation to do so is not immediately forthcoming.[30]

These proposals are intended to improve the lot of the individual citizen who has been wrongly treated by the police or unfairly prosecuted. Labour also intends to restore democratic control over police policy, which has been eroded by force amalgamations, the 1964 Police Act (which stated that operational matters are for the Chief Constable alone to decide and may not be challenged by members of the Police Authority) as well as by increasingly assertive and independent chief officers of police. Reducing police accountability to councillors has been justified largely in terms of preventing councillors interfering improperly with decisions to prosecute in individual cases but this problem would be eliminated by the creation of an independent prosecution service. Labour therefore proposes to establish elected Police Authorities throughout the country, including London, with statutory responsibility for determining police policy.[31] In addition, community police councils will provide an opportunity to discuss the quality of police provision at local level.[32] These proposals would in particular remove the anomalous situation in London, where the Home Secretary alone is the Police Authority. At present the Greater London Council has a non-statutory Police Committee with a staff but no formal powers, although it has campaigned vigorously for the changes it thinks necessary. The Labour Party also intends to remove magistrates from Police Committees (at present they occupy one-third of the seats) because accountability should be to elected representatives only.[33]

Now that Labour is likely to be in opposition nationally for some time, however, the Party may wish to review the use made of the existing Police Authorities, especially where local authorities are Labour-controlled. David Regan has conducted a national survey of Police Committees and has concluded that they do not fully use the powers they already possess. He believes that they could become 'major actors in the police service' by demanding information from the Chief Constable, pressing questions at Police Committee meetings and perhaps above all by the persistence of their members.[34] In addition, other councillors not serving on the Police Committee can ask questions of its chairman at full council meetings but very few do so. Again, the annual budget debate provides all county councillors with an opportunity to challenge almost any aspect of police work and policy because they are voting half the cost of the force. Labour Party organisations — especially County Labour Parties and Labour Groups — ought to address themselves urgently to making increased use of their existing powers as a prelude to the eventual implementation of the Party's wider proposals for reform.

To sum up, the Labour Party's proposals for police reform fall under three main headings. First, discretionary powers should be restricted and clearly defined in order to reduce the possibility that they may be wrongly used. Further protection will be afforded by the establishment of an independent prosecution service. Second, a fully independent complaints procedure should be established in order that aggrieved citizens may be sure that their complaints have been fully investigated and police wrongdoing dealt with. Lastly, the local accountability of the police must be strengthened in order to ensure that they do not alienate the public by heavy-handed methods and that contact with the community is strengthened. In the end, however, crime will only decline if its economic and social causes are eliminated. Social reform alone will cure the disease; better policing is only a treatment for the symptoms.

Further possibilities

The policies for law and order offered to the electorate in the Labour Party's 1983 election manifesto would improve the organisations involved fairly rapidly if implemented. Although Labour was defeated at the polls it seems likely that some of its policies will be implemented by the second Thatcher Administration. Others must await the next

160

election at least and the Labour Party now has a chance to review its commitments and consider whether other proposals should be adopted. There are several areas where further reform will be needed even if the policies proposed in 1983 are all carried out. Perhaps most fundamentally, the recruitment, training and methods of the judicial system should be reviewed. Magistrates should be appointed openly, not as at present by advisory committees reporting to the Lord Chancellor which are accountable to no-one and whose methods are totally secret. In the higher courts, solicitors should be made eligible for appointment to the Bench, thus doing something to reduce the domination of the higher judiciary by an exclusive educational and social elite.[35] Magistrates and judges should be given more initial and in-service training to increase their understanding of the causes of crime and of the range of treatments available for criminals. This might lead to fewer inappropriate custodial sentences, which will reduce the pressure on the prison service as well as saving some of the high costs of keeping offenders in prison. In the longer term, the nature of legal education should be re-examined but not only will this be a lengthy process; once a new system is introduced it will be fifteen or twenty years before its first products reach the Bench. Another strategy of reform would be to create a career judiciary. The coming establishment of a public prosecution service will provide an opportunity to offer prosecutors and others promotion to the Bench as stipendiary magistrates (largely replacing lay magistrates) and later to the Crown Court, County Court and High Court. This would both eliminate the present secretive and unrepresentative process for the selection of magistrates and widen the social base from which judges are recruited. However, in the short term steps must be taken to retrain existing judges and widen the judiciary's recruitment base as well. The system should be administered in the next Labour Government by a Ministry of Justice created by merging the Home Office and the Lord Chancellor's Department in order that policies for reducing the prison population, altering sentencing policy and changing the basis of judicial recruitment and training may be developed coherently.

One specific group of offenders — the young — is in particular need of attention. Retributive punishment is not only particularly inappropriate for young people who may not fully comprehend the consequences of their misdeeds; they are also the group which offer the best prospects for successful rehabilitation and retraining. In Scotland the juvenile courts have been replaced by children's hearings at which young offenders' needs and problems are discussed before a lay panel by teachers, social workers, the police and others involved as well as the child's family, in a non-adversarial setting. Only after a hearing has taken place may referral to the Sherrif's Court for a trial be considered.

This occurs in only a minority of cases.[36] The children's hearing is far more likely to produce an effective programme of treatment than a court. Frequently magistrates impose inappropriate or even damaging sentences because the aura of retribution moves them to do so. For young offenders in particular the reduction or elimination of custodial sentences is an urgent necessity because they are costly and unproductive. Intermediate treatment has a better success rate than Borstals and community homes but it is still regarded with suspicion by many magistrates. In any case, ignoring young offenders or simply reprimanding them has been shown to be the strategy most likely to avert recidivism.

Law and order policies must be assessed on the basis of their success or failure, not by whether they include popular forms of retribution or produce favourable publicity. Links between the police and the community must be developed and their accountability assured. Above all, we must remember that law and order is ultimately maintained by consent, not force and that the causes of crime are social as well as individual.

Notes

1. R. McGraw 'Beveridge and After: Has Social Policy Failed?' in H. Elcock (ed.), *What Sort of Society?* (Martin Robertson, 1982), pp.107-115.
2. European Commission, *Perceptions of Poverty* (EC Commission, 1977).
3. B. Wootton, *Social Science and Social Pathology* (George Allen & Unwin, 1959), p.329.
4. This analysis can be applied to racial problems. Mark Bonham Carter has argued that coloured people are the barium meal of society: quoted in D. Sheppard, *Bias to the Poor* (Hodder & Stoughton, 1983), p.10. Their colour simply highlights the poverty, poor housing, unemployment and other social problems of the inner city in which they mainly live. However, it is easier, more attractive and cheaper to pass anti-discrimination legislation and establish Government agencies to attack racial discrimination than to renovate the inner cities, thus solving the problems many black people share with their white neighbours.
5. K. Bottomley and C. Coleman, chapter 3 above; S. Cohen, *Folk Devils and Moral Panics: The Creation of the Mods and Rockers* (McGibbon & Kee, 1972); and S. Hall et al., *Policing the Crisis* (Macmillan, 1978).
6. A. Wildavsky, *The Art and Craft of Policy Analysis* (Macmillan, 1980).
7. A.R. Manser, 'It Serves You Right', *Philosophy*, 37, pp.293-306.
8. G. Perelman, 'Concerning Justice', in *The Idea of Justice and the Problem of Argument* (Routledge & Kegan Paul, 1963).
9. J.S. Mill, *Utilitarianism*, chapter 5.
10. *Commentaries*, Book 4, chapter 11.
11. Wootton, op.cit., p.329.
12. *The Brixton Disorders: 10-12 April 1981*, Report of an inquiry by the Rt. Hon. Lord Scarman, Cmnd. 8427 (HMSO, 1981).
13. The Labour Party, *The New Hope for Britain* (Labour Party, 1983), pp.27-28.
14. I. Taylor, *Law and Order: Arguments for Socialism* (Macmillan, 1981), p.138.
15. Ibid. p.141 ff.
16. Ibid. pp.142-143.
17. *The Guardian*, 13 July 1981.
18. *The Guardian*, 23 June 1981.
19. Labour Party, op.cit., p.28.
20. R. Hattersley, 'The Framework for a Labour Britain', in G. Kaufman (ed.), *Renewal: Labour's Britain in the 1980s* (Penguin,

1983), pp.125-138. See pp.134-135 for these points.

21. R. Baxter and C. Nuttall, 'Severe Sentences: No Deterrent to Crime?' *New Society*, 2 January 1975, pp.11-13.

22. R. Baldwin and R. Kinsey, *Police Powers and Politics* (Quartet Books, 1982), pp.2, 32-34.

23. P. Robinson, 'Is the Panda in Danger of Extinction?' *Police Review*, 30 July 1982, pp.1454-1458.

24. Baldwin and Kinsey, op.cit., pp.34-36.

25. M. Grigg, *The Challenor Case* (Penguin, 1965).

26. 'Deaths in Police Custody', *Third Report from the Select Committee on Home Affairs*, Session 1979/80, HC 631 (HMSO, 1980), pp.v-vi. Of the deaths, 138 took place in police cells and 136 in hospital.

27. Scarman, op.cit.

28. J. Alderson, *Policing Freedom* (MacDonald and Evans, 1979).

29. For example, the Northumbria Police have established consultative committees in selected districts. See W. Hartas, *Local Consultation Arrangements between the Community and the Police in the Northumbria Police Area* (Faculty of Professional Studies, Newcastle-upon-Tyne Polytechnic, 1983).

30. *The Guardian*, 23 June 1983.

31. Labour Party, op.cit., p.27.

32. Ibid.

33. See H. Elcock, *Local Government* (Methuen, 1982), chapter 7.

34. D.E. Regan, 'Enhancing the Role of Police Committees', *Public Administration*, 61, pp.97-110.

35. J.A.G. Griffith, *The Politics of the Judiciary* (Fontana, 1977).

36. See, for example, D. May and G. Smith, 'Gentlemen versus Players', *British Journal of Social Work*, 10, pp.293-315, and D. Dickie, 'The Social Work Role in Scottish Juvenile Justice', in D. Oakley (ed.), *The Social Worker and the Courts* (Heinemann, 1980), pp.53-70.

10 Alliance Attitudes to Law and Order

By S.J. Ingle

If asked what he might expect Alliance policy on law and order to comprise, the cynic would certainly answer: see what Labour has to say, see what the Tories think and halve the difference. If we start simply, by applying the cynic's rubric, we discover that the Labour Party, in both rhetoric and ideology, believes basically that in an egalitarian society crime would not be a major social problem, and all that is needed is a revolutionary transformation of society. Having failed to preside over such a transformation, Labour Government policy in the past has tended to follow the wisdom of the Home Office. As for the Conservatives, the rank-and-file attitude towards law and order is best summed up by the motion proposed for discussion at the 1982 conference by the Norwood Association, which read: 'That this Conference calls upon the Government to recreate the conditions in which a virgin leading a child and carrying a bag of gold could pass on foot from one end of the Kingdom to another without fear'. If all that is needed for a party to develop distinctive policies is doctrinal 'lebensraum' then it seems that a major area deaf to the tumbrils of the socialist revolution as well as to the siren songs of the Tory virgins is available to the Alliance of Liberal and Social Democratic Parties.

The fact of the matter, though, is that the Alliance has not so far turned its attention to this area;[1] to be plain, the Social Democratic Party does not yet have a 'policy', as such, on law and order.[2] This shortcoming has, obviously, influenced the shape of this chapter but in a sense not in a wholly disadvantageous way, for it allows me to make some more general points about the main emphasis of the Alliance political attitudes, which may be summarised here as 'community politics', and about how community politics provide a basis for a distinctive approach to the problem of law and order. The conclusion will indicate the limitations of the Alliance approach both in this broad sweep and more specifically in the field of law and order. For the most part, 'law and order' will be used as an umbrella phrase signifying that area of government policy relating to the maintenance of security of the person and property of the law-abiding citizen, and 'liberalism' usually to imply the doctrines and beliefs of the twentieth-century Liberal Party.

Participation and community

Participation is the keyword in modern Liberal politics and it stands in contradistinction to the bureaucratic elitism of scientific socialism and the social elitism of the major strands of conservatism. But equally important to an understanding of modern liberalism is the framework of participation, and that framework is provided by the community. Community is defined as 'a group of individuals with something in common: nationality, neighbourhood, religion, work, workplace or victimisation' and so on. In the pamphlet *The Theory and Practice of Community Politics*[3] the author claims:

> People establish identities in relation to the communities to which they feel they belong. Within them they establish a sort of role or status, a level of expectation or behaviour in their own and other people's eyes which they use as a measure of their own success and worth.

Moreover, membership of a community implies some responsibility for other members, thus communities possess a capacity for mutual care and support. But community does not necessarily imply neighbourhood, or geographical proximity; it might be based upon membership of some voluntary organisation for example, though it usually presupposes a local or regional setting.

Community politics contains a clear commitment to the dispersal of power and this, say Liberals, will enable society to react in a more flexible way to social and economic developments which might threaten a more centrally-controlled system. It entails a commitment to open government and it entails a commitment to the most thorough-going pluralism in order to create what is called a 'habit of participating, binding a community together in a constant relationship with power and decision making'.

166

Community politics, then, is seen to be both a means and an end. It is a means of creating a less unequal society superior to the state socialists' public ownership and it is an end in so far as participating in the decisions affecting one's own life is a goal of traditional Liberalism. Liberals reject the notion of class politics, claiming that the working class is not everywhere oppressed and exploited or indeed opposed to capitalism and is certainly not universally sympathetic to those who are oppressed and exploited. Moreover, the political 'mouthpiece' of the working class, the trade union movement, is regarded by Liberals as an increasingly unrepresentative vested interest which stands in the way of local industrial democracy. In a Liberal society, party politics (and thus class politics) would cease to dominate, giving way to group politics and community politics.

Moving on to the SDP, we find a similar preoccupation with these themes of community and participation. David Owen shows himself well aware of the historical origins of social democracy and clearly saw himself (if indeed he does not still see himself) as saving and not deserting socialism. He perceives essential divisions in socialism between revolutionaries and reformers, between centralisers and decentralisers. He sees himself as a champion of the tradition which, so he claims, seeks to revive the concept of 'fellowship and community within a participatory democratic society'. Socialism, he says, has become fixated with equality and yet 'the record of state-controlled societies in overcoming inequality is not such as to make any thinking democrat change his or her predisposition for liberty'.[4]

Owen feels that the scientific socialists have dominated the Labour Party, yet have failed to establish industrial democracy. He believes that the scientific tradition, established principally by the Fabians, has proved inadequate because of its faith in the expert as opposed to the public, and in centralism as opposed to participation. He stands four-square in opposition to Sidney Webb, who summed up the Fabian scientific attitude as follows:

> the great mass of people will always be found apathetic, dense, unreceptive to any unfamiliar ideas, and your eager spirit with the unfamiliar idea. . . frets and fumes at being held in check by this apathetic mass. . . You have got to work your government machine in some way that will enable you to get on notwithstanding their denseness.[5]

The Webbs not only despised the bulk of their fellow citizens but also quite a number of their fellow socialists. Beatrice differentiated between the A's and the B's, between the anarchists — who could hardly be trusted — and the bureaucrats. Owen, however, no doubt seeing himself as an A, refers to G.D.H. Cole's observation that Labour's post-1950 task should have been stimulating democratic activism, not trying to get round the stupidity of the masses, and yet this was precisely what the bureaucratic mind proved temperamentally incapable of doing.[6] Around the same time, R.H.S. Crossman spoke of a profound distrust of active democracy by Labour leaders. He believed that the next stage of socialism would lead either to some 'veiled form of totalitarianism' or to 'increasing, even at the cost of efficiency, the citizen's right to participate in the control of government and industry'.[7] According to Owen, Labour has not heeded Crossman's warning; probably Owen would argue that the veiled form has become a stronger possibility than ever and that, as an 'anarchist', he should seek to emphasise his faith in participation. In doing so, he distances himself, *ipso facto*, from former colleagues and allies himself with the Liberals. 'A true democracy', he claims, 'will mean a progressive shift of power from Westminster out to the regions, to the county and town halls to communities, neighbourhoods, patients, tenants, and parents'.[8]

Shirley Williams, too, argues for 'the need to strengthen the structure of self-government at lower levels'.[9] Power, she says, must be diffused through society. Industry must be democratised — by law — though a variety of options would be permitted, and a whole range of administrative bodies, such as school governors, hospital managements, housing estate managements, and so on would be open to wider democratic participation. The social services too could be 'given to the people', says Mrs Williams, 'through mutual help, family grouping, and the use of volunteers. . . If the welfare state is for the people, then people must not be reduced to being seen as claimants or clients'.[10]

Mrs Williams speaks of a new kind of political activist. 'He embodies the new romanticism compounded of concern for the environment, love of small communities, suspicion of centralisation and bureaucracy'.[11] This new kind of activist is deeply concerned about social issues, but does not see conventional party politics as a suitable vehicle for that concern. Hence, Mrs Williams correctly draws attention to the significant increase in the number of people involved in voluntary organisations of a political character and the significant decline in the number who are members of political parties. 'These voluntary organisations', she continues, 'are concerned with political objectives, usually in a single area, such as nuclear power, overseas aid, famine relief, child poverty, preservation of the countryside, abortion, women's rights, civil liberties, stopping motorways and unilateral nuclear disarmament. . . most of these politically involved people stay out of party politics; some would hold party politics in contempt'.[12]

In summary, then, the SDP like their Liberal Party allies seek to extend political participation by decentralising decision making and by emphasising wherever possible the sense of community. Before the founding of the Alliance, the SDP liked to see itself as saving socialism, but the socialist tradition which it wished to uphold was explicitly the communitarianism of William Morris (his avowed Marxism notwithstanding!) and not that of the Fabians. Shirley Williams quotes with approval Dahrendorf's maxim that life chances 'are a function of two elements: options and ligatures'. Ligatures, says Mrs Williams, are 'what fellowship and fraternity are all about'. Ligatures and options; community and participation: this is the main thrust of Alliance political attitudes.

Law and order

When we come to examine how community politics are applied to the specific policy area of law and order we must rely chiefly on Liberal sources, though there is no reason to believe that SDP policy would differ significantly. We may start confidently with certain assumptions about Liberal policy towards law and order. Being bound by common rationality, men will tend to act reasonably in a just society, or, to be more accurate, in a society they deem to be just. Good order, then, would be the normal condition of a liberal society and the law would exist chiefly to punish and if possible rehabilitate criminals; such punishment would need to be humane though that is not to say lenient. Liberals would recognise an immediate affinity with the guiding principles of the rule of the king of asteroid 325 in Saint-Exupery's *Little Prince* who, though an absolute ruler, based his laws on reasonableness:

> 'If I ordered a general to fly from one flower to another like a butterfly, or to write a tragic drama, or to change himself into a seabird, and if the general did not carry out the order that he had received, which one of us would be in the wrong?' the king demanded. 'The general, or myself?'
>
> 'You', said the prince firmly.
>
> 'Exactly. One must require from each one the duty which each one can perform', the king went on. 'Accepted authority rests first of all upon reason. If you ordered your people to go and throw themselves in the sea, they would rise up in revolution. I have the right to require obedience because my orders are reasonable.'

The reasonableness of the king's orders is the consequence of his infinite wisdom; the laws of a liberal society ought to be considered reasonable by virtue of the extent to which citizens might participate in shaping them; so far as is possible, they should reflect community values. Crucial among these values is seen to be social justice. As Emlyn Hooson writes:

> If a sizeable section of the community thinks the law is loaded against it. . . if it thinks that the economic and social conditions in which it lives will condemn it indefinitely to poverty and discomfort, that those who have the power and resources to do something about it simply do not care, then that section will feel few inhibitions about crime, whether it be theft or violence or generally behaving in an anti-social fashion.[13]

In his book *Policing Freedom*, ex-chief constable and Liberal Alliance candidate John Alderson also argues that social justice is a prerequisite to order and to enforcing the law successfully: 'if large gaps in the scale of wealth and social privilege are not narrowed from time to time, crime will flourish alongside prosperity'.[14] Although it is beyond the scope of this chapter to discuss them, Alliance policies on urban deprivation, unemployment and race relations contain clear statements on 'social justice'.

Emlyn Hooson attacks the sheer ugliness and inhumanity of modern collectivised society in which large amorphous organisations have displaced local communities. 'Town planners and architects have much to answer for in their erection of monstrous estates with no defensible space, and no sense of community.' These changes have been accompanied by others which have tended to displace individuals from their traditional social context: 'insofar as television in particular has desensitised people's reaction to violence and crime, insofar as it has presented a fantasy advertiser's world in stark contrast to the reality of modern Britain, insofar as it has been a contributory factor to the breakdown of family life, its influence is to be deplored'. The Liberal response (solution would be an inappropriate word) is to attempt wherever possible to promote community values. 'Children need to be shown that it is in their own interests that they act correctly, and for positive reasons, not because of a threatened beating.' A practical course in citizenship, says Hooson, based upon community service, should be part of the normal pattern of education, rather than something which, as at present, might or might not be taught.

Alderson argues along similar lines, quoting from *The Ecologist's Blueprint for Survival* to the effect that increasing crime rates are closely related to the decline in family life, both symptons of a disintegrating society. Alderson goes further, though, suggesting that what he calls the 'do-your-own-thing' society 'gradually reduces the consensus of right and wrong'. Bearing these factors in mind, he says, 'increased crime does not represent just an aberration, not just a chance pattern in a seemingly aimless movement, but it is a direct consequence of evolution and liberation itself. It might be seen as the price of an increasingly free and unfettered society and some would feel that if this is so, the price is too high and freedom has to be reduced in order to reduce crime.'[15] But if so, it is society itself that must decide and not some elite of specialists. In 1822 the Parliamentary Committee on the Policing of the Metropolis thought that an effective policing system for the capital would offer too great an intrusion upon individual liberty to be worth considering and so recommended against establishing such a system. The ordinary citizen in crime-ridden London was certainly not asked what he felt. It is a factor of the greatest importance to Liberalism that the 'voice of the people' be heard in such matters.

Having dealt with the social factors involved it will be appropriate to turn now to the police, for in policing policy we have a very clear example of community politics in practice. Many events in the recent past have made policing a major and emotive issue so that a sense of balance in judgement is not easy to achieve. What must be absolutely clear is that an ineffective police force would lose public confidence as soon and as completely as a force that had become a law unto itself, but as Alderson admits with considerable understatement, 'the balancing of the interests of the public generally, the sensible administration of justice and the rights of the suspected but unconvicted person is of considerable delicacy'.

Policing is concerned with social control, often against the will of individuals or groups. But the majority of offences are committed by citizens who are generally 'law abiding', so the police must exercise caution. Alderson says that those who insist that the job of the police is simply to know and enforce the law are arguing for a 'barren, unimaginative approach which can bring both law and the police system into disrepute and fails to exploit the potential of the law for soothing rather than irritating social maladies'.[16] Yet in deciding how to enforce the law the police have lost several clear advantages. In the nineteenth century they were not expected to enforce laws that did not command the general support of the law-abiding people who formed opinion in Britain. The police were there to control the lower classes — to the middle classes they were reassuring symbols of public order. But the development of the motor car has turned us all into potential criminals and social, political and environmental protest has involved all levels of society, including many who help to mould public opinion and who never before came into contact with the police. This represents a profoundly new situation.

Alderson considers the various styles of policing in relation to the new task of policing what he calls a free permissive and participatory society. The style he most favours is the communal-democratic, a style which allows for most of the techniques of policing of which he approves. Alderson reminds us that the link between the police and the individual citizen assumes equality of status. The Royal Commission on the Police in 1962 for example stated: 'The police of this country have never been recognised either in law or by tradition as a force distinct from the general body of the citizens'. Indeed, the duties of the ordinary police constable differ little from those of the ordinary citizen. But Alderson believes that the links between the public and the police should be made far more concrete. In order to achieve this he wishes to use existing community structures, both formal and informal, and where these no longer exist, or have never existed, they are to be built up with the local police force taking a lead. This approach found much favour in the Scarman Report and has subsequently been acted upon to some extent.

Community is defined by Alderson as 'a group of people who live in sympathetic proximity, with some significant factor in common', which suggests neighbourhoods as communities or perhaps churches, social clubs and so on. He suggests that the police should involve themselves in organising community meetings to discuss local issues of law and order and should try to promote a 'neighbourhood or community climate free from fear and uncontrolled delinquency and crime'. The local police should respond, he feels, to the character of the local community. He seems to be clear on one point in particular: being responsive to the local community means to the attitudes expressed at these meetings, to the views the representatives of local statutory agencies and voluntary bodies and local residents. He is interested, that is to say, in Shirley Williams's new politics, not at all in party politics.

Alderson's favoured techniques for community policing are basically what he describes as 'proactive', designed to penetrate the community in a number of ways in order to influence its behaviour. Proactive policing envisages a high degree of co-operation with other agencies — education for example. The educational setting, he says, offers an important non-conflict contact point in which a useful working human relationship can be achieved on issues affecting youth and the police. Proactive policing is described by Alderson as primarily preventive but he recognises the need for secondary preventive policing, of which an important feature is the increase of foot patrols, though he well realises the importance of mobile reactive patrolling too. His objection to what he sees to be the almost total modern reliance on reactive (fire brigade) policing is that it necessarily limits the contact between police and public to situations of conflict.

Alderson's ideas are very close to official Liberal Party policy. Liberals argue for increased police 'visibility', and this, too, is an argument for more foot patrols, and for the reopening of small local police stations. Moreover, Liberals are strongly in favour of increasing the number of special constables, whom they see as an invaluable link between the ordinary citizen and the police, with the specials' amateur status being regarded as an asset. At the least, it is claimed: 'It would be valuable simply having a large number of people trained to be aware of potential crime problems and preventive techniques'.[17] In the worst affected areas of London, Merseyside and Greater Manchester the proportion of specials to regulars in the late 1970s was under ten per cent compared to a national average of twenty-one per cent. But even the national statistics prove disheartening when further investigated. In 1938 there were 118,000 specials: forty years later there were 19,000. If crime can be prevented to any degree by making the police more visible then far greater use of the specials might prevent more crime. Special constables were used by Superintendent Webb in the Handsworth area of Birmingham during the riots of 1981 to great effect and particularly significant was the fact that many of his specials were recruited from the ethnic minorities in the area. Liberals' belief in the increased use of specials in this manner is endorsed by the SDP. In the party's policy statement *Urban Policy* an argument is also put forward for recruiting more from the ethnic minorities into the police cadet scheme. 'Our ultimate aim must be for the police to become the focus of a self-regulating society', say the Liberals. 'This means that the police must be seen to be enforcing the norms of the community.' There can be no doubt, according to the Liberals, that increasing the numbers and the use of the specials would make the police both more visible and more representative, thereby building the confidence of the community in such a way as to increase their support for the police and their commitment to the preservation of law and order. Liberals' faith in this kind of policing is shown by the fact that both Chief Constable Alderson and Superintendent Webb resigned their posts and fought the 1983 general election as Liberal candidates.

It is evident, then, how comprehensively the concept of community politics infuses Liberal/Alliance policy on law and order, or at least that crucial aspect of law and order, policing. Belief in community politics affects not only what the Liberals say but also what they do not say. For example, although Liberals are generally in favour of extending democratic control over police policy at all levels, they are less convinced than is the Labour Party that strengthening the hands of a police committee dominated by members of a ruling political clique supported by a small minority of the local electorate constitutes democratic control. Liberals and their allies are generally unconvinced of the representative qualities of the British electoral system and therefore put little emphasis upon this aspect of accountability. Liberals have expressed as much anxiety at the prospect of political control exercised by unrepresentative minorities as they have at police reluctance to conform to the general requirements of 'open government'. The SDP, too, has stressed the limitations of the present framework and argues that police authorities should comprise representatives of various local interests in each community, including voluntary and neighbourhood organisations. Only if the electoral system were more representative would 'democratic' control be viable. Under the present system, argues the SDP, it would be party political and hence ideological control.

Both parties are agreed, moreover, on the need to alter the present complaints procedure which they feel to be inadequate and illiberal. They seek an independent unit and a far more open *modus operandi* because, like Lord Scarman, they believe that the public has lost confidence in present procedures.

Limitations

Selective though this treatment of law and order has necessarily been, it may have served to give some flavour of community politics in this policy area. I should like finally and briefly in this section to consider some of its limitations.

To begin with what I take to be the broadest objections. Two fundamental assumptions may be seen to underpin community politics which perhaps should not go unchallenged. The first is that, given a suitable framework, the majority of citizens would positively wish to participate in the making of decisions. As a matter of fact there is no evidence whatever to support this assumption. Anthony Crosland, in *Socialism Now*, wrote rather despairingly: 'If what is meant by participation is an active and continuous process of participating in decision-making, then all experience shows that only a small minority of the population will wish to participate. . . the fact is that the majority will continue to prefer to lead a full family life and to cultivate their gardens'. Oscar Wilde made a similar point more pithily when he said that the trouble with socialism (of the social democratic kind!) was that it would take too many evenings. Now, if there is no widespread participation, community politics must fail, or so it would seem to me.

The second assumption is that, if allowed to shape their own circumstances, communities would act in a just, tolerant, reasonable — that is to say 'liberal' — manner. This is precisely what Jo Grimond

174

argued would be the case. He believes men to be bound by a common rationality; for him it takes the form almost of natural law. 'If you believe that people might freely choose such things as the legalisation of indiscriminate murder of one's children then there really is no basis for Liberalism at all.'[18] There is, however, ample evidence to show that some communities in the past have acted in repressive, intolerant and discriminatory ways. John Stuart Mill was so well aware of this possibility that he established a criterion for selecting those who might participate in self-government; those, that is, who were capable of moral self-development, a constraint so strong as to threaten the rationale of the whole enterprise.

Let me pass on now to what I take to be a less central but nonetheless important line of criticism of community politics, that it must tend to exacerbate and not lessen inequalities. As Shirley Williams reminds us: 'The ratio between the resources spent on a child in the poorest school districts of the decentralised federal US education system and the richest ones is in the order of six to one. In Britain, where education finances are funded as to 60 per cent from central government, the ratio is about 1.4 to 1.'[19]

Finally, to take a more specific criticism, if the police opt for a policy of community policing will this not inevitably lead to the toleration, in one area, of behaviour which would be acted against in another? Is this not an inevitable consequence and does it not place intolerable burdens upon a force whose primary task is to enforce the law without favour?

It would be naive to imagine that Liberals had not considered these objections, though how successfully they have countered them must be a matter of opinion. Taking the fundamental objections first, Liberals believe that as communities come increasingly under threat because of the state's inability to defend them, participation will begin to be seen as a necessary duty. They cite the example of residents' associations being reasonably successful in combatting vandalism. Moreover, if it were generally believed that participation might actually affect policies the Liberals believe as an act of faith that many more wish to participate. As for the potential illiberalism of communities, the Liberals realise that if virtue is to be spread it will require not only Mill's 'education-through-participation' but also Machiavelli's strong leaders and good laws. The Liberal Party sees its role in the community politics movement as being to stimulate and support communities but also to promote liberal values in society. Neither party of the Alliance is reluctant to use the state to help to create a more liberal society. For example, the previous Liberal-dominated Liverpool City Council announced its intention in 1983 of moving into inferior housing families who had been responsible for harassing immigrant families in their neighbourhood. The danger of using illiberal means to achieve liberal ends is plain to see but clearly Liberals and their allies feel that such nettles have to be grasped. All the same, both Alliance partners retain a basic faith in the reasonableness of their fellow citizens. Douglas Eden of the SDP has argued that on an issue like the restoration of hanging it is essential that Parliament listens to the voters. He envisages a public campaign of an educative nature which, he seems confident, would lead to the public's changing its mind. He cites in support of his argument the example of attitudes to the Common Market. Britain entered without a referendum and in opposition to majority public opinion. When, however, a referendum was held, after lengthy public debate, the majority supported the Community and Britain's continued membership.[20]

With regard to community politics fostering greater, not lesser, inequality Liberals would presumably want to make two points. The first is that vast inequalities exist in the present system. If we stay with the example of education, it can be pointed out that the quality provided in contiguous education districts within the same county in England and Wales may vary greatly, a fact easily masked by county-to-county comparisons of expenditure. All the same, ultimately the Alliance partners would have to come clean and repeat what they have said often enough: in the present circumstances, they attach more importance to participation than to equality.

Finally, would community politics lead to unacceptable discrepancies and place an intolerable burden of judgement upon the police? Alderson points out that at the moment the police do not enforce laws which they believe to be 'socially unacceptable', neither do they always and invariably enforce even those which they do regard as socially acceptable. 'Judgement, discretion and establishing priorities in enforcement become major police skills', he tells us. Obviously, even with community policing, serious offences would have to be punished wherever they occurred but large areas of discretion would have to remain with community policemen. It is no longer possible to police a modern society simply by force and the due criminal process. Community policing only adds significantly to the options open to the police in maintaining law and order.

Conclusion

Let me conclude briefly by stating that I believe it possible to argue that the Alliance does possess a distinctive and common approach to politics and I believe that in its approach to law and order this distinctiveness is readily apparent. Community politics suggests a relationship between the leaders and the led which is quite different from Conservative paternalism and scientific socialist elitism. It suggests a relationship between expert and layman in which the knowledge of the former is to be balanced with the wisdom and experience of the latter (a relationship which, had it been instituted in the 1950s, might have prevented the gross mistakes of city centre development which most acknowledge to have played such a large part in creating precisely those problems which we have been discussing). There is clearly a lack of precision about the concept of community politics but as the field of law and order shows, it represents a comprehensive and distinctive approach to some of the problems of the modern age; it represents not so much a solution to those problems as a method of approaching them, a method in which the individual citizen is expected to play a dominant and not a subservient part.

Notes

1. The Alliance manifesto for the 1983 general election, *Working Together for Britain*, contained no mention whatever of law and order or any similar issue.

2. However, two policy documents, *Urban Policy* (No. 9) and *Citizens' Rights* (No. 10), both published by the party in London through Jaguar Press, contain some comments on law and order issues, specifically relating to police powers and accountability.

3. Published by the Association of Liberal Councillors at Hebden Bridge, 1981.

4. D. Owen, *Face the Future* (Jonathan Cape, 1981), pp.5 and 9.

5. *New Commonwealth*, 28 November 1919.

6. See 'What Next? Anarchists or Bureaucrats?' *Fabian Journal*, April 1954.

7. R.H.S. Crossman, 'Towards a Philosophy of Socialism', in *New Fabian Essays* (Turnstile Press, 1952), p.29.

8. Owen, op.cit. p.14.

9. See S. Williams, *Politics is for People* (Penguin, 1981).

10. Ibid. p.205.

11. Ibid. p.42.

12. Ibid. p.177.

13. See E. Hooson, *Law and Order in a Civilised Society* (Liberal Party Publications, 1979).

14. J. Alderson, *Policing Freedom* (MacDonald and Evans, 1979), p.112.

15. Ibid. pp. 114, 115.

16. Ibid. p.29.

17. Hooson, op.cit. p.15.

18. J. Grimond, *The Liberal Future* (Faber and Faber, 1959), p.15.

19. Williams, op.cit. p.208.

20. D. Eden, *The Future of Social Democracy* (Jaguar Press, 1983).

11   Marxism and the Problem of Law and Order in Britain

By Martin Shaw

Introduction

This paper aims to discuss approaches to the problems of law and order in Britain deriving broadly from a marxist perspective. Marxism has become a theoretical mode as much as a practical orientation: a framework for debate rather than a rigid orthodoxy or a political line. There is therefore no single 'Marxist' explanation for law and order, and the aim here is to show some of the tensions in the application of marxist concepts to current problems. These tensions reflect, but may also help to illuminate, the difficult political choices facing not only marxists but all socialists, and indeed to some extent all democrats and libertarians.

Concepts of law and order in marxism

A major difference between marxism and most other political approaches is the elaborate theoretical structure with which it is endowed. Marxist theory is more refined, however, in some areas than in others, and even where the founding fathers were relatively clear, history has contrived great difficulties for the classical approach. This contradictory legacy of the marxist tradition has often been apparent in recent attempts to theorise law and order.

The very concepts of order and law are highly problematic — and separate — ones for marxism. Social order cannot be an absolute value: it is subordinate to social change, which clearly can be a disorderly process. The problem of order is moreover a historically specific one: marxists will locate it in the context of historically changing social formations. Capitalism is so inherently anarchic that the temporary accentuation of its disorderliness may be necessary to create a 'new social order', based on socialist relations of production.

Law initially played only a small part in marxist thinking about problems of social order. Law was, for Marx, part of the 'superstructure' arising on the socio-economic 'foundation'.[1] Even if, as Engels was later to suggest, it must be an 'internally coherent expression',[2] and thus possess some autonomy, it was widely supposed by classical marxists that law was a necessity only in class society. The abolition of conflicting class interests would make possible more spontaneous forms of social regulation based on common interests, beliefs and values.

Twentieth century history has forced marxists to re-think these early attitudes to order and to law, in the contexts of both capitalism and socialism. From the First World War onwards, marxists saw a new danger in the disorderliness of capitalism: the development of non-democratic, extra-repressive, even illegal forms of state power. Fascism was a directly violent, lawless monster, a form of order without law[3] — here the marxist critique shared common ground with liberalism, even if it went on to explain fascism in terms of capitalism which liberals generally did not.

Even more important, in forcing a revaluation of the role of law in social order, was the apparent 'lawlessness' of Stalin's regime in the Soviet Union. This experience of violent dictatorship pushed many marxists beyond the fragile concepts of 'soviet democracy' and 'soviet legality', understood as fundamentally distinct from the bourgeois variants, towards an attempt to incorporate into socialism much of the detailed framework of Western democratic and legal systems, for example political pluralism and the separation of powers.[4]

In defining their attitudes to law and order in contemporary capitalist societies, recent marxists have been greatly influenced by this contradictory legacy. On the one hand, they have maintained the classical marxist critique of the unequal, class-divided character of capitalist society, and have emphasised the limited character of its democracy. On the other, they have seen how threatened even this limited democracy is, above all by the state machine itself. They have tried to devise strategies which avoid the dangers of a simple collapse of the parliamentary democratic order, and of a loss of democracy in the construction of a revolutionary order.[5]

Attempts to theorise more concretely about law have strengthened this tendency towards revaluation. First, it has been recognised that the actual body of laws and legal practices in any given capitalist society is highly complex and variable, reflecting conflicts within as well as between classes, as well as a good deal of autonomous legal rationality.[6] Second, Gramsci's conception of the state as an organiser of consent as well as a source of repression has influenced marxists to see law in this dual role. And finally, the need for a rationale for defending existing rights has led as eminent a writer as E.P. Thompson to a celebrated — or to orthodox marxists, notorious — defence of the 'rule of Law' itself as 'an unqualified human good'. Thompson shamelessly interprets this hallowed and ambiguous concept in a one-sidedly democratic way, as 'the imposing of effective inhibitions upon power and the defence of the citizen from power's all-inclusive claims'.[7] This general view, necessarily controversial among marxists, has become increasingly influential in specific discussions of law and order in Britain.

Marxist analyses of law and order in Britain

If concepts of order and law can be distinguished in principle, contemporary marxists such as Thompson imply that they should also be strongly separated in analysing recent British developments. In effect, they invite us to see the situation as one in which the 'rule of law', in Thompson's libertarian definition, is threatened by the demand for order in the particular sense of a 'strong state'. It is not, of course, that any marxist, even Thompson, would dream of saying that the rule of law in this radical sense had ever been fully established. The state has ever harboured tendencies to secretive and arbitrary power. The argument is rather that a decisive shift is occurring in the balance between the power of the state and the framework of legal and wider social constraints within which it is exercised. The demand for 'law and order', which is an important but not the only part of this shift, is seen as a demand for coercive order, rather than specifically for law. Again, no serious marxist has suggested that the movement to a more coercive state is likely to reach the stage at which the existing framework of law is seen as wholly dispensable. The argument is rather that the demand for law is an ideological form of the drive to more coercive forms of social order, in which law and laws will be made to serve authoritarian ends. It is precisely to meet this ideology of law that Thompson has sought to claim the 'rule of law' for a more libertarian socialist tradition.

It must be stressed that the body of marxist writing about 'law and order' in Britain rests heavily on, and contributes largely to, the common sociological wisdom on this subject. Marxists have generally shared with radical sociologists the assumption that 'crime is not the chief problem to which the demand for 'law and order' really addresses itself. They have built on sociological analyses of the ways in which 'moral panics' are created about 'law and order' issues, tending in addition to locate these within the context of British economic and political decline. In this sense the work of Stuart Hall and his colleagues, already discussed in detail in the chapter by Keith Bottomley and Clive Coleman, has been seminal, and it is necessary to turn to it again.[8] In particular, we shall examine the way in which 'law and order' is presented as a part of a crisis of social order in a more general sense.

Hall draws closely on Gramsci, and suggests that British society is experiencing a 'crisis of hegemony', analagous in some ways to the crisis of capitalist order which between the wars produced the fascist 'integral state'.[9] I say 'in some ways', because Hall sees the British crisis as a specific historical situation, with its own emerging solution, which he calls 'authoritarian populism'. Like many other writers, he traces the long decline of the post-war social-democratic consensus, but Hall argues there has been a shift to a new consensus, which has been both a reaction to particular crises and something which has been consciously organised for. Referring to 'the powerful orchestration of a new authoritarian consensus', he sees the mass media as largely responsible for developing a 'disciplinary common sense' (which the police and Conservative politicians have also helped to construct).[10] While the new consensus has been under formation since the late 1960s, Thatcherism clearly represents for Hall a sort of interim climax to this process. Thatcher's 'law and order' and racist appeals of 1979 were the signals of a new authoritarian Conservatism with deep popular appeal to working class as well as middle class voters. Her seemingly brilliant evocation of patriotism in the Falklands war reinforced the view — most radically argued for by the marxist historian Eric Hobsbawm — that the new Right had struck deep and broad roots in popular consciousness.[11]

As Bottomley and Coleman have already discussed, Hall sees a general 'law and order' issue emerging out of the more isolated 'moral panics' about crime in the 1960s, becoming a new common sense in the 1970s, and articulated electorally in 1979. 'Law and order' is such a key facet of the new authoritarianism that Hall uses the terms almost synonymously, referring to the 'law and order consensus', the 'law and order state' and even the 'law and order society'. However, it is clear from the range of his discussion that the strengthening of 'law and order' involves far more than a tougher attitude towards crime, or even towards strikes and demonstrations which are increasingly linked with crime as problems of order. Indeed this is one of the recurring themes of the argument — that anxieties about crime, largely manufactured, are a peg on which a whole paraphanalia of coercion is hung.

182

The concept of 'law and order society' as a *process* raises difficult questions of the stage which this sort of development has reached, and also of course of the obstacles to it. This sort of analysis, especially when allied to a critique of the mass media, lends itself very easily to a premature closure, in which we are already living in a sort of police state and manipulated in the manner of *1984*. The sense of conflict and contradiction, surely essential to marxism, is lost. The danger of this conclusion will be very evident to anyone who has tried to use Hall's work in teaching undergraduates — for them the 'law and order society' is often well and truly established.

In this light it is useful that Ralph Miliband has recently provided a thumbnail sketch of a possible form of British 'conservative authoritarianism', and argued that the transformation of 'capitalist democracy' into 'capitalist authoritarianism' can be a gradual slide:

> In such a regime, trade unions might be allowed, provided they did not organize strikes. Parties might operate, provided they were not subversive. Political activity might be possible, provided permission had been obtained for it. Newspapers would be allowed, provided they did not foment 'class hatred' or 'spread disaffection'. Comment on radio and television would be free, provided it did not undermine stability. There would be censorship, but on a limited basis: on the other hand, self-censorship would be unlimited.
>
> Soldiers would play a much bigger role in all areas of national life than hitherto, but the regime would not necessarily be a military one. There would be plenty of civilians, of the most respectable hue, available to run the state, in partnership with military men and police chiefs. Police forces would be given much more extensive powers, and much more of a free hand to act as they thought fit. Nor, in the climate engendered by the regime and its propagandists, would they be disposed to ask anyone's permission to do so.
>
> Nevertheless, much of the state would function more or less normally. A dismal aspect of such conservative authoritarianism is precisely the normality which endures, and which provides reassurance to many people who want a quiet life that things are not all that different, really, except of course for activists and others in gaol or rehabilitation centers of one sort or another ('concentration camp' evokes the wrong memories). There would be cricket on the green, and at Lord's; Derby Day at Ascot; the football season and the FA Cup; comedy on television; the same announcers blandly

reading the news; the Queen's Christmas Broadcast; even the House of Commons, minus some unpatriotic MPs, temporarily detained.[12]

What is more important to note here is that despite Miliband's attempt to anglicize the authoritarian danger, and to distinguish it clearly from classical facism, we are still, with Mrs Thatcher, well short of the sort of state which Miliband describes. Even the worst prognosis of Mrs Thatcher's second term still leaves the British state, on Miliband's definitions, clearly within 'capitalist democracy'. The 'strong state' is for Miliband neither here, nor inevitably coming, but 'prefigured by the widening ambit of repressive state power'.[13] He argues that (in sharply deteriorating economic conditions, with exacerbated class conflict, it *could* occur.) One might add that it is equally, if not more likely to result from a sharpening international situation, in which war in Europe came to seem possible.

Miliband, although writing in 1982, could almost be said to be using the worst-case 'ideal type' of an authoritarian state to evade the more pressing issue of whether there is an 'interim climax', and if so of what kind. Other marxists have not been so coy, but it seems that two main sorts of case have been made, the connections between which have not always been clearly defined. On the one hand, an impressive array of academic writers, political research groups such as the editors of *State Research* (now unfortunately closed down), and civil liberties groups, have identified trends in legislation, the administration of the legal system, and above all in policing, as creating a state which, if not 'the strong state' in the fullest sense is demonstrably a dangerously stronger state. On the other, authors such as Hall, who returns time and again to this theme in polemical as well as academic writing, and also Hobsbawm, have emphasised the ideological shift which has taken place. As we have already seen, they have emphasised the development of authoritarian ideas, and the contribution of 'law and order' demands to a new consensus.

There is obviously no inherent contradiction between these two strands of analysis, stressing respectively the material and ideological dimensions of the demand for law and order. The two processes which are identified may largely complement each other, as in Gramsci's analysis of the integral state under fascism. But unless the connections are clearly argued, there is a danger of onesidedness which can be seriously misleading. For example, prior to the riots of 1981, radical analyses of developments in the police, such as the *State Research* paper 'Policing the Eighties', overwhelmingly stressed the development of reactive or 'fire-brigade' policing, the dramatic rate of technological development and arming of the police, and the reorganisation of special forces such as the SPGs. 'The present "debate"' they wrote, 'between preserving policing by consent. . . or the adoption of "fire-brigade" (or reactive) policing has, in practice, *already been resolved*.'[14] 'Community policing', as advocated by John Alderson, tended to be treated as marginal, its marginality confirming the strength of the main trends in policing.

There was, it seems to me, nothing wrong with this analysis as a description of trends. But by focussing on developments within the police in isolation, there was a danger of neglecting or simplifying the social and ideological conditions for them. So that when the riots of 1981 exposed the weakness of the ideological rationale for narrowly reactive policing, indeed its straightforwardly counter-productive character, radical analysts were rather unprepared for the sudden promotion of 'community policing' and the quasi-liberalism of the Scarman Report. Two alternative responses seemed to be available: to stick to the earlier line of analysis, emphasising the whole superficial nature of the new enthusiasms; or to respond to the apparent one-sidedness of the earlier positions by seeing in 'community policing' a more dramatic shift than in fact it represented. The reality of the situation is more complex than either of these responses allow. Here we should distinguish, as P.A.J. Waddington argues in chapter 5, between the concepts (or ideology) of community policing and the specific practices to which they often refer. The ideology is certainly loose and potentially contradictory, providing both a cover under which the police may adapt their practices without any major change of orientation, and a space in which alternative liberal or even socialist concepts may be advanced. The current practices to which the concept is widely applied — often little more than 'bobbies on the beat' and 'consultation' in selected areas — are not so much a radical return to traditional policing, or a new strategy, as a re-emphasis on some sides which have always been present in police practice. The British police today sometimes remind one of those NATO strategists of 'flexible response' who want to improve their conventional forces while maintaining their full battery of nuclear options.

This analogy with the military is put forward half seriously to illustrate another issue in marxist analysis. Just as critics of nuclear weapons sometimes criticise what they see as the 'technological imperatives' of the arms race, so critics of the police sometimes refer (as Joe Sim does in the 1982 *Socialist Register*, for example) to 'the technological imperatives of the force'.[15] While any sort of technology has its own logic, and a dramatic raising of their technological level is certainly an important feature of recent police history, it seems mistaken to see this (as Sim does) as the main thrust of police development. Technologies only come to the fore when social conditions (such as that of military competition between two roughly equally protagonists) require them to do so. In the case of the police, the driving force of policy is not technology itself but the need to respond to the crisis of social order, which writers such as Hall have analysed.

This argument may explain why the danger of one-sidedness seems much greater in accounts of 'law and order' based primarily on developments within policing, than in those which emphasise the overall ideological crisis. Of course, there is always a danger in the latter of minimising the concrete effects of repressive police tactics. But this does not seem one into which writers such as Hall have often fallen. And in any case, it seems valid to state that what keeps the working class, and even ethnic minorities, in their place is not mainly the enhanced fire-power of the police but the success of the ideological offensive for 'law and order' and 'the resolute approach' (not to mention, of course, the dull compulsion of the dole queues). Guns and CS gas are as much symbols of tougher authority — to use the military analogy, they are the domestic 'deterrent' — as they are concrete weapons for use in conflict situations. This is why E.P. Thompson is so right to see the threat of jury vetting and other so-called 'reforms' of the jury system not so much in terms of the number of additional convictions which may ensue, as in terms of a general tendency to undermine the limited democratic element in our legal system.[16] It is also why the emergence of the Police Federation and the Chief Constables as political forces concerned with law and order is at least as important as changes in police tactics and weaponry. Here we have a very significant group, the 'new men of power' in our society, and one is reminded of C. Wright Mills' attempt to point up the role of the military in US society in *The Police Elite*.[17] While one would not suggest that the British police are quite on a par with the US military (and indeed one might look first at the British military themselves, especially since the Falklands war), the same problem of flexibility in marxist concepts of power seems to be indicated.

If there is an 'interim climax', then, in our progress towards a 'law and order society', it is marked by the consolidation of a new ideological consensus and a new hierarchy of the powerful — trade union leaders out, police and military chiefs in. Its physical manifestations are there — the armouries of the police, their enhanced powers and pay, and the legal restrictions of new industrial relations laws. But for the moment, the ideological success of law and order and Thatcherism in 1983 is in itself one of the factors making the full-blooded authoritarianism of *1984* both unnecessary and unlikely.

Marxist responses to 'law and order'

Increasingly marxists have attempted to offer answers to the problems of 'law and order' in Britain today, and it is to these that we must now turn. In referring to the 'consolidation' of a new ideological consensus, it is necessary again to qualify any suggestion of closure. Even the most pessimistic of marxists — and Stuart Hall, for example, was an early realist, arguing in a pre-election issue of *New Socialist* that hopes of defeating Mrs Thatcher were illusory[18] — reject the idea that the 'law and order' consensus need have any long term stability.

Marxists generally argue that the same economic trajectory of British capitalism which is the underlying reason for the transition from the 'social democratic' to the 'law and order' consensus, creates the conditions in which an alternative solution can also be posed. For some marxists, such as the Socialist Workers Party, this will of course develop directly out of industrial class conflicts and the struggle against a more repressive police force. Others, such as Hall, will argue that the last decade has proved that a solution will arise neither automatically from economic crisis nor from the narrowly political agitation of marxist sects. Instead the attempt to pursue more authoritarian policies, within a state which retains a substantial democratic framework (including ideas about the rule of law), will create its own contradictions to which a socialist response is possible. Hall argues in a Gramscian vein that the left needs to construct a popular and democratic socialist consciousness to answer the populism of the Right.[19] This is, in its nature, a long term task — as Hall recognised before Mrs Thatcher won her 1983 landslide — and neither an escalation of industrial militancy, advocated by the revolutionary left, nor a short-term electoral defeat of Thatcherism, which would satisfy many in the Labour Party, will solve the fundamental problem.

One part of the answer offered by marxists to the problems of law and order is then, to say that 'law and order' as an ideology requires us to offer an alternative vision of society. Hall's argument is that socialists of all kinds, revolutionaries as well as reformists, have effectively ceased to provide such a vision, thus creating the space for the ideologies of the Right. At the same time it is clearly not enough to respond to the demand for law and order, which claims to be based on specific problems of crime, with a general vision of a society based on more equal and humane social relations. More specific answers are needed, and socialist writers and activists have increasingly put forward more immediate proposals to meet these demands.

One interesting feature of recent debate has been a return to the most basic of all issues, the problem of crime itself. Here there is a potential divergence between the labelling theories of the radical deviancy sociologists and the requirements of a 'socialist criminology'. Ian Taylor has been foremost in arguing for the need 'to take popular anxieties about crime and social order seriously'. Taylor is not disputing that real increases in crime are magnified by increased reporting or by the presentation and propaganda of the 'law and order' brigade, the police included. Indeed he argues that 'we cannot uncritically accept the conventional "state" definition of crime': we should critically examine the conventional categories, and if necessary define new ones. On the one hand, 'only a proportion of the behaviours which are currently classed as "criminal" are seriously harmful to working-class and popular interests'; on the other, we have to retrieve a concept of crime (originally argued for by Hermann Mannheim) 'as involving both social *and* economic offences *against the common interest*, committed by the advantaged and disadvantaged alike and requiring an equal level of attention by the public and by a socially-response police force.'[20]

Nevertheless, such a conception of crime must still recognise that many categories of conventional crime, from burglaries to street attacks and rapes, do represent real problems which directly affect and concern millions of working class people. Taylor argues that not only do we have to point up the broad economic and social causes of these 'crime rates' — causes which after all are more complex than popular socialist arguments often suggest — but we have also to propose interim measures to deal with what they represent. Socialist proposals for democratising the courts, police and penal institutions may be put forward to counter the danger of the strong 'law and order' state, which is of paramount importance to activists in the labour and socialist movements. But they must also connect with the real anxieties which exist among working class people, anxieties on which the ideologies of 'law and order' constantly feed in order to justify repressive policing. The argument must be that more democratic and accountable forms of policing will mean more attention to the real problems which concern ordinary people on a day to day basis. A wedge must be created between this popular need and the demand of the police for increased armaments, special forces, etc.

Taylor's contention that 'law and order' can even be turned around to become 'arguments for socialism' is a radical one, in the context of both sociological and marxist debate.[21] For marxists, it involves a much greater recognition of the necessity for police, a point which is even less conceded within the classical tradition than the necessity for law itself. Indeed Taylor argues for the renewal of 'a social democratic conception of crime', playing a good deal on the ambiguities of 'social democracy' which was originally, of course, a term for revolutionary marxism rather than pragmatic reform. Clearly Taylor is effecting the transition from far-left to Labour Party politics like so many marxists today. At

188

the same time he is recognising that faced with the 'law and order' state and the need for renewal of popular socialist politics, it is necessary to make interim demands for democratic reform. In this sense a marxist approach to law and order is not so much an independent political perspective, as a contribution to a broader debate among civil-libertarians and socialists. Some of the thinking behind this approach has been developed in *Marxism Today*, the journal of the Communist Party, but its most natural political expression — given the ever-increasing marginality of the CP — is in the Labour Left.[22] The best practical embodiment of the sort of approach which Taylor advocates is probably the work of the Greater London Council Police Committee and its support unit — although few if any GLC members would actually consider themselves 'marxists'.[23]

Obviously there is an 'orthodox' marxist objection to this, represented politically in Britain by the SWP. For them, it may certainly be legitimate to recognise the real social problems of crime, and to argue that only socialism will remove their causes. But it is a dangerous illusion to rely on reforming the police and legal system through parliamentary and municipal action. While not unwilling to use the courts and the police in specific instances, as a matter of strategy the only defence which can be countenanced — against racist attacks or police violence, for example — is the self-defence of working class and black communities. Reform of the law or police, whatever its short term effects, only ties the working class to the state which it must in the end overthrow if it is to create socialism.

This difference among marxists seems to boil down to the schism between reform and revolution, and theoretically to different conceptions of the state. For classical marxists and their revolutionary descendents today, law, the police, government and prisons are all parts of the fundamentally coercive apparatus of class repression. In the long term they can only be abolished, by mass revolutionary action, leading eventually to a law-less and state-less communist society. To revolutionaries anyone who rejects this approach is by definition a reformist, or at least veering in that direction. To most of the marxists we have discussed in this paper, this is however a false polarisation. The state is a complex and contradictory set of institutions. In the short and medium term they can and must be wrestled with to produce the most favourable balance in society. Direct, mass action and political reform are not alternatives but complementary. In the long term, the process of socialist transformation will require an immense work of deepening political democracy into social and economic democracy. In this process, law and law-enforcement must equally be fully democratised and transformed. The lessons of past attempts at socialist transformation are that law is not an optional extra for socialism.

This argument is obviously not just about general perspectives, it derives very much from the analysis of the 'law and order' consensus and 'authoritarian populism'. The main marxist writers, E.P. Thompson, Stuart Hall and Ralph Miliband, are all relatively pessimistic about the current drift. Long gone is the revolutionary optimism of the late 1960s. We are invited to renew the struggle for socialist transformation, starting with a long hard look at the dangers of the present.

Notes

1. Karl Marx, 'Preface to A Contribution to the Critique of Political Economy' in Marx-Engels *Selected Works*, Vol.1 (FLPH, 1950), pp.575-8.
2. Friedrich Engels, 'Letters to Schmidt', Marx-Engels *Selected Correspondence* (FLPH, 1960), p.540.
3. Franz Neumann, *Behemoth* (Harper, 1966).
4. On the need for pluralism, Ernest Mandel, *Revolutionary Marxism Today* (NLB, 1979), ch.1; on the separation of powers, Ken Coates, *Heresies* (Spokesman, 1983) ch.5.
5. See Ralph Miliband, *Marxism and Politics* (Oxford University Press, 1977) ch.VI; Nicos Poulantzas, *State, Power, Socialism* (Verso, 1978), Part Five.
6. See for example Hugh Collins, *Marxism and Law* (Oxford University Press, 1982).
7. E.P. Thompson, *Whigs and Hunters* (Allen Lane, 1975), p.266.
8. Stuart Hall et al., *Policing the Crisis: Mugging, the State and Law and Order* (Macmillan, 1978).
9. For an explicitly Gramscian presentation, see Hall, 'Popular-Democratic *vs* Authoritarian Populism: Two Ways of "Taking Democracy Seriously"', in Alan Hunt, ed. *Marxism and Democracy* (Lawrence & Wishart, 1980).
10. Hall et al, op.cit., p.217.
11. Eric Hobsbawm, in *Marxism Today*, March 1983.
12. Miliband, *Capitalist Democracy in Britain* (Oxford University Press, 1982), pp.154-155.
13. Ibid., p.156.
14. 'Policing the Eighties: The Iron Fist', *State Research*, 19, August-September 1980, p.146 (emphasis in original).
15. Joe Sim, 'Scarman: The Police Counter-Attack', *Socialist Register 1982*, p.57.
16. E.P. Thompson, *Writing by Candlelight* (Merlin, 1980), section on 'The State and Civil Liberties'.
17. C. Wright Mills, *The Power Elite* (OUP, 1956). When Mills' concept is compared in purely formal terms with the marxist concept of 'ruling class', it is forgotten that the thrust of his work was an attempt to argue that there had been a radical concentration of power in American society in the then recent past. The prime cause of this was, he suggested, the role of the US in the international arena, hence the importance of the military alongside the economic and political elites which are more conventionally given prominence.
18. Stuart Hall 'Whistling in the Void', *New Socialist*, 1983.

19. Hall, 'The Battle for Socialist Ideas in the 1980s', *Socialist Register 1982*, pp.1-20.
20. Ian Taylor, 'Is crime here to stay?', *New Statesman*, 12 Nov. 1982, p.12.
21. Ian Taylor, *Law and Order: Arguments for Socialism* (Macmillan 1982). This contains a much fuller exposition of the arguments summarised in his *New Statesman* article.
22. *Marxism Today* has served as a focus for intellectual debate, especially before the launching of the Labour Party's *New Socialist* in 1981. But many of the writers in it have not actually been members or supporters of the Community Party.
23. The GLC Police Committee has published its own bulletin and reports as part of its campaign to gain control over the Metropolitan Police by accountable local representatives.

12 Conclusion

By N.C.M. Elder

This final chapter falls into three sections, designed as a coda to what has gone before. The first section reflects upon the significance of the contrast between the prominence of the law and order issue in the 1979 election campaign and its virtual disappearance from the scene in the general election four years later. In part, therefore, this section is intended to provide a fresh perspective on some of the background factors which prompted this whole study in the first place. The second section looks briefly at the older and newer currents that have been influencing the policies of Conservative administrations in the criminal justice sector since Mrs Thatcher first took office in 1979. It links with the first section in considering the areas of convergence and divergence between the Conservative and Labour Parties in this area of the law and order problem. The concluding section broadens the sweep, to draw out characteristically modern aspects of the law and order problem, taking up some of the themes from earlier chapters for consideration from a fresh perspective.

1979 and 1983: consensus broken, consensus restored?

In the 1979 general election the law and order issue featured prominently, but not so in the election campaign of 1983. A Fabian tract published in 1983 censured the Conservatives for breaking a consensus between the two major parties in 1979 upon this matter: it was curiously, but illuminatingly, entitled 'Law and Order: Theft of an Issue.'[1] Since the author is a member of the Howard League for Penal Reform and a founder member of the Labour Campaign for Criminal Justice, perhaps the strongest implication here is that criminal justice administration requires a cool and dispassionate approach, a *professional* approach, insulated from the emotional shock-waves associated with public opinion. Certainly the Conservatives are indicted for exploiting the genuine anxieties of the people about crime in 1979 so as to pave the way for a more authoritarian society. Labour, it is argued, got the worst of both worlds in 1979: it had a 'soft' image and a 'hard' policy. It is acknowledged that the statistics for *serious* criminal offences, with all due allowance made for elements of uncertainty, have shown a marked secular increase in the post-war period as compared with the inter-war years before 1939. But the record shows that Conservative Governments have had, to say the least, no better success than Labour Governments in the containment of the *serious* crime rate. So the Conservatives are attacked for falsely suggesting that increased police forces and stiffer sentences are the proper remedies for an intractable problem.

This line of argument gives rise to a number of reflections. First, it might be argued, if there was consensus, how could there be an issue to be stolen? But the fact is rather that Labour could never *make an issue of* a 'hard' policy on law and order, for such a policy runs counter to the party's natural grain. Contrast the frequency with which law and order motions feature at Conservative Party conferences — 99 in 1983, for example, as compared with 55 on employment and industrial relations and 27 on defence[2] — with the infrequency of the appearance of such motions at Labour Party conferences. The Labour Party's general sympathy for the underdog in society leads it to identify instinctively with Richard Hoggart's 'Us' against 'Them'.[3] In 1958 the 'Them' included public officials, the bosses, the police, magistrates and teachers; in 1984 some public officials and most teachers have probably dropped off the list, but the others remain. So Labour Party conference motions tend to reflect anxieties about the behaviour of police forces rather than anxieties about prevailing levels of lawlessness.

Second, the official statistics for serious crimes continued to show an annual increase during the 1979-83 Thatcher administration[4] with a levelling-off for 1983 revealed in the figures released in March 1984. Yet public concern about the crime rate was not evident in the 1983 election, contrary to what had been the case in 1979. Does this, then, reflect cynical Conservative electoral manipulation in 1979? It rather reflects the more immediate readiness of the Conservatives to respond to the perceived requirements of the electorate as consumers of security. Labour, by contrast, readily accepted the expert view that to increase

194

the size of police forces was unlikely to make a significant dent in the crime rate, and that to stiffen sentencing policy was unlikely to act as a deterrent. The most effective deterrent would be to improve the detection rate for crime. The difficulty for Labour was that this analysis left it bereft of any security policy at all. In short, the Conservatives were bound to win the competition between the two major parties to satisfy the genuine fears of the electorate; there was, indeed, no real competition, and it was no accident that this was so.

Third, Labour found itself in a similar position in 1979 in respect of penal policy. The high hopes which had been placed in rehabilitative treatment for prisoners in the 1960s by liberal reformers and professionals in the field had been in large measure disappointed. In default of any coherent penal policy, Labour felt reluctantly driven back to the traditional recipes for the administration of criminal justice. But these too went against the party's grain, and the Fabian pamphlet represented an attempt to begin the resolution of a perceived dilemma. The charge that the Conservatives in 1979 were moving towards a more authoritarian society — synonymous with a 'law and order' society in the view of the National Council for Civil Liberties — partly reflects the fact that any inter-party consensus on penal policy was felt to be uncongenial and hoped to be temporary. The burning question for resolution was what might constitute a coherent penal policy comformable to the best party principles?

Fourth, the law and order issue in the 1979 elections was closely interlinked with the political hot potato of trade union reform. The winter of 1978/79 was 'the winter of discontent' and of union militancy under the Callaghan Labour administration. As Andrew Cox has noted earlier in this volume, what is new in the strikes of the 1970s and the 1980s is the hazard to essential services and the readiness to question the legitimacy of Government decisions.[5] These considerations helped to push the question of union reform to the very forefront of the 1979 election campaign. As to essential services for example, a good deal of the 'head of steam' generated in the Conservative campaign came from condemnation of the actions of a relatively small number of National Health Service workers who were apparently prepared to act as judges of the medical priorities and to endanger the welfare of the sick in the course of their protest about low pay. At one level, the argument was about who bore the responsibility for these actions — the government or the strikers. The Conservatives held strongly that those who willed the action could not be exonerated of responsibility for the consequences of that action. At a different level, the dispute was about what constituted fair play, with the electorate as arbiter. It was also about civil tranquillity, with the question of the legal restraint of unions hovering in the wings. Thus the Conservatives highlighted the law-breaking associated with violence on the picket lines in the course of the long-running Grunwick dispute. Labour characteristically focussed on the behaviour of the police at the scene of the action. In short, the major issue between the parties in the 1979 campaign was seen by the main contenders as either the defence of voluntaristic union process from legal attack, part of the move towards a more authoritarian society, or the exercise of power by the state to check the abuse of power by the unions. So in this respect — to revert to the title of the Fabian pamphlet — there most certainly was an issue between the parties, and the question of 'theft' was irrelevant.

By the time of the 1983 elections, the Conservatives had got the 1980 (Prior) and the 1982 (Tebbit) Employment Acts on the statute book and addressed themselves to the question of union reform by that combination of voluntarism and scaled-down legal restraint outlined by Andrew Cox in chapter 7. The activation of legal restraint has been left to the employers. Sometimes they have used it, as in the case of Eddie Shah's 'Stockport Messenger' dispute with the National Graphical Association over the closed shop, but more often not, as with the National Coal Board's decision in 1984 that 'it would not be constructive' to proceed with the action for contempt of court against the Yorkshire miners for defying the court order to desist from secondary picketing. The Conservative calculation has been to seek to minimise the chances of direct challenges to government authority through order-defiance by attempting to particularise the economic considerations relevant to each case and so reduce the ideological content of industrial disputes. Thus common law provisions, for example, have been relied on to prevent mass picketing from degenerating into effective intimidation. But naturally the 1983 election gave the Labour Party occasion to promise the repeal of Conservative industrial relations legislation upon returning to power, and it was mainly thus that the issue of union reform featured in the 1983 election campaign. For the rest, the election that year centred on the government's management of economic policy: was a renewed mandate appropriate in order to continue the austere course that had been charted, or were the Conservatives to be adjudged guilty of 'cut and run' tactics in view of the economic disasters predicted by the opposition?

A few brief observations may be permissible, to round off this section, about the Brixton and Toxteth riots of 1981 which occurred midway between the two general elections and which have attracted so much attention earlier in this work. These riots, as Fishwick and Dixon make clear in Chapter 2, were by no means the first examples of public order disturbances in Britain giving rise to fears about inter-racial discord. It might, however, reasonably be argued that the massive immigrations of the late 1950s and the 1960s transformed the matter of race relations from a *local* to a *national* preoccupation. This is reflected in the fact that Race Relations Acts were then for the first time thought necessary, with new official bodies and new voluntary organisations coming into being in order to safeguard the rights and promote the peaceful integration of the new populations in British society. These people had been encouraged to come; they had the right to expect the state to fulfill its obligations. Now that the dust has settled, it is clear that early analogies with the US experience in the 1960s were misleading, not only in respect of the scale of the problem but also because the fear that the riots were racial in character has been proved groundless. Equally it is clear that the police have had to develop new levels of sensitivity and sophistication in order to handle the special problems of policing areas with high ethnic minority concentrations. But the point in the present context is that no backwash from the traumatic events of 1981 was apparent in the elections two years later. That this was so probably depended less upon the intervening Falklands conflict erasing memories than upon the large degree of inter-party consensus that race relations questions are best handled in a non-partisan spirit and with due reference to the views of experts in this field.

1979-1984: more of the same?

Conservatives are often typified as sharing the ancient retributive justice approach to law and order as a problem for the state with an ignorant and atavistic electorate, essentially composed of an almost infinite series of Alf Garnetts on Clapham omnibuses. Perhaps the thought is not often expressed thus, but such is the essence of the characterisation. The experts who work at the sharp end of criminal justice research are thus tempted at intervals to resurrect the approach of Edwin Chadwick as counterweight: 'The law must be made to conform to public opinion, or the public opinion must by means of public instruction be made to conform to the law.'[6]

There is something in the characterisation, but the truth is perhaps both more prosaic and more complex. Thus the Conservatives on taking office in 1979 with William Whitelaw as Home Secretary, could argue that they were in large measure simply attending to the intimations of existing arrangements in accordance with the best Oakeshottian principles. As to the police, they were at last bringing establishments up to strength and remedying the grievances over pay which had caused the Police Federation to withdraw from the pay negotiating machinery by the beginning of 1977. So Whitelaw's first act in the new post was fully to implement the recommendations of the Edmund Davis inquiry into this area, the inquiry itself having been set up by Merlyn Rees under the previous Labour administration in November 1977.

As to penal policy, the Conservative administration is clearly acting in general conformity to what Bottomley and Coleman have noted as a contemporary West European trend, namely the 'bifurcation' of policy between severe penalties for serious criminal offences and a measure of increased leniency towards 'ordinary' offenders.[7] In respect of serious offences, Conservatives tend to feel a close affinity with the sentiment expressed by the narrator in *The Great Gatsby*: 'Conduct may be founded on the hard rock or the wet marshes, but beyond a certain point I don't care what it's founded on.'[8] So, for example, Leon Brittan, succeeding as Home Secretary after the 1983 Cabinet reshuffle, has indicated minimum 20-year prison terms for the killers of police or prison officers, for terrorist murders, for the sexual or sadistic killers of children, and for those who commit murder using firearms in the course of robbery. The maximum sentence for those carrying firearms in the course of crime is to be increased from 14 years to life. Legislation is foreshadowed to empower the Attorney-General to refer what appear to be over-lenient sentences to the Court of Appeal for *future* guidance — possibly this was prompted by the case in which the rapist of a girl hitch-hiker escaped with a fine of £2,000 on the grounds that the victim had been guilty of contributory negligence. In April 1984, incidentally, the Criminal Law Advisory Committee recommended that the maximum penalty for attempted rape should be increased from 7 years to life and for indecent assault from 5 years to 10. 'Members of the public', said the chairman (Lord Justice Lawton), 'clearly took the view that some of the indecent assaults are terribly serious. . . so clearly something had to be done.'[9]

At the same time Conservative policy on serious crime has also shown the impact of utilitarian rather than retributive considerations. This appears with particular clarity in the divergence between a sizeable segment of the party's parliamentary representation on the one hand and a majority of the electorate on the other over the issue of the reintroduction of capital punishment. A MORI poll of June 1981 had shown up the familiar pattern of public opinion on this topic, with 78 per cent expressing themselves in favour of capital punishment 'sometimes' and only 19 per cent opposed to its use in all circumstances.[10] Despite a significant measure of Cabinet support, and despite a vigorous mass media campaign by the Police Federation, proposals to bring back the death penalty for certain categories of murder were decisively rejected on the customary free vote in June 1983. The large new intake of Conservative MPs proved more liberal than had originally been expected. It seems quite likely that the June 1983 division has finally killed off this particular aspect of the law and order issue, quite likely also that the uncertain evidence about the deterrent effect of the death penalty was a factor weighing with some of those who voted against its reintroduction.

At the opposite end of the spectrum governmental penal policy is showing some influence from Western European practices in respect of 'ordinary', and especially the youthful, offenders, although such influence is not uniform across the board. Pragmatic considerations undoubtedly weigh heavily here, not least the desire to reduce the serious overcrowding in prisons — publicity about which must have contributed to the salience of the law and order issue in the public mind at the time of the 1979 elections. Hence the Conservative Government's speedy implementation of the recommendations of the May Inquiry into the Prison Service[11] for measures to clear the jails of petty offenders, in combination with a major programme of prison building and modernisation. Professionals in the criminal justice field are well aware of the fact that the prison population in many West European countries is significantly lower, on a per capita basis, than in Britain despite no great difference in the incidence of criminality.[12] The new prison building programme can be regarded as an instalment of 'more of the same', along with the increased police forces and stiffer sentences for serious offences. So, for that matter, can the 'short, sharp shock' treatment for young offenders, introduced by William Whitelaw, the efficacy or otherwise of which is currently under scrutiny: this innovation certainly squares with that belief in the value of discipline which is always more marked in Conservative than in Labour or Alliance circles. But at least this expedient is in accord with the objective of preventing the contamination of young offenders by contact with the hard cases among the prison population.

The 1982 Criminal Justice Act reflects the influence of the bifurcation of penal policy in its impact on non-serious offences. It significantly increased the range of options available to courts and magistrates as alternatives to jail for young offenders, and it cleared the prisons of the not very numerous categories of people convicted of vagrancy and of soliciting for the purposes of prostitution. Following the same line of reform, Leon Brittan as Home Secretary has announced his intention to do likewise for the larger categories of drug addicts and, much more significant numerically, of people who have defaulted on fines.[13] Here community service orders offer a likely alternative, now that objections from the probation service about 'buying out' appear to have been resolved. Again, the option of weekend detention is under consideration for minor offenders, following contemporary Dutch, Belgian and West German precedent.

This both avoids jeopardising the job of the offender and enables him/her to contribute towards household expenses and possibly also towards the cost of detention.[14] Similarly, in Sweden, some minor offenders are permitted to obtain outside jobs while they are under sentence, returning to jail at night after the day's work.

The 1982 Criminal Justice Act is also of interest because it reflects to a modest extent the steadily increasing significance of the *restitutive* principle in modern penology. Courts are empowered by the Act to make a compensation order without other punishment, and if in addition they levy a fine then the compensation order takes precedence if the offender is unable to meet both in full. In March 1984 Leon Brittan, speaking to the Holborn Law Society, urged the courts to make greater use of these powers. He also promised funding for local youth support scheme experiments of the type practised at Exeter and South Shields. Under these, young offenders carry out repair work to make good damage which they have caused. Thus, as the Home Secretary put it, 'the offender is made to confront what his action means in human terms'.[15] Similarly, from the opposing political camp, David Downes: 'By agreeing to make restitution to the victim, and by the victim agreeing to accept such restitution, the offender is arguably brought to a sharper realisation of the harm done, and given an opportunity to expiate his guilt more fully, than by feeling himself victimised by imprisonment.'[16] So here a genuine consensus is visible, and one which is likely to have general popular backing. It may perhaps be characterised as being based on an extention of the principle of equity in the system of criminal justice, the correction of an imbalance between victim and offender. The rapid growth of the National Association of Victims' Support Schemes testifies to the need, and the Home Secretary has given clear evidence of his desire to press further along the same road by projecting new legislation in respect of criminal injuries. The intention here is partly to give victims of violence a statutory right to compensation from the long-established Criminal Injuries Compensation Board, and partly to seek to ensure that the offender is made personally liable to pay compensation so far as is practicable.

Inter-party consensus tends to wear very thin, however, when the focus moves to that complex of law and order problems styled problems *of* the state, rather than *for* it. This becomes particularly apparent when the role of the police is under consideration. A partial exception to this generalisation is the matter of *preventative* policing, on which increased stress has been laid in the last decade. Thus, for example, the rapid growth of neighbourhood watch schemes in parts of London and scattered communities elsewhere in the country has attracted a measure of cross-party support, although Labour inclines towards the view that these are least likely to work where they are most needed. However, party differences have surfaced particularly sharply over the Police and Criminal Evidence Bill which is currently nearing the statute books.

The essential point to be made in respect of the Police and Criminal Evidence Bill is that it proposes to strike a new balance between the desire to improve the efficiency of police forces in the detection of serious crime, on the one hand, and to safeguard the liberties of the citizen — and notably of the citizen as suspected person — on the other. In view of the rare complexity and sensitivity of the detailed provisions — e.g., a new Code of Practice to replace Judge's Rules for the regulation of police powers of search, arrest, questioning and detention — it is hardly surprising that this measure has occupied a record number of standing committee sittings. The Bill would make an excellent case-study of how a government seeks in practice to resolve the condundrum posed earlier in this work by Bottomley and Coleman and set out significantly by Philip Norton at the end of the introductory chapter.[17] Here it is perhaps enough to say that the different balances proposed by Conservative and Labour are very revealing in their different perspectives on the problems of reconciling citizens' liberties with police efficiency.

To sum up the argument of this section, the Conservatives in their five years of office have indeed provided 'More of the Same' in the sphere of criminal justice administration, but equally there have been significant pragmatic modern influences in evidence in their policies. Here there is much inter-party common ground: the differences tend to show up most on nuances and matters of detail. Thus Conservatives are apt to favour determinate minimum sentences for serious crimes, Labour incline towards determinate maximum sentences. Conservatives finally are much less worried than their opponents by laying on 'More of the Same' and perhaps less inclined to search for what they instinctively regard as the chimera of a *coherent* penal policy.

Law and order in the modern state

It is now time, in conclusion, to look at law and order in the modern state in a longer perspective. The preservation of civil tranquillity against internal and external threat is the most ancient and, in a sense, the most primary function of any state: it is equivalent to self-preservation. In pre-modern times law, as Robert Berki observes, was congealed in order, so that particular status/rank relationships were elevated to the universal level. The prevailing order is no longer, of course, regarded as part of a great chain of being, hierarchically arranged under Divine providence. On the contrary, 'The modern state (as we know the story by heart) emerged as a kind of raging tempest. . . bringing with it social mobility, legal emancipation and equalisation, abstract political liberty, and the elevated position of the individual, rational, good, competent to govern and to judge the actions of governments.'[18]

The Cromwellian interregnum, it may be suggested, from this perspective prefigured the modern state in some respects, and it came into being in 'a raging tempest' more violent than anything seen in Britain since. In more modern times the fluidity of the relationship between law and order noted by Berki is attributable in part to the rise of left-wing political movements and programmes for the recasting of status/rank relationships in a new order. In general, the political scene in contemporary Britain may be characterised as one of competition between alternative varieties of order moderated and mediated through the agency of the ballot-box. As one moves towards the radical left end of the political spectrum, however, so the tendency strengthens to regard the liberal democratic state as exhaustively definable in terms of an instrument of oppression for the continued subjection of the working-class. In A.J.P. Taylor's words 'Marx jeered at the "night-watchman" theory of the state, but the only difference in his conception was that it stayed awake during the day-time.'[19] Given this view of things, the inclination to order defiance increases, and the resemblance to the secretaries of the Cromwellian era increases the further leftward one travels: exclusivity, zeal, a strong sense of fraternity, intolerance of opposition, iconoclasm, and, rather paradoxically, an anti-materialist spirit.

The Labour party in general, and in this respect also the partners of the Alliance, belong to the libertarian tradition. They thus worry constantly about the emergence of a more authoritarian society and focus upon the cluster of problems associated with law and order as a function *of* the state rather than as a function *for* the state.[20] This focus may itself be regarded as an aspect of modernity, and virtually the whole of Part 2 of this volume (chapters 4-7 inclusive) bears witness to its significance. When the major parties in the political system shared a common concern for the defence of propertied interests, there was little scope for the advocacy of more sensitive policing methods or for the establishment of pressure groups in defence of citizen's rights. Ideological influences naturally also colour perceptions, in particular the tendency on the left to go more whole-heartedly along with the view of the individual as 'rational, good, competent to govern and to judge the actions of governments'. Sometimes this shows in a readiness to reach for the catapult, so to speak, in face of authority, as perhaps when the Young Liberals elected Sarah Tisdall as honorary Vice-President after her conviction for breach of official secrets. It also shows in a tendency to stress individual rights without reference either to corresponding obligations or to the position different individuals hold in society in relation to others.

When the field of vision is narrowed to the contemplation of the problem of lawlessness, to law and order as a problem *for* the state, it is perhaps worth noting that the Labour Party's preoccupation with the environmental conditions in which criminality and delinquency flourish coincides with the focus of the new professions and disciplines concerned with behavioural analysis of these phenomena. The juxtaposition here is not intended to imply that the professionals are Labour supporters, merely that those concerned with environmental factors share a common orientation to that extent with the Labour Party. Here again is an essentially modern dimension of the subject matter under review, although it might be argued that it is a continuation of the humanitarian tradition of the great 19th century prison reformers, whether Christian or secular in inspiration. Social workers, for example, began to form a profession in Britain in the 1930s, following the American precedent. The therapeutic value of non-judgmental acceptance of the client by psychiatrists, probation officers, etc. has become universally accepted among those working at the sharp end of the criminal justice system on the welfare side. Sociological analysis of the relationship between e.g. delinquency patterns and inner-city areas of deprivation, and criminological analysis of delinquency have tended to bear out one type of grass-roots observation, namely, that some children hardly have a chance. From this angle, 'the slum is to the offender what the poisoned well is to the typhoid sufferer.'[21] Here statistical evidence is central to attempts to get at empirically verifiable 'causes' of crime and so, hopefully, to reduce its incidence. The 'causes' here are statistical probabilities.

Labour's instinctive tendency to take a more roseate view of human nature than their opponents can sometimes lead, in the more artless versions of their thinking in these matters, to the hope that criminality might be effaced in a society without economic deprivation or social injustice — another vision characteristic of modern times, although there have been occasional earlier philosophical glimpses of Utopia. Their approach to this aspect of the law and order problem tends also to be coloured by the nature of their constituency. For they are aware that the less well-off sections of the community are simultaneously those who suffer most from the incidence of petty crime and those who are least ready to report minor offences to the police. They also naturally tend to see themselves as the protector of those who feel the scales of justice are weighted against them.

The professionals in the investigation and treatment of criminality may or may not subscribe in practice to one of the reductionist varieties of ethical theory which themselves are a modern philosophical phenomenon (if one takes the long view). According to these constructions 'good' and 'right' acts are to be interpreted psychologically or sociologically.[22] But the point is perhaps worth making that the logic of reductionist theories entails a *relativistic* world-view. 'Evil' has no place in the vocabulary of progressive philosophy. The case is similar with positivistic theories in law.

All of these considerations make their contribution to the intense diversity and plurality of modern society in which governments of whatever political complexion grapple with the problems of maintaining law and order. For Conservatives, obviously, traditional strands of thought are as a rule much more influential in colouring the approach to such problems. Largely as a result of this, they see themselves as the *populist* party whenever this issue becomes salient, and on the whole the electoral dividends have borne out their self-image.

Conservatives, in the first place, tend to be more sceptical about environmental explanations of crime. In practice of course they acknowledge a degree of validity in this approach. Thus the disturbances of 1981 resulted in the government's approval of an annual £380 million urban renewal programme and establishment of an inner city directorate within the Department of the Environment. But no interministerial meeting took place on inner-city problems for at least 2½ years after the autumn of 1981.[23] More generally research has indicated for example that the relationship between crime and unemployment appears to be unknowable.[24] So 'dole-inquency' is still delinquency and it is fallacious to assert that wrong-doing is *caused* by relative deprivation. In any case is relative deprivation genuine deprivation? Crimes, even minor crimes, are the actions of individuals *as* individuals directed to personal gain. To turn a blind eye even to minor offences would be unfair towards those similarly circumstanced who do not commit offences. Conservatives too, tend to take a more serious view of offences against property, as they always have done. At root this is because property is seen as the fruit of hard work rather than of exploitation; hence anger is readily aroused by those who seek a quick way of transferring it to their own advantage. A new dimension has entered here with the widespread growth of insurance cover, but the same principle holds in diluted form — the cost of policies rise, and honest folk are penalised by the misdeeds of the amoral.

These considerations find a ready cross-class echo in the electorate. Conservatives tend to a more pessimistic — they would say realistic, view of human nature, and are less inclined to see the individual as 'rational, good, competent to govern and to judge the actions of governments.' They do, however, follow the Aristotelian dictum that the best judges of a meal are the diners, not the chef: in this narrower sense individuals are competent to judge the actions of governments. They also concede that the electorate is composed of political equals, so that a central problem of law and order in the modern state is the maintenance of social discipline between political equals.[25] Now that authority derived from a static hierarchical order of society has vanished for ever, the authority necessary to social cohesion must be functional in character, and demonstrably so. From this in part flows the Conservative stress on personal responsibilities as the correlative of individual rights.

But how, it may be asked, can Conservatives posit a 'settled polity' in a modern society so diverse, fragmented and fluid? A large part of the answer to this question is contained in chapter 8 of this volume. Here it is perhaps sufficient to underline that the concept is both a political guideline and a political resource, and that we are in the realms of political finesse as a counter to potential order-defiance. Thus measures to encourage the maximum spread of personal property ownership are designed, among other things, to promote the spread of a sense of having a stake in the existing order. The concept perhaps becomes hardest to operationalise when the appeal is to economic rationality in times of acute economic depression. Thus the bitter miners' strike of 1984 was about jobs rather than about pay, with undertones of a challenge to the capitalist market order, belief in which is common to both the Government and the N.C.B. The Conservative response is to insist upon the liberal democratic legitimacy of their tenure of power, the maintenance of which is a shared 'settled polity' interest of all parties in the political system, until the next election falls due to pass judgement on affairs, and also to insist upon the managerial autonomy of the NCB in the handling of the conflict.

Three last questions merit a brief consideration to end this summary review: tensions between public and professionals in the area of criminal justice, the role of the mass media as another specifically modern problem in the law and order field, and finally, the salience of youth criminality or delinquency in the general phenomenon of lawlessness.

The public do not, of course, confront the professionals at all in the ordinary course of events in the area of criminal justice — unlike, say, with crumbling tower blocks, the effects of expert decisions are seldom felt with immediacy. So here the question upon which to focus is that alluded to in the introductory chapter, namely the belief that liberal Home Office policies are vote-losers. One might, perhaps, start with the observation made many years ago by Lord Salisbury, 'You should never trust experts. If you believe the doctors, nothing is wholesome; if you believe the theologians, nothing is innocent; if you believe the soldiers, nothing is safe. They all require to have their strong voice diluted by a very large admixture of insipid common sense.'[26] But what in contemporary Britain is 'common sense' in a highly pluralistic society?

'We deal with subjects', a Deputy Secretary in the Home Office is quoted as saying, 'on which the man on the Clapham omnibus thinks he's an expert. It is difficult to know what the real demands of the community are.'[27] The difficulty would seem to be more acute at the less serious end of the criminality scale. Thus on the one hand only a half of those questioned in the British Crime Survey for 1981 wanted the people who had committed offences against them to be jailed: many simply favoured a fine.[28] On the other hand, for example, birching finds many advocates among the public for soccer hooligans who perpetrate violence. Similarly, many on the Isle of Man were bitter about the end of birching there in 1978 as a result of the European Court ruling that the practice was degrading and unlawful. A threefold increase in incidents of wounding on the island in 1978-82 was seen by these as a predictable consequence of the ruling.[29] In respect of serious crimes, as Bottomley and Coleman have pointed out, public opinion favours severe punishment: the poll figures given earlier on public attitudes towards the death penalty illustrate the point.

Much of the tension between public and experts in the field of criminal justice would appear to spring from divergences in the setting of the balance between victim and offender. Criminologists, sociologists, probation officers etc. tend to share a common humanitarian concern to return offenders to society as useful members in the shortest possible time. Sometimes they are misperceived (though sometimes not) as ready to explain away delinquency as being *determined* by socio-economic circumstances. They professionally adopt utilitarian criteria based upon statistical analysis. They are apt to evolve orthodoxies which are regarded as unquestionable until disproved by experience: in the process, they may regard the opinions of others as not worthy of consideration, viewing their own research as the centre of all relevance. Because emotional involvement is a barrier to professionalism, they tend to be contemptuous of its public manifestations and of the (self-) righteous anger of the 'moral majority'.

The public are first and foremost, perhaps, consumers of security. Consider, for example, a report in 1983 from Dr John Coker, deputy chief probation officer for Hampshire, containing the findings of a seven-year study of 239 'lifers'. The worst risks and the most horrific murderers were unlikely ever to be released. The average time spent in prison by the others was 9.2 years, under the system then in practice. 221 had committed murders before sentence, only 2 after release. The effect of the prospect upon behaviour in prison was concluded to be beneficial.[30] But in the public mind it is the two murders committed by 'lifers' on release which count: two people are dead, it is argued, who would probably have been alive had so much consideration not been paid to those undeserving of it.

This is a good point at which to raise briefly the question of the significance of mass media impact on the law and order issue in the modern state, for it is the two murders which get the publicity, not the rest of the equation in the mind of the professional. This topic has received some attention earlier in this volume in connection with the generation of 'moral panics',[31] undoubtedly with justification. The tendency of the media to sensationalise follows the same principle as the high-circulation daily (not to mention Sunday) papers: good news is no news. Often this has its funny side, as when what goes on on a football pitch is entirely ignored in favour of what goes on off it (one is reminded of the legendary definition of a Beethoven concert by a St. John's Ambulanceman as 'something at which nothing ever happens'). Sometimes it has more undesirable consequences: witness the complaint of the Age Concern organisation that it was bedevilled by the mistaken idea that violent attacks on the elderly are a commonplace, whereas most such attacks are on the young. Again, the exploitation of the media by terrorist movements is another characteristic of modern times which has been well documented. Those who complain most bitterly about media bias are sometimes those who would introduce rigorous censorship had they the power to do so. Coverage of crime is rare in the media of the USSR, and audience surveys there have shown that many viewers would like more attention paid to items of human interest.

Moral outrage at popular level is, of course, a different matter from a moral panic, and it can spring from fellow-feeling for the victim. From this perspective some of the recent developments in the field of criminal justice which were alluded to in the previous section of this chapter might help to narrow the gap between public and professional standpoints — in particular, the moves towards redressing the balance between victim and offender and the slow spread of the restitutive principle.

In conclusion, one or two additional comments may be made on the high incidence of youthful crime and delinquency in the general crime figures. The young are classed by Berki as one of society's disadvantaged groups, along with ethnic minorities, the poor and the uneducated.[32] The point is not developed in the context in which it is raised, but it suggests the thought that 'disadvantage' is an umbrella term covering a number of ambiguities. Youth unemployment is clearly a disadvantage: the extent of the state's responsibility for it is a central issue of political debate. Is youth unemployment a correlate of youth delinquency? The relationship between unemployment and criminality in general has been found to be wavering and uncertain. To come from a broken home is a disadvantage. A happy family life was regarded as the best safeguard against delinquency by the Labour Party study group whose report *Crime: A Challenge to us All* was presented to the party's Home Policy Committee in May 1964. This group championed the idea of a family welfare service against the background of child delinquency figures running in the early 1960s at double the rate for the years immediately preceding the Second World War. They followed the Webbs in holding that, quite apart from poverty, unemployment and poor housing, serious personal inadequacies, tangled personal relationships, etc. are productive of child neglect and juvenile delinquency. By 1983, 80 per cent of children in the 10-15 age bracket were reported to be living with both their natural parents, and the annual divorce rate for England and Wales showed a sixfold increase over a 25-year span at the rate of approximately 150,000 cases a year.[33] It is scarcely surprising, then, that the Commons' Select Committee on Social Services should have concluded in April 1984 that prevention, where practicable, was better than patching up after breakdown and that in the long run 'parenting skills' should form part of the school curriculum.[34] The contemporary Swedish poet Per Gunnar Evander served a spell in his country's probation service and discovered that all the cases with which he dealt came from an unhappy and disturbed home background.[35] Is the state, then, to be considered responsible in any degree for the disadvantage of broken homes? The idea is far-fetched. Society, then? If so, in what sense, and to what degree? The idea is nebulous formulated thus.

We are here on the threshold of complex questions which cannot be pursued in the present context. Can it be said, for example, that the young are disadvantaged by a sense of rootlessness? Is the recession by a small minority into a kind of tribal violence caused by the disadvantage of lack of guidance? Certainly the growth of more humane attitudes in the educational and penal systems has been unable to prevent an increase in violence in society, as the figures for serious crime testify. But even to suggest the possibility of disadvantage through lack of guidance brings us back to the conflict between anti-authoritarian and traditionalist attitudes which is one significant strand in contemporary pluralism in society and which continues to contribute towards tensions between segments of professional and segments of public opinion. A distinction should in any case probably be drawn between 'anti-authority' and 'anti-authoritarian': the two are far from identical, and the terminology has been much muddied by misuse.

In March 1982 the Home Office celebrated its second centenary as a kind of combined Ministry of Justice and Ministry of the Interior. The political visibility of the minister at its head has increased strikingly in the five-year period primarily under review in this volume. Both the law-breaking and order-defiance aspects of the law and order issue have contributed to this: the salience of each in the 1979 election has been followed by Embassy sieges, continued intermittent terrorist attacks, the long and bitter miners' strike, significant reforms in the area of criminal justice and, more in the minor key, measures to combat increased heroin smuggling and to regulate the video recording market. With the modern state, the functions of welfare provision and economic management have become steadily more prominent. With economic recession, the charge is heard from left-wing critics of the Conservative administration that Britain is regressing from a welfare to a police state. It is a weapon drawn from the armoury of political combat.

Notes

1. D. Downes, *Law and Order: Theft of an Issue*, Fabian Society Tract No. 490 (Fabian Society, 1983).
2. Figures in *The Times*, 12 October 1983.
3. R. Hoggart, *The Uses of Literacy* (Pelican Books, 1958), Ch. 3 passim.
4. Downes, op.cit., table at p.2.
5. Chapter 7.
6. Sir E. Chadwick, 'Police', quoted in S.E. Finer, *The Life and Times of Sir Edwin Chadwick* (Methuen, 1952), p.477.
7. Following Professor Tony Bottoms. See above ch. 3.
8. F. Scott Fitzgerald, *The Great Gatsby* (Penguin, 1954), pp.7-8.
9. *The Times*, 13 April 1984.
10. *The Times*, 17 June 1983.
11. *May Inquiry into the Prison Service* (Cmnd. 7676) (HMSO, 1979).
12. See for example the table in Downes, op.cit., at p.18.
13. 'Law and Order', *Politics Today* (Conservative Research Department, 1983), table at p.408.
14. Ibid. Also R. Kilroy-Silk M.P. in *The Times*, 3 February 1983.
15. Report in *The Times* by its Legal Affairs Correspondent, 15 March 1984.
16. Downes, op.cit., p.29.
17. See ch. 3 and p.16.
18. R.N. Berki, 'Considerations on Law and Order', *Hull Papers in Politics No. 35* (Hull University Politics Department, 1983).
19. A.J.P. Taylor, *Englishmen and Others* (Hamish Hamilton, 1956), p.77.
20. See the Introduction to this volume.
21. E.J. Sacher, 'Behavioural Science and Criminal Law', *Scientific American* November 1963.
22. See, for instance, M. Ginsburg, *On Justice in Society* (Penguin, 1965).
23. *The Times* leader column, 'Whitehall's Urban Blight', 23 April 1984.
24. *The Times*, 10 March 1984.
25. There is an illuminating discussion on this point in P. Norton and A. Aughey, *Conservatives and Conservatism* (Temple Smith, 1981), pp.45-52.
26. A.L. Kennedy, *Salisbury 1830-1903: Portrait of a Statesman* (John Murray, 1953), p.106.
27. T. Brennan, *The Times*, 24 March 1982.
28. *The Times*, 25 February 1983.

29. E.M. Taylor M.P., *The Guardian*, 20 May 1983.
30. Reported by P. Evans, Home Affairs Correspondent, *The Times*, 10 October 1983.
31. Chapter 3.
32. Berki, op.cit.
33. Reported by J. Witherow, *The Times*, 21 November 1983.
34. *The Times*, 27 April 1984.
35. Lecture given in Scandinavian Studies Department, University of Hull, 10 May 1984.

The Contributors

The Editor

DR PHILIP NORTON is Reader in Politics at the University of Hull. He is the author of *The British Polity* (1984), *The Constitution in Flux* (1982), *The Commons in Perspective* (1981), *Conservatives and Conservatism* (with A. Aughey, 1981), *Dissension in the House of Commons 1974-1979* (1980), *Conservative Dissidents* (1978) and *Dissension in the House of Commons 1945-74* (1975) and has contributed widely to political science journals. He serves on the executive committees of the Political Studies Association of the United Kingdom and the British Politics Group in the United States and is academic secretary of the British Study of Parliament Group.

Other contributors

ARTHUR AUGHEY is Lecturer in Politics at Ulster Polytechnic. He is co-author (with P. Norton) of *Conservatives and Conservatism* (1981) and has published articles on Conservative philosophy and also on Ulster loyalism.

DR KEITH BOTTOMLEY is Reader in Criminology at the University of Hull. His publications include *Understanding Crime Rates* (with C. Coleman, 1981), *Criminology in Focus* (1979), *Criminal Justice* (ed., with J. Baldwin, 1978), *Decisions in the Penal Process* (1973) and *Prisons Before Trial* (1970) and has contributed widely to journals on criminology.

CLIVE A. COLEMAN is Lecturer in Sociology in the Department of Social Administration at the University of Hull. His publications include *Understanding Crime Rates* (with K. Bottomley, 1981) and various articles on the role of the police.

DR ANDREW COX is Senior Lecturer in Politics at the University of Hull. His publications include *Adversary Politics and Land* (1984), *Politics, Policy and the European Recession* (ed., 1982), and *The Politics of Urban Change* (with D. McKay, 1979). He has contributed numerous articles to political science journals.

DAVID DIXON is Lecturer in Law at the University of Hull. His publications include 'Gambling and the Law' in A. Tomlinson (ed.), *Leisure and Social Control* (1981) and various articles in sociological and legal journals.

DR HOWARD ELCOCK is Head of the School of Government at Newcastle-Upon-Tyne Polytechnic. His publications include *Local Government* (1982), *What Sort of Society?* (ed., 1982), *Political Behaviour* (1976), *Portrait of a Decision* (1972) and *Administrative Justice* (1969) and he has contributed numerous articles to political science and public administration journals. He served on Humberside County Council 1973-77 and 1978-81 and was chairman of the Council's Planning Committee 1975-77.

NEIL ELDER is Reader in Politics at the University of Hull. His publications include *Government in Sweden* (1970) and (with D. Arter and A. Thomas) *The Consensual Democracies* (1982). He has also published various articles on Scandinavian politics.

ELAINE FISHWICK undertook research, from 1979 to 1982, on the history of policing, at the Centre for Socio-Legal and Criminological Studies at the University of Sheffield.

DR STEPHEN INGLE is Senior Lecturer in Politics at the University of Hull. His publications include *Parliament and Health Policy* (with P. Tether, 1981) and *Socialist Thought in Imaginative Literature* (1979), as well as various articles in political science journals.

JOHN LAMBERT is Lecturer in Law at the University of Hull. He is the author of *Police Powers and Accountability* (1984) and various articles on the police in legal journals.

PROFESSOR JOHN REX is Director of the ESRC Research Unit on Ethnic Relations at the University of Aston. His numerous publications include *Social Conflict, A Theoretical and Conceptual Analysis* (1981), *Colonial Immigrants in Great Britain — A Class Analysis* (with S. Tomlinson, 1979), *Sociology and the Demystification of the Modern World* (1974), *Discovering Sociology* (1970), *Race, Colonialism and the City* (1970), *Race Relations in Sociological Theory* (1970), *Race, Community and Conflict* (with R. Moore, 1967) and *Key Problems in Sociological Theory* (1961), as well as numerous book chapters and articles.

MARTIN SHAW is Lecturer in Sociology at the University of Hull. He is the author of *Socialism and Militarism* (1981) and *Marxism and Social Science* (1975), and editor of *War, State and Society* (1984). He has contributed articles to various sociological and socialist journals.

P.A.J. WADDINGTON is Lecturer in Sociology at the University of Reading. His publications include *The Training of Prison Governors* (1983) and *Are the Police Fair?* (1983). He is the author of various articles and is a regular contributor to *Police*.

Select Reading List

Some recent works on Law and Order

The Police

J.C. Alderson, *Policing Freedom* (Macdonald and Evans, 1979).

J.C. Alderson, 'Comment — Scarman: to be or not to be?' in *Report of the Chief Constable of Devon and Cornwall 1981* (HMSO, 1982).

J. Brown, *Policing by Multi-Racial Consent* (Bedford Square Press, 1982).

M. Brogden, *The Police: Autonomy and Consent* (Academic Press, 1982).

P. Hain, *Policing the Police*, 2 vols. (Calder, 1979).

Lambeth, Borough of, *Final Report of the Working Party into Community/Police Relations in Lambeth* (Lambeth, 1981).

R. Mark, *In the Office of Constable* (Collins, 1978).

R. Mawby, *Policing the City* (Saxon House, 1979).

D. McNee, *McNee's Law* (Collins, 1983).

D.E. Regan, 'Enhancing the Role of the Police Committee', *Public Administration*, 61, pp.97-110.

R. Reiner, 'Fuzzy Thoughts: the Police and Law and Order Politics', *Sociological Review*, 28, pp.377-413.

Report of the Commissioner of Police of the Metropolis (HMSO, annual).

Crime Rates and Penology

A.K. Bottomley and C. Coleman, *Understanding Crime Rates* (Gower, 1981).

A.E. Bottoms, *The Coming Penal Crisis* (Scottish Academic Press, 1980).

M. Hough and P. Mayhew, *The British Crime Survey: First Report*, Home Office Research Study No. 76 (HMSO, 1983).

H. Jones (ed.), *Society Against Crime: Penal Theory Now* (Penguin, 1981).

R.D. King and R. Morgan, *The Future of the Prison System* (Gower, 1980).

Riots and Conflicts

J. Benyon, *Scarman and After* (Pergamon Press, 1984).

D. Cowell et al. (eds), *Policing the Riots* (Junction Books, 1982).

E.W. Evans and S.W. Creigh (eds), *Industrial Conflict in Britain* (Cass, 1979).

M. Kettle and L. Hodges, *Uprising! The Police, the People and the Riots in Britain's Cities* (Pan, 1982).

National Council for Civil Liberties, *Southall 23 April 1979: Report of the Unofficial Committee of Enquiry* (NCCL, 1979).

The Brixton Disorders 10-12 April 1981, Report of an Inquiry by The Rt. Hon. Lord Scarman (Cmnd. 8427) (HMSO, 1981).

Political Attitudes to Law and Order

R. Baldwin and R. Kinsey, *Police Powers and Politics* (Quartet Books, 1982).

H. Collins, *Marxism and Law* (Oxford University Press, 1982).

Conservative Research Department, 'Law and Order', *Politics Today*, 22, 19 December 1983 (Conservative Research Department, 1983).

D. Downes, *Law and Order: Theft of an Issue* (Fabian Society, 1983).

S. Hall et al., *Policing the Crisis: Mugging, the State and Law and Order* (Macmillan, 1978).

E. Hooson, *Law and Order in a Civilised Society* (Liberal Party Publications, 1979).

P. Johnson, *A Tory Philosophy of Law* (Conservative Political Centre, 1980).

J. Sim, 'Scarman — the Police Counter-Attack', *Socialist Register*, 1982.

I. Taylor, *Law and Order: Arguments for Socialism* (Macmillan, 1981).
I. Taylor, 'The Law and Order issue in the 1979 British General Election and the Canadian Federal Election 1979', *Canadian Journal of Sociology,* 5, pp.285-311.
P.A.J. Waddington, 'Are our politicians chasing an illusion?' *Police,* 15 (3), pp.24-26.
J. Wheeler, *Who Prevents Crime?* (Conservative Political Centre, 1980).
J. Young and J. Lee, *What is to be done about Law and Order?* (Penguin, 1984).

Index